From Sea to Sea

River Plate To Lake Michigan

by
Nelda Bedford Gaydou

RISING PHOENIX PRESS

Text Copyright © 2018 Nelda Bedford Gaydou

All rights reserved.
Published 2018 by
Progressive Rising Phoenix Press, LLC
www.progressiverisingphoenix.com

ISBN: 978-1-946329-41-7

Printed in the U.S.A.
1st Printing

Cover Illustration and book layout by Sabrina Bedford
Visit www.msgbedford.com

For my parents, with love and gratitude

Acknowledgements

I would like to thank my brother, David A. Bedford, for all his practical help and encouragement and my niece, Sabrina Bedford, for her delightful artwork.

Table of Contents

"He will proclaim peace to the nations. His rule will extend from sea to sea and from the River to the ends of the earth."
Zechariah 9:10, NIV

Shellbacks and Pollywogs

Nancy's eyes grew wide and she clapped her hands in excitement as the waiter set the cake with two glowing candles on the table and her one hundred and twenty fellow passengers broke into a rousing chorus of "Happy Birthday." Every night for the remainder of the voyage she expectantly awaited a repeat performance.

Sailing from New Orleans to Buenos Aires was sheer luxury for the entire Bedford family: three whole weeks of rest and relaxation. For Ben, the gangplank onto the ship was a release from his indentured servitude to higher education (two years crammed with classes, dissertation and oral examinations to earn his doctorate in theology), although he was still bound by one paper chain—he boarded with a sheaf of finals to be returned to the professor for whom he had been grading. For La Nell, it was literally a chance to catch her breath after having a lung collapse during a bout of double pneumonia brought on by the stress of keeping the family going while Ben studied, typing his endless papers and dissertation, seeing her teenage son through painful knee surgery and, most of all, dealing with the death of her only sister. The graded papers and mandatory medical reports would be mailed from the first port of call. They were taking no chances on delaying their return to the mission field.

The month of pampering after their breakneck pace and the penny pinching required by nearly half a year off salary was simply delightful. There was no housework, no cooking and no errands to run. Their spacious cabin was kept in order by a steward whose performance rose from merely perfunctory to devotedly assiduous as the end of the voyage and the hope of a good tip approached, while delicious meals were served at their assigned table in the dining room by a charming and efficient waiter, except for the days when abundant and delectable buffet lunches were offered in the lounge. Trays with tempting delicacies were passed around in the afternoon to bridge the gap until dinner.

They were traveling on the S.S. Del Sud, one of Delta Line's "Del Triplets" (Del Norte, Del Sud and Del Mar) that carried passengers and cargo between New Orleans and eastern South America. The vessels were 495 feet long and 70 feet wide, capable of traveling at 17 knots and accommodating 120 passengers and 367 crew members. Built some fifteen years earlier, in the late 1940s, they were the last word in comfort for the time. Their distinctive appearance included tall twin smoke uptakes just behind a squat dummy funnel that housed two decks of officers' quarters, the radio room and the emergency generator. The forward superstructure was almost circular, giving a wedge shape to many of the staterooms, all located on the outside and equipped with private facilities and air conditioning. Each ship had a Grand Lounge, library, deck café and domed dining room as well as a large salt-water swimming pool on a spacious deck.

The passengers soon settled into comfortable routines. Those who felt the need for something more than reading, napping and talking to while away their time could choose from board and card games, ping pong, putting and shuffleboard, to name a few of the options. La Nell won the table tennis tournament despite her respiratory problems and Ben met some fellow golf enthusiasts, one of whom recommended links in the general vicinity of the Bedfords' new assignment. David chatted with everyone and picked up a smattering of Portuguese from the polyglot voyagers, besides taking the time to teach his ten-year-old sister to play ping pong and shuffle a deck of cards. Nelda spent most of her days roaming the ship with a new-found friend her age and most nights babysitting Nancy while the older members of the family took in movies at the lounge.

The first week they sailed some 2,000 miles through the Gulf of Mexico and the Caribbean to reach Barbados. This beautiful little island in the Lesser Antilles lies just outside of the Atlantic hurricane belt, 250 miles northeast of Trinidad and Tobago and almost due north of the border between Venezuela and Brazil. The Spaniards who named the island were the first Europeans to land there and its name, which means "the bearded ones," may refer to the hanging roots of the bearded fig tree that is indigenous to the island or to the allegedly bearded Caribs who once inhabited it. It was the English, however, who first settled there permanently in 1627 and made it a colony. In 1966, two years after this trip, it became an independent country and a member of the British Commonwealth of Nations.

During their short stay the Bedfords did some rapid sightseeing in the capital city, Bridgetown, taking in their stride the traffic that circulated on the left side of the road, British-style. They dutifully mailed their medical reports and graded papers to the U.S. and found a cobbler for David. He had boarded the ship on crutches, recovering from surgery intended to stop the growth in his left knee joint, thus allowing a polio-induced difference in the length of his legs to be shortened and the consequent deviation in his spine to straighten out. Struggling up the gangplank and catching a glimpse of the number of stairs on the ship, he instantly decided to forego the crutches. Now he needed an insole and a lift for the heel of his right shoe to even up his legs, and the friendly cobbler soon had him ready to go. Thanks to his timely operation, David never developed a limp and his spinal column recovered its rightful shape.

They reached the Equator approximately 1,000 miles further along, an event known as "Crossing the Line," which has traditionally involved initiation rites in many of the world's navies. It usually takes the form of a "Court of Neptune," in which Trusty Shellbacks (veteran sailors) induct Slimy Pollywogs (first-time crossers) into "the mysteries of the Deep," and generally involves an increasingly embarrassing series of ordeals similar to fraternity hazing. Shellbacks are allowed to capture pollywogs, interrogate them and crack eggs on their heads or whatever else strikes their fancy. Passengers often celebrate with a considerably scaled-down version of the initiation rites. The S.S. Del Sud was no exception: there was a costume party complete with heavy teasing of the pollywogs that included a race in which they had to push ping pong balls with their noses along the floor of the Grand Lounge. Fortunately for the Bedfords, they were all confirmed shellbacks except Nancy, and she was too small to be hazed.

David attended the festivities as one of the newly famous Beatles and sang *She Was Just Seventeen* to the accompaniment of a table tennis paddle guitar. Afterwards, the inductees received certificates with the name of the vessel and the date on which they had crossed the Equator.

The long, lazy days also gave the Bedfords time to prepare themselves for their new assignment in Argentina. The entire first term and part of the second had been spent in Rosario, the great port city on the mighty Paraná River. They had loved it there and formed many close ties until they felt called to do pioneer work in Comodoro Rivadavia, the Oil Capital on the Atlantic coast, deep down in Patagonia. There they had fallen in love all over again and had been looking forward to going back. However, while they were on furlough in the U.S., the Mission informed them that there were so many needs around the country that there could only be one set of missionaries in Comodoro. Ben and La Nell offered to leave the choice up to the other family, which had arrived there shortly before they themselves had left, and the Pippins chose to stay. A long period of praying and soul-searching began. Among the many requests for help, the Bedfords received an invitation from the South Zone Association in the Greater Buenos Aires Metropolitan Area. Multiple letters were exchanged between them, the Convention, the Association and the Mission, and they gradually became convinced that it should be their new place of service. Just about when they had made their peace with the idea, the Mission wrote that the Pippins had decided not to return to Comodoro after all and the slot was still open. It was a great struggle between heart and mind: if they had been guided by the heart alone, they would have returned like a shot; however, the church had called a capable national pastor and they knew that they were not needed there nearly so much as in Buenos Aires. So, they accepted the South Zone's invitation, with the proviso that at first they would continue to have some responsibilities as interim area missionaries for the Comodoro area.

By the time they reached Rio de Janeiro, 2,700 miles after their first brief stop, everyone had to get used to walking on land again. As in 1957, the Bedfords were met and shown around by friends, this time the Gray family. Dr. Jack Gray had been one of Ben's Missions professors and he was in Brazil gathering first-hand information and perspective on the field.

Rio is a fascinating city. It took over colonial administration from Salvador in 1763 and in 1808 the Portuguese royal family and most of the aristocracy fled there from Napoleon's invasion, making it the only European capital outside of Europe. Prince Pedro proclaimed the independence of Brazil in 1822. Rio was the administrative head of the nation, first of the empire and then of the republic, until Brasilia was made the new capital in 1960.

The Bedfords took in as many sights as they could, crowned by the magnificent view from the enormous art deco Christ the Redeemer statue that overlooks the city, before going on to the next stop in Santos, the busiest container port in Latin America. Ben took advantage of the opportunity to get his hair cut. He was feeling quite pleased with the flow of bilingual conversation with the gregarious barber. He pondered out loud on the fact that the Portuguese-speaking Brazilians tend to understand the Spanish-speaking Argentines better than the other way around, attributing it to the pronunciation characteristics of the respective languages. Spanish has only five vowel sounds and is timed so that all syllables are of equal length, while Portuguese has a much broader range of vowel sounds that can be loosely categorized as open, closed, reduced or nasal and is timed so that stressed syllables are longer than the others. The barber cut into these linguistic musings, allowing his professional courtesy to slip and unmasking the deep-seated Brazilian-Argentine rivalry with a curt:

"Não, é porque argentino é máis burro!"[1]

Ben manfully swallowed this insult to his beloved adopted country and continued to try to understand as much as possible on a bus trip to São Paulo, the largest city of Brazil, with a local church member as tourist guide. The only significant breakdown in communication was when he mistook the Portuguese *falar* ("to speak") for the Spanish *fallecer* ("to die") and wondered who had passed away.

The weather had been turning increasingly cooler as they advanced southward and eventually turned into full-fledged winter.

---

[1]"No, Argentines are just dumber!"

As they rounded Uruguay, they met the waters of South America's second largest drainage basin.[2] Some geographers consider the Río de La Plata a gulf or marginal sea of the Atlantic Ocean, while for others it is a river, the widest in the world, reaching as much as 120 miles across. It behaves like an estuary where freshwater and seawater mix. The huge discharge of its tributaries prevents salt water from penetrating the inner Río de La Plata. The capitals of Uruguay and Argentina are both important ports flanking the river, Montevideo on the east and Buenos Aires on the west. The shipping route is kept open by constant dredging.

The next-to-last port of call was Montevideo, with an overnight stay. The Bedfords were received and shown around by their longtime friends the Bartleys. The family's excitement reached fever pitch: tomorrow they would once again be on Argentine soil!

---

2 It covers an area roughly equal to one fourth of the surface of the entire continent. It includes areas of southeastern Bolivia, southern and central Brazil, all of Paraguay, most of Uruguay and northeastern Argentina. Its main rivers are the Paraguay, Uruguay and Paraná, the latter being its main tributary and one of the longest rivers in the world. These waterways carry an estimated 57,000,000 cubic meters of silt into the Río de La Plata every year, where the muddy waters are stirred up by winds and tides

The Good, the Bad and the Ugly

What kind of vehicle would they be assigned this time? So far, their experience had been mixed. On their first term in Rosario, it had been an ancient and arthritic Humber that forced the family to get around mostly by bus, streetcar and bicycle. During the second term, they had negotiated the long, dusty distances of Patagonia in a sturdy and utterly dependable little Opel station wagon. They had experienced the good and the bad. Now came the ugly: a 1960 Rambler Cross Country station wagon. Pre-power steering and pre-power brakes, it had a three-on-the-tree manual transmission, that is, with the shifter on the steering column, so that it required wrestling rather than guiding. On the other hand, its tank-like design and strength could be a distinct defensive advantage, for this would be traffic on an entirely different level.

Although Argentina was the country with the seventh largest territory in the world, at that time it had only 20,000,000 inhabitants, of which one third, 6.6 million, lived in the Greater Buenos Aires area, making it the sixth largest megacity in the world, after Tokyo, New York, London, Paris and Shanghai. Besides cars, the streets of Buenos Aires teemed with pedestrians, buses, streetcars, trucks and trains. With the port and downtown at its apex in the east, Buenos Aires fanned out beyond the Federal Capital into mile upon mile of solid city in three large administrative areas: North, West and South.

For the first two months, until their assigned house was ready, the family's center of operations was the Capital, in a Mission-owned apartment on the same block as the International Baptist Theological Seminary. They had arrived at the end of June, right before the winter break from school and just in time for Mission Meeting, where Ben was promptly elected president. They enjoyed showing off Nancy and got acquainted with several families they had not yet met. For the older children, all missionaries who arrived in Argentina after they went on their second furlough were forever "new." David was enrolled at Lincoln, the American Community School in the North Zone, and Nelda met with a tutor every morning to catch up on the first half of fifth grade.

Ben had made his initial forays by train, but now he was running up the mileage on the Rambler. Right away he met with the Executive Committee of the South Zone Association, which represented nineteen congregations and was presided over by Francisco "Pancho" Pluís, pastor of the church in Rafael Calzada, but he was shown around mostly by Pastor Quattrocchi of the Avellaneda Norte church, who was quite a character. He confided that he had practically been ordered into the ministry by former missionary Martin Blair. Despite being considered somewhat of a stickler for the rules, he was one of the biggest-hearted of men and was known to travel whatever distance was required to offer consolation when anyone in the Baptist world passed away. The Association asked for Ben and La Nell's help in emphasizing and promoting evangelism, Christian education, fellowship, church planting and Seminary extension programs. At first, every Sunday the family visited two different churches of the Association and soon *Bienvenidos* ("Welcome") became Nancy's favorite hymn, which she could belt out with the best of them.

Frequent trips were also required to supervise the repair and paint jobs at their future residence, recently vacated by the Mills family, now reassigned to Jamaica. It was located in Adrogué, head of the seventh of ten districts south of the Capital.[3] The usual way there was by Avenida Pavón, originally the *Camino Real*[4] that had been used mainly to transport cattle to the stockyards in the early nineteenth

---

[3] These were, north to south, Avellaneda, Lanús, Lomas de Zamora, Esteban Echeverría, Ezeiza, San Vicente, Almirante Brown, Quilmes, Berazategui and Florencio Varela.

[4] A principal road or highway financed by the State, literally "Royal Road," a term left over from the days when the government was the Kingdom of Spain.

century and was now a wide and extremely busy thoroughfare.

The house was very attractive and comfortable, facing a cobblestone street in a pleasant residential area, with neighborhood stores and the railway station within easy walking distance. In fact, the whole town was quite attractive. It had been conceived with an advanced urban design—generous tree-lined streets in a grid, intersected by diagonals, parks and boulevards—whose plans were approved in 1873. Esteban Adrogué donated lands for the railroad, city hall, town square and several important buildings. He wanted to call the train station "Almirante Brown" but the name was already taken. Since it was customary to honor the person who donated the land, it became "Estación Adrogué," and the moniker extended to the town itself, although the name was not legally adopted until the late 1990s. Many of the original buildings, designed by a renowned Italian architect, are still standing today. It became a cultural center and was nicknamed "The Pearl of the South." A great number of the original country houses remained, large buildings in the English or Spanish style, with ample grounds, ornate dark green or black iron gates and fences, and, everywhere, huge shady trees. Jorge Luis Borges, the great Argentine poet and master of the short story, spent a great deal of time there in his childhood and once said: "In whatever part of the world I find myself, when I come upon the scent of eucalyptus, I am in Adrogué."

Humpty Dumpty

Only Nancy regretted the change of furniture. When they unpacked their belongings that had been in storage in Comodoro Rivadavia during their furlough, the Bedfords enjoyed being reunited with so many familiar objects that had represented continuity throughout their numerous moves, but there were some disappointments.

One had to do with Nelda's dolls. She had amassed quite a respectable collection by the time they left Comodoro. There were dolls of all sizes, colors and materials, from babies to brides, miniature to life size. There was even a boy doll whose entire outfit—shirt, shorts, belt, hat and shoes—had been made by La Nell. The little girl received dolls every birthday and Christmas and sometimes in between, for example, when her father returned from a trip. She took turns playing with them all and put them on loving display in a bookcase. Although she had outgrown the tea-party stage, she looked forward to decorating her room with them and enjoying the memories.

The dolls had been carefully packed and placed in storage cabinets above and separate from the closets in the Mission house in Comodoro. Box after box and barrel after barrel were unloaded from the moving van, but the doll boxes were nowhere to be found. Finally, an old suitcase was opened and there were the remains of the collection: perhaps three whole dolls and random pieces—a leg here, a head there—of a few others. They could not be put together again. It remained a sad and rather disturbing mystery.

Another disappointment was the condition of the living-room furniture, which could best be described as pitiful. The Patagonian climate had taken its toll and replacements would have to be found. In the meantime, Nancy enjoyed the indoor sport of jumping up and down on the couch, for once unhindered by her parents, who knew she couldn't make it any worse.

So they began the search. Not far from the Seminary was the furniture district and they found a shop on Avenida Rivadavia that made pieces to order. Except for the beautiful set in Rosario, the Bedfords had always had to settle for basic functionality. Now La Nell chose elegant Louis XVI in walnut, with olive green upholstery for the living-room group and forest green for the dining-room chairs. They were able to order everything but the *bargueño*,[5] for which they would have to wait several years, until the exchange was favorable enough for a reasonable price. This furniture was to accompany them on every move for the rest of their lives.

It was the golden age of antique shopping, with amazing bargains to be found. Over the years La Nell gradually added just the right accessories: light fixtures, lamps, a *dressoir*[6] and even a telephone. It was all beautiful and perfect for entertaining their frequent guests— but Nancy's days of jumping on the couch were over.

---

[5] China cabinet
[6] Small wall-mounted marble-topped shelf and mirror

Solar System

Each family member settled into an orbit that revolved around the home, where, sun-like, La Nell's gravitational pull kept their paths on track. She ran the house, kept everyone's schedules straight and seconded her husband, all the while somehow carrying out her own personal tasks in Christian Education, the Women's Missionary Union, the Association and the Convention.

Nancy was of course the nearest planet and spent most of her time at home, entertaining herself with toys and books indoors, or with the swings in the big back yard, or relaxing in the shade of the lemon tree with its heady fragrance. Most days she wore her hair pulled up into a ponytail, but on Sundays and special occasions it was let down with only a barrette to keep it from falling in her face. Her big sister liked to take her to the neighborhood merry-go-round because she enjoyed it so much, its operator shamelessly favoring her in catching the ring,[7] and because of the sensation she always created. When the sun shone, the little girl's waist-length hair would glow in living gold, silver and copper, so beautiful that people would stop and stare, often with their mouths open.

Nelda's personal orbit extended to a radius of a little over three city blocks. She spent much of her weekends exploring the neighborhood on her mother's old but dependable bicycle from Rosario. She was enrolled at St. Michael's College, a bilingual institution within easy walking distance. In the morning, the school offered the Cambridge program and taught all things British. Nelda

---

[7] It was customary for merry-go-round operators to hold out a ring that the children would try to grab as they went around; the child that caught the ring got a free ride.

acquired a lifelong fascination with English history and was soon able to mimic an upper crust British accent perfectly, but she reserved it for private entertainment. She had been deeply offended by her Language teacher, Mrs. Hall, who on her first test marked her American spelling wrong and perpetually winced at her vowel sounds.

"Can't you at least *try* to sound British?" demanded Mrs. Hall in a maddeningly condescending manner.

"No, I *can't!*" replied Nelda with the most American "a" possible.

Mrs. Hall would grind her teeth and grudgingly give her Colonial pupil high marks because her performance was unobjectionable in all other respects.

Nelda's feelings were somewhat soothed by the attitude of Mrs. García, the school's Anglo-Argentine founder and principal, who was thrilled to have a living example of the wonderful variety of the great English language.

In the afternoon, the school followed the national education program. Nelda's first teacher was amazed that she achieved perfect Spanish in less than a month and La Nell was forced to dispel the idea that they were in the presence of a linguistic genius. She explained their long absence and that re-immersion into Argentine culture had brought it all back.

The school uniform was typically British: white shirt; dark green tunic, sweater, blazer, neck scarf and hat; green and silver tie and knit belt; gray pullover and knee-high socks; brown leather shoes; and abominable green bloomers for physical education.

David's orbit was more elliptical and extended all the way to Olivos, in the North Zone where his school was located. It offered a first-rate U.S. college preparatory education. Initially he lived in a boarding house during the week and went home on weekends. The pension was a large two-story house run by a single middle-aged German surnamed Vieler whom David suspected of being a former Nazi officer, a hypothesis supported by the Mauser rifle mounted on the drawing-room wall. Over a dozen boys from the interior lodged there, half of whom went to Lincoln and half to other schools. There was one bathroom on each floor and showers were taken according to a strict schedule. David was fortunate enough to have a room all to himself on the top floor, and shared breakfast and dinner with the other lodgers. An elderly Swiss or German woman was in charge of cleaning and cooking. She summoned them to meals by rapping out *"Zu Essen!"*[8] There was a train station nearby, Estación Borges, but it did not carry passengers as it belonged to a freight line called Tren de la Costa[9], so the landlord drove the boys to school in his Estanciera,[10] holding the steering wheel Continental-style.

David finally decided that he would rather live at home and make the trip to school every day by public transportation. This merely involved walking three blocks to catch the 7:28 a.m. train, riding to the end of the Roca Line at the Constitución Terminal, catching the subway to the Retiro Terminal, taking a train from the Mitre Line to the Olivos station, and then walking fifteen blocks if time allowed and the weather was fine, or riding a city bus that dropped him off two blocks from school. The reverse process got him home at 4:50 p.m.

However, David did not mind this seemingly onerous program. On the contrary, he took advantage of the opportunity to acquire an intimate knowledge of the place he wholeheartedly adopted as his own. It was fabulous to live in a world-class city. He studied maps and buildings, thereby developing his native bump of locality even more and gaining a working knowledge of a variety of architectural styles. This fascinating melting pot, of a predominantly European and Middle Eastern mixture, connected him with the whole world. He felt a heady sense of freedom: for a few pesos he could go just about anywhere.

Ben's duties covered an area perhaps not as long as David's but considerably wider. He visited all the pastors in the South Zone individually to hear their concerns and learn what he could do to help, and his duties in the Convention and the Mission often took him to the Capital.

The Associational pastors were an outstanding group of gifted, energetic and committed men, most of them close to Ben's own age, many already known by him, some all the way back from his first term. One of these was Daniel Gaydou, who had moved from the

---

8 Time to eat!
9 Train of the Coast
10 Wyllis Jeep Station Wagon

South to lead the church in Adrogué and was generally considered the most handsome pastor in the nation. He and his wife Dolores now had three stair-step boys. The middle son, Alberto, was Nelda's age and usually delivered the messages sent to the parsonage because the Mission house did not yet have a telephone. The infrastructure was old and woefully inadequate, often forcing people to wait for years to get a line. The Bedfords joined the local church right away and the rest of the family attended there while Ben made the rounds of the other congregations and was often invited to preach.

A Monument to Cooperation

As when they were assigned to Comodoro Rivadavia in 1959, the Bedfords were commissioned to start a new church in an area with no Evangelical presence. Apart from tremendous prayer support, the experiences were very different.

In Comodoro they had been forced to "wing it," so to speak. There was no plan and only one family of believers to help. They visited neighbors, handed out fliers and put an ad in the newspaper, meeting first in their home, then in rented quarters and finally in their own church building. When they left after three and a half years, there were two thriving congregations and a school. This time around there was an abundance of planning and support. Within one year, where there had been nothing, a vigorous thirty-nine-member congregation was meeting in its own building.

At their annual session in December 1964, the nineteen churches of the South Zone Baptist Association unanimously voted to begin a new work and requested that Ben be its pastor. They decided that it should be in the Quilmes District, specifically in San Francisco Solano, a place that in the space of ten years had gone from being mostly open country to a city of nearly one hundred thousand inhabitants.

The town's name was due to the fact that its lands had been bought by the Franciscan Order in the mid-1700s and used for plantations called Chacras de San Francisco.[11] They were sold to two private individuals in 1826 and in turn by their heirs to the Tulsa Company in 1948. In December of that year the Government of Buenos Aires authorized their subdivision and sale as well as the foundation of a town. At that point, it consisted of a collection of empty blocks and

---

11 Farms of Saint Francis

dirt roads covered with thistle patches, dotted here and there with lonely little houses. There were no shops, no schools, no medical or postal service, no police and no fire department. As people flocked to Buenos Aires in search of work during the industrial boom, workers began building their houses. The brick-and-mortar type of construction allowed them to do so in stages. Many started with a basic living area and bathroom and, once they moved in, they could use the money that had gone to rent for gradual expansion. The town square with the first park was built in 1958. In 1963 the neighbors formed a commission to work toward municipal autonomy.

A church-planting plan was soon put into action. The project kicked off with a ten-day revival on the main street. Permission was obtained from the owner of an empty lot to set up the Association's tent, which could hold up to 200 persons. The nineteen churches took turns watching the tent overnight, setting up the chairs and sound system, and preaching. They all pitched in to visit the neighbors, hand out fliers and paste posters on walls. Attendance was very good and decisions of faith were made every night.

The next step was to set up a smaller tent loaned by the Emanuel Baptist Church on the permanent site and begin to hold regular services. The lot was only two blocks away from the paved main street and had been bought at a very reasonable price from a widow who belonged to the Quilmes church, pastored by Juan Cornaglia. Materials from shipping crates donated by the Ford Motor Company were used to build a small temporary wooden building. A new missionary family, the Davenports, contributed the container in which they had brought their belongings and it was used as a Sunday School classroom.

Construction soon began on an 850 square-foot auditorium, which required approximately 9,000 U.S. dollars. The Mission loaned $2,000 and the Association and budding congregation raised the remainder while labor was contributed by the new believers and members of other churches. The Woman's Missionary Union (WMU) of the Association collected money for the pews and pulpit. These were made by Pastor Daniel Gaydou, who had grown up in his father's carpentry shop and put his considerable manual skills at the service of

17

all who needed them. A member donated sheet metal from his shop for the baptistry and one of the new converts welded it into place.

The building was dedicated on the first Sunday in October 1965; fifteen persons were baptized in November; the First Baptist Church of San Francisco Solano was organized early in December with thirty-nine members; and it was formally received into the Association at the very next annual meeting after the one in which the project had been voted. A layman who was sitting behind Ben leaned forward and tapped him on the shoulder. He whispered, "I will donate a parcel of land in Solano for new work."

The Association's dream of sparking enthusiasm for opening new works had come true. A mission point was started in the donated lot. Young people from the Association's churches led the effort, beginning with a tent revival in April 1966. Another gift of wood from packing crates was received, this time from the Chrysler Motor Corporation.

The lead article of the May 1967 issue of *The Commission*, the Southern Baptist Foreign Missions Journal, was called "A Monument to Cooperation." It summed up the history of the Solano church and ended with these words on the mission points that grew out of this effort:

> *On the Sunday before Easter a group of men and boys, none of them residents of Solano, gathered at the site. After Bible reading and prayer, they spent the day mixing mortar and laying a foundation for the chapel, though there was not a professional bricklayer among them.*
>
> *Sunday School attendance increased quickly to more than 30. Bible study was begun on Wednesday evenings. A seminary student, Augusto De la Calle, assisted with the services. To the small chapel building three classrooms soon were added. The association provided all the money for this project, and the chapel became a mission of the young church in Solano, with associational young people cooperating.*
>
> *While all this was developing in one suburb, at least 11 other mission points were being established by individual churches in the area, and five of these new works were provided permanent buildings in which to meet. In addition, almost every one of the*

[now] 21 churches was involved in some type of building project for its own growth. Many of the churches have conducted these building programs without outside financial aid, and others have put in a sizable portion of the total cost. It is reassuring to witness the effort these churches put forth on their own.

Who Is Going to Help You Now?

When the project began, the participants had no idea how it would snowball. At the end of the initial revival, participants from the various churches helped take down the tent and put away the equipment. Ricardo Kölln, from Florencio Varela, was helping Ben stack folding chairs in the back of the Rambler.

"Who is going to help you now?" he asked.

"So far, my wife and my children!" answered Ben ruefully.

"You know, I've been thinking and praying about this, and I believe that God is calling me to serve here."

This was wonderful news for the Bedfords, but it was with very mixed feelings that Pastor Schmunk watched this faithful deacon and trustworthy treasurer, a veritable pillar of his congregation, take up the challenge. Like Ben, Ricardo was in his late thirties. He had recently been widowed and had three children—two daughters whose ages matched those of the two eldest Bedford children and a son who was several years older than Nancy. Silvia and Nelda clicked from the very first and soon became inseparable, the beginning of a life-long friendship. Ricardo, son of World War I immigrants, had been born and raised in a German colony in the Province of Entre Ríos, but he had long since gone to Buenos Aires to seek his fortune. He was now the owner of a prosperous small business that anodized and galvanized metal parts. Honest and hardworking, he was always willing to help and many young men got their start working with Ricardo. Later he was instrumental in starting two more new works that became churches.

As the regular meetings got under way, new and old friends joined the effort. The mostly do-it-yourself construction generated a lot of camaraderie and not a few humorous situations. Ben long had a vivid image of himself staggering slightly under the weight of yet another two pails of mortar, preparing to hand them off to the three men plastering the tall brick wall from the makeshift scaffolding. The one on the near end took a step to the right, leaning slightly to catch the hook dangling at the end of a long rope on the handle of the first pail with the confidence born of multiple flawless executions of the maneuver. Yet something must have been different, for the board tilted, slowly at first and then gaining momentum. The first man slid off, the second rolled down the board, and the third was launched into a spectacular summersault high in the air before crashing to the ground, while mortar flew in every direction, generously spattering them all. Thankfully, no one was seriously injured and the incident soon became legend. Ben was irresistibly reminded of one of his little daughter's favorite shows, *The Three Stooges*. They were among the most enthusiastic and generous members of his congregation—Baez, Albornoz and Loberche, the first two new Christians and the third a volunteer from another church in the Association.

The Baez and Albornoz families were the first to be baptized in Solano. Mrs. Baez was pregnant at the time and was later to joke that her son was baptized twice—once with her and once on his own. Mrs. Albornoz was so eager to learn that she volunteered to act as secretary for the Auxiliar de Niñas,[12] the girls' missionary activity, not only to help out but to soak up every bit of instruction.

Mrs. González became a Christian at the mission point and proved to have exemplary faith. Her favorite Bible story was that of Paul and Silas with the Philippian jailer. She took for her own the promise "Believe in the Lord Jesus, and you will be saved, you and your household" (Acts 16:31), and she lived to see it fulfilled as one by one her family members became believers.

Not only did the Bedfords come to know and love a new group of people, they also got to renew cherished bonds. The plans for the worship center and the designs for the pews and pulpit were prepared by none other than José Ragni, the architect with whom they had teamed

---

[12] Girls' Auxiliary, better known as G.A.'s in the U.S.

up for a series of building projects in Rosario and who, together with his wife Delia, had been the first to be baptized in the new building of the First Baptist Church of that city.

The Marzocchis, the family that had helped them pioneer the new work in Comodoro Rivadavia, had recently moved back to Banfield and soon offered their services. They faithfully rode a bus for thirty to forty-five minutes over badly potholed roads in all weathers to teach Sunday School. Although the pavement was only two blocks away, the walk to the church building could be quite hazardous, since the streets turned into squelchy rivers of mud whenever it rained. Even those who went in cars were forced to park on the pavement and go the rest of the way on foot. Umbrellas and galoshes were standard equipment.

Another welcome addition, a little later, was Mercedes Pitoiset, the teenager who had lived with them in Comodoro while she finished school and was now a Seminary student. She struck up a close friendship with Esther Roberto, surgical nurse and sister of the lady who had lent her empty lot for the initial tent revival, and both sisters eventually became believers. Esther's husband Julio was at sea most of the year as chief engineer on a merchant ship, so she attended with her seven-year-old daughter Patricia. This was to prove to be a most important connection for the Bedfords, particularly David.

Par for the Course

Shortly after arriving in Buenos Aires, Ben and La Nell tried an alternative route to the South Zone. It was called the *Camino de Cintura,*[13] and was reached by a continuation of the Federal Capital's ring-way known as the *Camino Negro,*[14] a veritable "black belt" of a road. It had been paved that very year, and the complete absence of lighting made it pitch black at night.

Signs indicating that they had reached Lomas de Zamora rang a bell:

"Didn't that guy on the ship say that there was a golf course around here?" asked Ben.

"Let's find out!" answered La Nell.

They stopped the car, got out and inquired of a passerby if he knew where the Lomas Golf Club was.

"You mean where the *ingleses*[15] play? Sure."

Following his directions, they were soon in open country. It transpired that what the *ingleses* were playing there was not golf but polo, a sport which has been dominated by Argentina since the 1930s. As they pondered their next move, a man approached and asked if he could help. He turned out to be the Vice President of the Lomas Golf Course who just happened to be watching polo that day.

"The golf course is actually right outside of Ezeiza," he explained.

He went on to say that the membership drive had just closed but the Club had a tradition of extending free membership to ministers and their families who lived in the South Zone. The Bedfords became

---

[13] Belt Road
[14] Black Road
[15] English

honorary members, complete with IDs, even for little Nancy, and full access to all benefits, including use of the golf course and swimming pool.

Except for a brief period in Rosario, Ben had not golfed regularly since he had stopped caddying when he was fourteen. He had not been able to practice the sport at all for ten years, until they were in Costa Rica to learn Spanish before going to Argentina. There he played once, with borrowed clubs. His game was somewhat rusty.

"Have you ever seen anyone play worse?" he ruefully asked his caddy.

"Yeah—the guy who owns those clubs," was the dry response.

Before they left the U.S. in 1953, one of Ben's speaking engagements took him through Amarillo, Texas. He stopped at the golf course and purchased a partial set of clubs. During their first term, he played once at the Rosario Swift packing plant's course and once at the country club, but it was expensive.

An interview with a psychiatrist was part of the missionaries' complete periodic medical exams. During their first furlough, the doctor told Ben that he needed to take up an activity to help him relax. Golf was the most attractive possibility, but he felt that it would eat away even more of the little time he had to spend with his family. La Nell offered to learn so they could play together, and they bought a set of clubs each.

When they returned to Rosario and moved from the apartment to a house, they discovered that there was a nine-hole golf course close to them, near the Belgrano railroad. They found that they could just fit in a quick round about once a week during the siesta when no one else was around. La Nell proved to be a natural and looked forward to their outings just as much as her husband. Ben began to regain and build upon the skills he had acquired as a child and teenager, to the point that one day the caddy asked if he had been a professional player. The only appointment Ben ever missed in his life was when he was playing golf and forgot a meeting with the senior area missionary, Thomas Hawkins.

They also initiated their good friend Bill Ferrell into the game. On his very first round he hit a really beautiful spoon shot. Later that evening as he relaxed in an armchair at the Bedfords' house, a dreamy look and wistful smile would steal across his face every time he thought about that ball curving gracefully onto the green. He ended up playing more frequently than they did, on the lush fairways of Córdoba.

In Comodoro Rivadavia Ben played only once, on a dry bumpy course where oil pipelines marked the hazards and the "greens" were made of sand, much like a golf course he had once seen in Odessa, Texas, but on their second furlough they played on several occasions. Once they were in Arlington, and the three college students ahead of them waved them through. La Nell was a bit embarrassed and self-conscious at having to make her next shot under their watchful gaze. Her ball was some thirty or forty feet away from the green; she swung and it arced up into the air, landed on the green and rolled gently into the hole.

"Get out of here!" exclaimed the young men.

Ben even played a couple of times with a broken hand at a golf course in Fort Worth which later became the site of the TCU baseball stadium and tennis courts.

La Nell had learned to play with pointers from Ben but now was able to take advantage of the availability of a pro at the Lomas Golf Club for a few lessons.

"*¡Brava, Señora!* But the follow-through is not so good," he said as he helped her correct her tendency to slice.

One day they gave him a Bible and when they got back from their eighteen holes he had already gone through much of the New Testament.

As far as possible, they tried to play once a week. When they left the South Zone, they informed the Club because they did not want to abuse its generosity. It responded by making them members as long as they lived in Argentina. When they retired, they received a letter giving them access and reduced rates at private golf courses around the world.

Yet another benefit was that they could take paying visitors, who otherwise would not have been allowed to play at all. They often treated friends and overseas guests. Ben and La Nell got to where they were pretty much par for the course, and their children became well acquainted with the language of bogeys, birdies and even eagles.

25

AWOL

"The best laid schemes o' Mice an' Men gang aft a-gley"[16] was a very fitting motto for the Bedfords in 1965.

During the first term of service in Argentina, the Bedfords and their best friends the Ferrells had purchased a lot together with the intention of building a little getaway. Every time one of the couples thought they could manage it, the other was in a particularly tight spot. The two families were now in their third term and had yet to do anything about it.

"At this rate it will never get done."

"Then let's just close our eyes and do it!"

"Okay!"

So they had carefully drawn up their budgets to pay for plans and permits, bricks and mortar, wood and labor—tightening their belts to the very last notch. It was the only time in the Bedfords' forty-year missionary career that the dollar fell and became weaker than the peso, so they were pretty much broke for a good while and had quite a struggle to make ends meet.

But it was worth it—in spite of everything it was definitely worth it, and they were able to use it the very next summer, January of 1966. A local architect by the name of Bonamico drew up the plans for a very serviceable house that made the most of every inch of available space.

The center of the structure was open for the kitchen and dining areas, forming an L to the right at the back with the den. Halfway down on the left the wall opened up onto a small hall with a bathroom in the middle, flanked on either side by a bedroom—to the left Bill and Opal,

---

16 "The best laid plans of Mice and Men go oft astray" (Robert Burns)

to the right Ben and La Nell. Across the hall was the bedroom for the four girls (Lynn, Betty, Nelda and Nancy), just large enough for two built-in sets of bunk beds, each with two large drawers underneath. All three bedrooms had a small open closet as well as a triangular slab of marble rescued from the leftovers of grander building projects and shaped to fit into a corner with a mirror hung above to create a "dresser." Immediately to the right of the front door was another small hall, with a tiny bathroom and a tiny bedroom with bunkbeds for David and Curtis. There was a fireplace in the corner of the living-dining area and a door that opened onto a small porch and stairs leading down into the back yard.

After dismissing the carpenter, whose incompetence literally made La Nell cry, Bill, who was handy with tools, built the cabinets and finished the baseboards. They soon realized that something was wrong with the adhesive that had been used to lay down the vinyl tiles. It began squirting out at the joints whenever weight was applied. They were forced to take up all the tiles, soak them in thinner, scrub them clean, wash and dry them, and then re-lay them with proper adhesive after scraping and cleaning the cement floor to obtain a smooth surface. This involved practically every member of the two families in a veritable assembly line where practice made perfect, although quite a number of rubber gloves were ruined in the process.

The location and the view were fabulous. Not only were they in La Falda, a little jewel of a town in the heart of Córdoba's Punilla Valley, reputed to have the third healthiest climate in the world, they were perched on a hill looking down toward the east onto the town and across to *Cerros Banderita* and *Cuadrado*,[17] with turquoise skies by day and velvety black star-studded skies by night. There were charming walks in every direction and the swimming pool at the Baptist campgrounds was only ten minutes away by car.

The two families were to spend a good part of their summer and winter school vacations there for years, although Ben and Bill had to go back to work in Buenos Aires after a few days and make quick trips whenever they could get away.

---

[17] Mount Flag and Square Mountain

At that time, most of the houses in the area had names rather than numbers, and the new owners went back and forth a good deal trying to come up with just the right thing. In the end, it was Ben (Allen Benjamin) who hit the nail on the head.

"I've got it! We'll name it for all of us: Allen, William, Opal and La Nell. Let's call it AWOL!"[18]

Although it puzzled their Spanish-speaking neighbors mightily, they always got a kick out of the wrought-iron name proudly affixed to the front wall. They had told the Foreign Mission Board's Area Secretary, Dr. Frank Means, about their plans and were able to take him there on a visit. When he saw the sign he chuckled, "You really did it!"

---

[18] Absent WithOut Leave

Gaining Traction

The children soon grew used to seeing their mother hanging from a door. It was one of the few things that could relieve the pain.

La Nell had been in full swing. Besides running the house, keeping all the family members on course with their schedules, hosting innumerable dinners and acting as secretary for her husband, she had an impressive list of activities of her own. At their local church in Solano, she taught Intermediate girls in Sunday School, organized and led the activities of the Girls' Auxiliary, and headed the Women's Missionary Union. In the South Zone Association, she promoted the WMU. In the Convention, she served on the Christian Education Board and represented the WMU on the Executive Committee. In the Mission, she held various positions, from committee member to recording secretary to vice president and acting president.

In the midst of all this hustle and bustle, she began experiencing pain in her lower back and neck, at times very intense and often shooting down her arms and legs. When it persisted over several weeks, it was time to get medical advice. They consulted Dr. Jack Edward Davis at the British Hospital, recommended by their friends Charles and Bernadine Campbell, who had been missionaries in Bahía Blanca, the physician's home town.

Dr. Davis, a second- or third-generation Anglo-Argentine, was a renowned plastic surgeon who had trained under leading doctors in that field in England. He was a founding member of ISAPS (the International Society of Aesthetic Plastic Surgery), of which he was president in 1979 and from which he received two of its maximum awards, for his work on Dupuytren's contracture and on the reconstruction of the auricular pavilion. He was the first surgeon in

Latin America to perform microvascular anastomosis in toe-to-hand transfer, but he had started out as a general practitioner, earning his medical degree in Córdoba, and was an excellent diagnostician. He had become interested in plastic surgery in his native southern Buenos Aires Province from seeing field workers crushed and maimed by farm animals and machinery.

Dr. Davis diagnosed rheumatoid arthritis. This condition would require inactivity during the painful periods of inflammation and contracture, and preventive measures in between. As far as possible, the movements required by sweeping, mopping and ironing were to be avoided. Golf would provide the right kind of exercise when the painful symptoms abated.

He recommended buying a home neck traction unit. A metal support was placed over the top of a door. It held and guided a rope and pulley system with a bag full of water on one end and a heavy-duty cloth halter on the other. La Nell would sit in a straight-backed chair against the door with her head cradled in the halter. The weight of the bag would stretch out the vertebrae, separating them and giving relief to the sciatic and cervical nerves pinched by inflamed tissue.

The initial bout with arthritis kept La Nell in bed for several months. Although Ben was pretty handy around the house, learned how to make biscuits for breakfast (later adding brownies and a few other recipes to his repertoire) and got the kids off to school, his hectic schedule kept him out of the house most of the day. They were forced to admit they needed help and finally hired a young woman from the Province of Santiago del Estero who went by the nickname "Pechi." She lived with them for nearly three years, helping with housework, cooking and babysitting. Nancy spent the most time with her, and it was Pechi who taught her to drink mate. Yerba mate is a green tea drunk from a gourd through a metal straw, with or without sugar. More than a beverage, it is a social ritual for most Argentines. Pechi also introduced the girls to the world of the *novela*, basically soap operas in magazine form, arranged like comic books, with photographs instead of drawings.

The humid weather of Buenos Aires made La Nell's condition worse so that now AWOL, located in the perfect weather of the

Córdoba mountains, became a veritable godsend. Every few months La Nell and Opal would take an overnight bus to La Falda and spend several restorative days there reading, playing cards and relaxing, while they basked in the warmth of the fireplace.

At home, La Nell's bed became the family conference center, where the children would take turns gently sitting or lying down at its foot to go over the day with their mother or join her in a game of gin or canasta. On one such occasion, Nancy and La Nell heard a loud siren. The little girl wanted to know what it meant and her mother explained about ambulances, police cars and fire trucks. They talked about different kinds of accidents and Nancy wondered which would be the most painful way to die. She mused that knives or bullets or fire would hurt.

"I'd rather die from old age," she decided. "But it will be a long time before that happens."

She looked earnestly at La Nell as she unconsciously switched languages: "*¡Pero a vos no te falta tanto!*"[19]

Nancy was quite offended when her mother reacted to her existential ponderings with whoops of laughter.

---

19 "But it won't be that long for you!"

Business as Usual

The little clouds of condensed breath and the proliferation of transistor radios pressed up against the commuters' ears as they waited for the train that cold June morning in 1966 were nothing new. What struck David as unusual as he neared the platform was the intensity on the listeners' faces. When he got within hearing range, he realized that nearly everyone was tuned to the same station—Radio Colonia from Uruguay.

"Something big must be going down!" he thought.

A newspaper vendor who was hawking *La Razón* by blaring "Grampa ousted!" informed him that a widely expected military coup must have taken place. He decided he'd better go home.

After listening to the official announcement that confirmed the removal of President Illia and urged the population to carry on business as usual, Ben drove David across town to school and arranged to have him spend the night with the Ferrells to avoid potential trouble. As it turned out, there were no major disturbances and life went on with barely a ripple, at least on the surface.

Once again, the Bedfords marveled at the way Argentines on the whole took the changing fortunes of their country in their stride and forged ahead. Recessions, devaluations and price hikes alternated in a bewildering and unpredictable manner with social and economic improvements and gains.

Since their arrival in the country in 1953, Argentina's government had gone through an impressive number of changes. They had been in Rosario when Juan Domingo Perón, who had himself risen to power through the military only to establish his own party and be elected democratically, was deposed by the military in the so-called

"Liberation Revolution." General Pedro Aramburu became the de facto president in 1955 and banned the Peronist party.

Elections were held in May of 1958, a few months before the Bedfords moved to Comodoro Rivadavia. These were won by Arturo Frondizi, of the Intransigent Radical Civic Union, aided by a pact with Perón, who was pulling his underground party's strings from exile in Spain. During the next four years, Frondizi managed a wobbly balance on the political tightrope at times twitched and at others yanked by Peronists on one end and the military on the other, but ultimately pleased neither. When Frondizi lifted the ban on the Peronist party in the 1962 elections, it won ten of the fourteen governorships at stake. In March, about four months before the Bedfords left Comodoro, the military decided to take charge and ousted Frondizi, who said he would not resign, commit suicide, or leave the country.

Senate President José María Guido was appointed as Frondizi's successor, while the military once more proscribed the Peronists and dealt with its own internal rivalries between the far-right "red" faction and the relatively moderate "blue" faction, which eventually prevailed and named General Juan Carlos Onganía as Chairman of the Joint Chiefs. A period of "normalization" followed and elections were finally held in July of 1963, while the Bedfords were on furlough. The Radical Civic Union's candidate won with about one fourth of the vote, most Peronists having turned in blank ballots. In the first round of the Electoral College, he was seventy votes short of the required number, but it was finally reached with the support of three small centrist parties.

Arturo Illia, a moderate pragmatist, was a physician with a long and distinguished history of social and political service. Although organized labor initially supported him, secret plans for Perón's return turned it into opposition. Big business was made nervous by his economic and social measures[20] and the military feared the political freedom[21] he allowed. A media campaign was orchestrated to make Illia seem slow, dim-witted and inefficient, and to encourage a coup.

---

[20] Including minimum wage, price control of basic foodstuffs, drug quality and price control and 23% of the national budget dedicated to education
[21] For example, lifting restrictions on Peronists and Communists

Although many years later he was vindicated as one of the most honest and hard-working presidents in Argentine history, political cartoons of the day portrayed him as a turtle or a kind but bumbling grandfather.

With the military running things again, much of what was going on was not made public. Newspapers, radio and television focused on non-controversial topics. Argentines were up to date with sports, books, movies, music and fashion from around the world—no sooner was something new out in New York, London or Paris than it appeared in Buenos Aires. International political news stories were given prominence and often chosen so that careful readers who looked between the lines were able to make interesting parallels with the domestic front.

When their hectic schedules allowed it, perhaps two or three times per year, the Bedfords would make a family outing downtown. It was fun to dress up, because everyone was expected to look their very best. Calle Lavalle was known throughout the twentieth century as the "Movie Street" due to its large number of theaters, and that is where they saw such iconic films as *My Fair Lady* and *The Sound of Music*.

However, once in a while something would happen that hinted at the hidden depths. A case in point occurred on one of the numerous occasions when Ben was headed to a committee meeting of some sort. This time he was in a taxi with two old friends, Ignacio Loredo and Ananías González. They were just passing the Congress building, deep in talk, when a Molotov cocktail exploded right behind them. It hadn't been meant for them; they were unharmed and never knew what it was all about.

Quite an Impact

The vortex of activities into which the Bedfords had been spun was not random. It became apparent that they were merely in one of the hotspots of a complex system. In Rosario, they had seen their church's Sunday School enlargement program expand into a citywide campaign with unexpected offshoots that spread across the country. They were now at another such moment of convergence and expansion.

Ben's election as President of the Mission in 1964 automatically placed him in the Convention's Coordinating Committee for that year. It consisted of an equal number of national and missionary members. Once again he was privileged to be working with an outstandingly talented, committed and visionary group. It came up with a bold idea for growth on a national scale and created the Commission for a Decade of Advance to work on it. Ben was one of its members.

A ten-year plan was put into action immediately. The goal was to grow from 200 churches and 15,000 members in 1964 to 400 churches with 30,000 members by January 1, 1974: 10 new churches in 1964 and 10 more in 1965; 15 new churches each in 1966 and 1967; 20 each in 1968 and 1969; 25 each in 1970 and 1971; and 30 each in 1972 and 1973. These ambitious numbers might not quite have been reached, but there is no doubt that the program had amazing success and gave shape to Baptist work for many years.

Growth was to be achieved through a series of efforts to strengthen the churches' evangelistic spirit; retain new converts; choose strategic locations for new works; have pastors support a circuit of churches near their own; encourage field missionaries to go to new areas with no work; inspire mission points to become autonomous churches; make financial plans for aid, equipment, prefabricated chapels and building loans; deploy Seminary professors and students; and carry out intensive lay training programs for both men and women. All Convention and Mission activities would be geared to support this plan, under the supervision of the Convention through its Executive Board.

It also went hand in glove with the preparations for the continent-wide 1969 Campaign of the Americas whose slogan was "Christ the Only Hope." At that time Jacobo Vartagnan was Chairman and Ben Vice Chairman of the Convention's Evangelism Committee. Vartagnan was ill for a time so a good bit of organization and legwork fell to Ben. Together with Ananías González, he co-authored a practical guide for the churches of the Buenos Aires area for the Simultaneous Campaign of 1968, a lead-in to the Campaign of the Americas the following year.

Meanwhile, encouraged by the success of its initial coordinated effort in Solano and the upsurge of new works, the Buenos Aires South Zone Association planned and executed a Stewardship and Mission emphasis in 1966 and set its sights on opening new home Bible studies as possible mission points and future churches: 66 in '66, 67 in '67, 68 in '68, and so on. Courses were offered throughout the area to prepare laymen, and Ben was pressed into service as a teacher. Enthusiasm was so great that, at the conclusion of his report to the National Convention, Francisco "Pancho" Pluís got a bit carried away: "In the South Zone we have the best association, the best churches, the best pastors and the best missionary!" When Ben returned from a furlough several years later, Daniel Gaydou, who had been in charge of Evangelism that year, caught him up on the South Zone's progress: "I'm afraid we didn't start 68 new home Bible studies in '68," he said very seriously, before breaking into a huge grin. "There were 84!"

The Mission duly went about gearing its efforts toward supporting the Decade of Advance. At the July Mission Meeting following its implementation, Ben declined reelection as President, but he did offer the suggestion of doing something along the lines of a very successful program carried out in São Paulo, Brazil that he had been privileged to hear about on a bus trip between Santos and that metropolis during a stop on the way back to the field. He was asked to present a proposal the next day, so he and his fellow members on the Evangelism

Committee, Charles Campbell and Bill Ferrell, were forced to pull an all-nighter.

What they came up with was a plan to concentrate staff, money and resources in one place to create a veritable "impact." They suggested Córdoba, with the largest metropolitan area in the country after Buenos Aires and Rosario as well as the advantage of already having several missionaries and quite a few resources. The Mission liked the idea but felt that it was a lot of money to put into only one place so it proposed dividing it into two: Córdoba and Tucumán. A committee was formed to coordinate the "Impact Program" and Ben was elected chairman.

The kickoff would take place at the National Convention in Córdoba in April of 1967, with simultaneous revivals in ten places in that city, and thirty couples would be prepared to do personal work. Tucumán's kickoff would be in September. Some missionaries were already in place and others were appointed as they arrived: Córdoba had the Malones, Mines, Taylors, Saunkeahs and Johnsons, while the Baileys and the Reeves went to Tucumán.

The Bedfords were able to participate in both initial campaigns. Since it was before the seatbelt law was in force, Ben managed to cram about eight Seminary students into the long-suffering Rambler for the trip to Córdoba, but it was in Tucumán that the appositeness of the program's name was borne in upon him in a forceful and tangible manner. They were staying with the Baileys and the men left to pick up Pastor Horacio Juárez at the train station. On the way they were struck by another vehicle.

"You go on ahead in a taxi while I deal with this," suggested Doyle.

Ben flagged down the next cab and climbed in. It had barely gotten under way before it was involved in a second crash. In the end, he and Doyle arrived at the station at about the same time. Ben had received a double impact in less than five minutes!

37

Rail Jockeys and Dragons

"Why don't you run on up while I find a place to park the car?" asked Ben.

"No, I'd rather go with you," replied Nelda.

As usual, getting to the appointment with the orthodontist on time was going to be a very close call. Choosing the method of transportation and the time to leave home was always somewhat of a gamble.

Sometimes they went on public transportation, which usually ran pretty much on schedule, but took a very long time and was a bit wearing. They had to walk several blocks to the station in Adrogué, take a train to the end of the line in Constitución, walk through the huge station to the subway, transfer to another line and then walk the rest of the way to the doctor's office. It was located deep in the heart of the Capital, in the "Once" [22] neighborhood, part of Balvanera, one of the forty-eight legal divisions of Buenos Aires.

The other option was to drive, thus avoiding all the walking, crowds and clouds of cigarette smoke that billowed through the rail cars. However, it was not without drawbacks. They had to traverse the entire South Zone on the very busy Avenida Pavón until they reached the Riachuelo, the river that separates the Province from the Capital. The river had been spanned there by one bridge after another since the late eighteenth century. Several of them fell victim to flooding and one was purposefully set on fire to stop the British from crossing in 1806.[23] The latest, from the 1930s, included a swing bridge to allow

---

[22] Eleven
[23] During the first of the two British Invasions

larger ships to pass. It was usually plain sailing, but if the bridge was up, they were in for a long wait and an impressive buildup of traffic.

Once across the river, there was a series of challenges to be faced apart from the breakneck speed and the lack of anything resembling lanes. Although today Buenos Aires has traffic lights on some 3,500 street corners, more than any other city in the Americas (even New York) or Europe, at that time they were just beginning to appear. The first one was installed in 1958. Most people thought they would never work and, in fact, they were removed for a time but eventually prevailed. Meanwhile, on busy intersections policemen wearing white elbow-to-wrist sleeve covers directed traffic, blowing shrill blasts on silver whistles from elevated platforms that were often protected overhead from sun and rain. Even so, tremendous bottlenecks could form, forcing motorists into exasperating stops and crawls.

Cars vied for space with black taxis with yellow roofs, buses and trucks. Although many commuters traveled by train and subway, the most common form of public transportation was the bus. Originally called a *taxi colectivo*,[24] it was dreamed up in 1928 by eight enterprising taxi drivers over coffee at their favorite café. Because of the economic situation at that time, few could afford taxi fares. They decided to offer to take several passengers at the same time at a reduced rate. The route was down Avenida Rivadavia, from Primera Junta to Flores. At first people were skeptical but the idea soon caught on. Women's initial reluctance was overcome by a clever marketing ploy: free rides for girlfriends and sisters. Regular taxis began by accommodating three passengers in back, one in front and two on the side seats. The vehicles evolved until the average *colectivo* had room for thirty-three seated passengers and the same number standing. Eventually there were 200 routes, distinguished from each other by the buses' numbers and bright colors.

The streets of Buenos Aires were paved, some with asphalt but many with cobblestones.[25] The process began in 1783 and the first cobbles came from Colonia del Sacramento in Uruguay and Martín

---

[24] Collective taxi
[25] Even today, fifteen percent of the streets of Buenos Aires are of cobblestone.

García, an island in the middle of the Río de la Plata. In the mid-nineteenth century, many stones came from Ireland and Wales as ballast in ships from Great Britain that went home loaded with grain. A whole industry grew up in the early twentieth century in the quarries of Tandil, in southeast Buenos Aires Province. The first skilled laborers were immigrants from Italy, followed by others from Spain and Yugoslavia. This age-old trade had at least fifteen specializations, including stonecutters, drillers, stone splitters and draymen. The average output was 250 cobbles per man per day, and the stones were transported to Buenos Aires by train.

Trams had run throughout Buenos Aires, first pulled by horses in the 1870s and later driven by electricity. At their height in 1950 there were sixty-seven lines, but they were gradually phased out in the mid-1960s. However, the rails remained and Ben, like many other drivers, grew quite adept at riding them at top speed, achieving a smooth ride in the midst of bumpy cobblestones.

The length of the trip in terms of time thus depended on the volume of traffic, the position of the drawbridge over the river and how many trains had to be waited for at the crossings. Nevertheless, Nelda preferred being late to going into the office alone. The orthodontist himself, nearing the end of his career, was not only an excellent professional but a sweetheart, exuding grandfatherly charm and benevolence. He was Dr. Ramón Torres, who had developed a very effective treatment for correcting misaligned teeth with removable braces. The front desk, run by his wife-cum-receptionist-cum-accountant, was another story: she was a veritable dragon. Although they had never seen her spout actual flames and smoke, her blistering remarks and stony expression terrified patients and parents alike. She was particularly fierce with any who were tardy or missed appointments.

Appointments with Dr. Torres were a fixture in the Bedford family for many years because, although David's teeth were perfect, first Nelda and then Nancy required lengthy treatments. Eight years of faithfully paying orthodontic bills did not soften Mrs. Torres. She sounded grumpy and skeptical when Ben informed her that he needed to cancel Nancy's next appointment because of a family health emergency. A couple of months later she grudgingly asked about the relative's health. Ben told her that, unfortunately, she had passed away. Mrs. Torres gasped and her face became a mask of anguish.

"I am terrified of dying! I don't sleep at night because I'm afraid I might not wake up."

"I know someone who can help you not to fear death and a book that tells you why," Ben told her.

"I'd like to read that book. Could you get me one?" she asked.

"I'll bring it next time," he promised.

At the following appointment, Ben gave her a New Testament and recommended that she start by reading the Gospel of John. He told her that he and La Nell would be glad to explain anything she did not understand.

"I'll read it and call you when I want you to come," said Mrs. Torres.

A few days later the phone rang.

"I have read the book and I'm very interested. When can you come?"

They arranged to go on Thursday afternoon when the office was closed. Mrs. Torres took them back to the apartment where she and her husband lived.

"Where is Dr. Torres?" they wanted to know.

"You just explain it to me and I will explain it to him," she countered.

After they had answered all her questions and talked a while, they asked if she would like to attend a church service with them. They agreed on the next Sunday evening.

Ben talked to Dr. Tinao, pastor of the Once Baptist Church, the congregation nearest to the Torres' home, so they were expected. Mrs. Torres was amazed at the warm greeting from so many persons who didn't even know her.

"They are nicer to us than at our club!" she exclaimed.

They occupied a whole pew: La Nell at one end, followed by Mrs. Torres, Nelda, Nancy, Dr. Torres and Ben at the other end, so that the couple could not see each other when they sat down. At the end of his sermon, Dr. Tinao made an invitation, and both Dr. and

Mrs. Torres raised a hand in a public profession of faith. They left the church armed with goodwill, offers of help and contact information.

When the Bedfords took them home, La Nell got out of the car to say goodbye. Mrs. Torres turned to her and, to everyone's amazement, embraced her warmly.

"I'm at peace. For the first time in years, I can sleep!"

The dragon had been tamed.

Westward Ho!

Disgruntled muttering hovered in the air as the entire family, on hands and knees, cleaned and waxed the vast expanse of parquet floor. They had just finished this process in the house in Adrogué, leaving it spotless and ready for the new occupants to step in, although when they returned for the last few items that had not fit into the moving van they found Ben's sermons, which had been neatly arranged by books of the Bible and dates, strewn all over the house by disappointed thieves. Now they—the Bedfords, not the thieves—were whipping their new home into shape.

And there was a lot of it. In fact, it was the largest house they ever lived in: entrance hall, living room, dining room, kitchen, breakfast room, three bedrooms, two bathrooms and a garage/boiler room downstairs, plus two attic bedrooms and one bathroom upstairs, to say nothing of a patio and an immense backyard. It belonged to the Mission and had been unoccupied for some time.

They had had to vacate the house in Adrogué so that the new South Zone area missionaries could move in—Charley and Darlene Westbrook with their three children and German Shepherd—because the Bedfords had a new assignment: although Ben would continue to pastor the church in Solano, he would be leaving his Associational responsibilities for a position at the International Baptist Theological Seminary.

The invitation had been made and accepted several months before. On June 6, President Jack Glaze had written:

Dear Ben:

> *The Board of Trustees of the Seminary has requested that a Director of Practical Activities be secured to intensify this phase of training the Seminary now offers.*
>
> *The Director will assume the status of professor on the Faculty after official approval by the Board of Trustees in their called meeting of November 9-10, 1966. In addition, the position will entail an initial teaching assignment as needed while the approach to the area of "Practical Theology" is being undertaken. Eventually, the permanent field of teaching will center in that which is currently known as "Teología Pastoral",[26] or the academic discipline that complements the practical application of "Obra Práctica".[27]*
>
> *After much prayer and consultation with the Faculty and individual members of the Board of Trustees, I would like to offer you this position in a full time capacity, beginning at least by the first of next calendar year. This would enable the preparation of materials and approach for the academic year of 1967.*
>
> *It is with pleasure that I can report a unanimous desire on the part of the Faculty that you join the staff directing the urgently needed "in-training-program". Rest assured that our prayers will accompany you as you consider this invitation.*

The newly assigned residence was in the West Zone of Greater Buenos Aires, roughly a twenty-minute drive from the Seminary. David would have a shorter commute to Lincoln, while the girls would be within easy walking distance of their new school, where Nancy would begin kindergarten and Nelda high school.

This was Colegio Ward, named after George Ward[28] and founded in 1913 with the support of the Board of Foreign Missions of the Episcopal Methodist Church. It opened in March 1914 in the Capital barrio of Flores with three students from Santa Fe Province. In the

---

26 Pastoral Theology
27 Practical Work
28 A U.S. businessman from New York who donated funds to establish a school in honor of his mother Nancy, who had recently passed away and had been passionate about the education of children

beginning, it emphasized business disciplines. An English division was established at the same time—the American Grammar and High School (AGHS), which eventually broke off in the mid-1930s and evolved into the Lincoln School or Asociación Escuelas Lincoln, the only school in Argentina accredited in the U.S.

Over time, Colegio Ward achieved official accreditation from the Ministry of Education and grew to offer classes from kindergarten through high school, with college prep and teacher training programs. It developed a school magazine, literary society, music department with a highly regarded band, philosophy club, student center, sports program and boarding facilities. It progressed steadily toward self-support, until the faculty became wholly national (that is, of the country) and the first Argentine director, Dr. Ernesto Bauman, was named in the early 1960s.

In 1926, the school bought a handsome property in the West Zone, with what was probably the oldest building still standing in the area. It had been the country home of Marta Ramos Mejía, whose ancestor Gregorio had immigrated to Argentina from Spain in 1799, raised a large family and, after a short but productive stint in Upper Peru, bought extensive lands in La Matanza, the first district immediately to the west of the Capital. The property was handed down to his descendants, who eventually had the area mapped and plans drawn up for future subdivision into city blocks. The railroad arrived in 1858 and the family donated four square blocks for the station. Seventeen years later Ferrocarril Oeste was electrified and allowed commuters to pass conveniently from train to subway, promoted with the rhyming motto *"del subte al tren sin cambiar de andén."*[29] Ramos Mejía received city status in 1964.

However, all that mattered to the girls was that they felt very much at home in the school that, like them, was Argentine with an Evangelical background and a love of English. Enrollment was so high that year that a fourth first-year secondary division of the national program had to be created by taking students from the three

---

[29] From sub to trains without changing lanes

overcrowded ones, resulting in a class of twenty boys and five girls, including Nelda.

At that time, the twelve years of school in Argentina were divided into seven years of primary and five years of secondary. High schools had one of four orientations: national (college prep for arts and sciences); normal (certified elementary teachers; college prep for secondary teachers); commercial (certified secretaries and bookkeepers, college prep for accountants and administrators); and industrial (certified builders, electricians and mechanics; college prep for engineers or architects). The first three years shared a basic curriculum and it was possible to change tracks.

Nelda's class remained in the same room while the teachers came and went. The list of subjects was long: Spanish Language, History (Ancient), Geography (General, Asia and Africa), Math (Algebra and Geometry), Botany, Political Science, English, Music, Art, Practical Activity and Physical Education. Core subjects were taught four or five times and the rest once or twice per week. The school year was divided into three quarters and at the end of each there were comprehensive written examinations on three subjects, which the Ministry of Education determined randomly, lottery style, by taking three numbered balls from a sphere that held one ball for each subject, after several brisk turns of the handle.

Kindergarten was in the morning only, so Nelda walked her little sister to and from school, and returned by herself after lunch. She got to know many of the kindergarteners' mothers and could hardly believe her ears when one of them identified her son as "Félix," clearly considering her choice of name very clever since their last name was *Gato*.[30] The poor child was actually called "Félix Gato," like the cartoon. Nancy was thrilled to be going to school, at long last, like the big kids. She was to attend Ward until the middle of the fifth grade. Among other things, her contact with many students from various Christian denominations gave her a broader experience of Argentine Protestantism than her siblings, whose acquaintances were almost all either Baptist or Catholic. Further down the line, this proved to be a source of many fruitful connections for her.

---

[30] Cat

Matchmaker

"Excuse me, Ben," interrupted Foreign Mission Board Area Secretary Frank Means during a briefing with Mission officers held in the Seminary's Board Room, "is there something you don't want me to know about?"

"What do you mean?"

"Well, for starters, you've been giving your report in Spanish."

"Oh!"

The thing was, there were so many committees and so many meetings that sometimes it was hard for Ben to know if he was coming or going. His office in the Seminary was the scene of a daily struggle to keep track of requests and assignments for the Decade of Advance. He could hardly complain because he had been in on the whole thing from its design and launching in 1964. He had scarcely stepped off the ship after the furlough in which he had earned his doctorate when he was elected President of the Mission. As such he became a member of the Convention's Coordinating Committee, which proposed the creation of the Commission for a Decade of Advance, an ambitious program to double the number of churches and members in Argentina in ten years. Ben worked both in its planning and execution as part of the Commission and pastor of a new church in the South Zone Association, where he was area missionary and promotor of new works.

One of the key components of the Decade of Advance was the training of pastors and lay people for the evangelistic effort. The Seminary was to play a leading role by strengthening existing programs, offering new courses for lay people, and putting students and professors out in the field.

The International Baptist Theological Seminary had been established in 1953, the very year that the Bedfords had first arrived in Argentina. It was not really a new institution, but rather the culmination of a long process that had begun at the turn of the century with the first Baptist missionaries who, besides planting and pastoring churches, dedicated a significant amount of time to teaching everything from the basics to systematic theology on an individual basis. The fledgling Mission saw the wisdom of prioritizing education and in 1912 the Theological Training School opened classes to nine students, two of them by correspondence. It was led first by J.M. Justice, until 1917, and then by Sydney Sowell until his retirement in 1942. The institution gradually became known as the Baptist Seminary.[31]

The Mission purchased property at the corner of Ramón Falcón and Bolaños in the barrio of Floresta in Buenos Aires and gained permission for the Seminary to meet there. Outstanding students became leaders in the Baptist work and some of them went on to be professors. There were women students practically from the start and soon they represented half of the enrollment: missionaries, church workers, writers, teachers and directors of departments of theological institutions, as well as pastors' wives.

An Education Board oversaw the institution, first under the leadership of Santiago Canclini and then William Cooper, until it was replaced in 1953 by a Board of Trustees with members from Argentina and the bordering countries of Uruguay, Paraguay and Chile. The Baptist Bible Institute and the Women's Bible Institute from Rosario were incorporated, and the Foreign Mission Board set about recruiting missionary professors with graduate degrees in various fields. The reorganized and renamed International Baptist Theological Seminary soon became the preferred institution for training Christian workers in the South Cone.

Dr. Cooper resigned as Seminary president in 1966 to finish off his missionary career in the field, in the Province of Misiones. Dr. Jack

---

31 See *Mi vida en mi patria adoptiva: 51 años en Argentina [My Life in My Adopted Country: 51 Years in Argentina],* by Luisa Elena Combs (Louisa Combs Hawkins)

Glaze was elected in his stead and Ben officially welcomed him in his capacity as President of the Board of Trustees. Ben was President of the Board and of the Mission when a proposal was submitted to have half the members of the Board of Trustees elected by the Mission and half by the Argentine Convention. The nationalization process continued to advance as more qualified Argentine professors became available and began to occupy an increasingly higher proportion of the faculty and staff positions. The first Argentine president, Dr. Daniel Tinao, was named in 1975 and all twelve members of the Board were elected by the Convention by the end of that decade.[32]

But now the Seminary professors were stretched to the limit and decided that a full-time coordinator was required to keep up with the challenge of the Decade of Advance. They invited Ben as Director of Practical Activities and Professor of Practical Theology beginning in 1967. He used the months between the invitation and the beginning of the school year in March to contact and meet with the pastors and representatives of all the Associations of the Capital and Greater Buenos Aires to learn their requirements.

When classes started, it was his job to find places of service for around 100 students and pass on requests for help from the professors, as well as to coordinate logistics. Some of the students were ready to pastor and others to preach, teach or lead worship. Some of the churches were able to cover the students' weekend travel and boarding expenses, while others required help finding funding, for example through the Fraternal Aid program. Constant contact had to be maintained both with the churches and the students to ensure that things were running smoothly and make adjustments on the way. Ben's filing cabinet filled up quickly.

---

[32] Stanley D. Clark, Sr. "Theological Education in Argentina" in *100 Years of Ministry in Argentina,* Argentine Baptist Mission, 2004.

Just Be Natural

"But, Professor, shouldn't the Holy Spirit be the one leading us to witness?"

This argument was put forth by nervous students in Ben's Evangelism class to cloak their reluctance to speak to strangers in a mantle of spirituality.

"Of course, but I'm sure that you will have many opportunities every week and will be led to act on at least one of them. It will soon become natural."

In addition to writing, each student was required to witness to at least one person during the week. They were then to recount their experiences on tape, so their professor could hear all of them, and take turns sharing with the whole class. The initial grumbling was gradually replaced by excitement as they began to gain confidence and see the fruits of their efforts in many who listened to what they had to say and came to know Christ personally. They also learned to deal with rejection and became more sensitive to when people were ready or willing to listen.

Ben himself never left home without some kind of literature to give away and his trusty little Agenda Bautista, a yearly pocket planner put out by the Publication Board of the Convention that included a directory of all the churches and pastors in the country. If he took a taxi, for example, he almost always found some way of bringing the conversation around to Christ, give away a portion of the New Testament and write down the name, address and telephone number of the nearest church or pastor, or, if the driver wished it, take down his name and information to pray for him and help put him into contact with a church.

Students shared their weekend experiences in the various churches where they were assigned in the Practical Work class. Here, among other things, they learned the nuts and bolts of ministry: how to visit, baptize, give the Lord's Supper, officiate at business meetings, perform wedding ceremonies, dedicate children, organize church ministries, and so forth.

Ben had all the Seminary students in Practical Work and Evangelism, whether they were working toward a degree or a special diploma, and taught other classes as needed. Some courses were designed by track so that, for example, for Old Testament Jack Glaze taught the degree students and Ben the special diploma students.

They had just really gotten into the routine of the school year when the Foreign Mission Board reported that the Sunday School Board wanted to produce a film portraying the fictitious story of a young man from his calling to ministry through his preparation at the Seminary. Several scenes were shot there, including one in the Practical Work class. Ben's was the only voice not dubbed by actors. The film was used countless times to promote missions and Christian education in the United States.

The producer, Don Fearheiley, wrote the following letter on October 31, 1967.

Dear Ben:

Let me thank you for your contribution to the film, FOR MANY TOMORROWS. I believe you did a fine job for us in the film, as we were able to get into your classroom. It isn't easy to act in such a situation. But a great part of acting is just to be natural. And being natural, I feel you came across as good as any other teacher I have photographed. Not only in this film, but others that we have made through the years.

Colleagues and Coworkers

Coordinating Seminary student and professor placement throughout the churches of the Greater Buenos Aires area took networking to a whole new level. Building on skills acquired over years of associational and area missionary work, Ben kept the telephone wires humming, clocked up the miles on the car and public transportation, and sent La Nell's fingers flying over the typewriter keyboard.

There was already a good working relationship with many pastors, especially in the South Zone, and now the circle was broadened. Heretofore most of Ben's contacts with other missionaries had been on committees, but now he saw those who were professors on a regular basis and pressed them into service where there were empty pulpits.

Jack Glaze was President and taught Old Testament. Interestingly enough, Ben was President of the Board of Trustees when Bill Cooper resigned. Up until then the Foreign Mission Board had nominated new presidents and the Trustees had simply approved the candidates. Ben and Secretary José Missena now argued that if the Board was truly to be the governing body it should elect the president. The FMB agreed and Jack Glaze was the first president both nominated and approved by the Seminary Board of Trustees. He had a unique way of admonishing his students to "Take care!" (aiming a finger at them in the manner of a pistol) that was wickedly imitated in many skits. Once, early in their missionary careers, he and Ben were at the market searching for popcorn kernels, but neither of them could remember how to ask for them in Spanish. In their defense, the variety of terms used by Argentines can be confusing: *maíz pisingallo, pochoclo, palomitas de maíz, pororó* or even *pururú*. Finally, Jack told the vendor, "You know, corn that explodes!" That did the trick.

Cecil Thompson was Dean and taught Theology and Ethics, while his wife Jean taught Pedagogy and participated in musical events playing the violin. At one point, they lived next door to the Bedfords and one Sunday Jean sent their son Andy to borrow a bit of butter. He returned with amazing news: "Mommy, Mommy, guess what? The Bedfords are eating in the dining room and using the good dishes, and they don't even have company!"

It was indeed a Sunday lunch tradition at the Bedford home to use a nice tablecloth and set the dining-room table with china, silverware and crystal. The usual menu was eye of round roast (which had been gently cooking while they were at church), rice or mashed potatoes with homemade gravy, and fresh green salad.

Then there was Dan Carroll, who taught Christian Education and was known for his beautiful chalk-art evangelistic presentations. His wife Betty Alice initiated her students into the mysteries of Greek. Back in the Bedfords' Rosario days, Dan and Ben had made a trip to close a property deal in Junín, in northwest Buenos Aires Province, in a venerable old Jaguar formerly assigned to the Watsons. Dan suggested a cross-country short cut, part of which was over an unpaved road. Unfortunately, an axle broke and the time required for repairs forced them to make their separate ways home considerably later than originally planned.

Justice Anderson taught History and Homiletics and had covered Pastoral Ministry before Ben's appointment to the Seminary. The two men shared a profound love of evangelism. Justice crisscrossed the country with mission teams and was instrumental in encouraging home mission pioneers Alba Montes de Oca, Miriam Brunner and Gladys Greca. His wife Mary Ann's many talents included organizing memorable social events. She was the unforgettable roastmaster of a party honoring a Mr. Underwood, who had given a series of lectures on evangelism and publicity. Her imitation, complete with board and diagrams, had them all, roastee included, breathless with laughter. After the furlough in which Justice earned his doctorate, a spoof graduation ceremony was held at the Mission's New Year's Eve party.

Former president Bill Cooper did the honors, capping the presentation in his deep Mississippi accent: "Some people graduate magna cum laude, but in your case, it's 'Lawdy, how come?!'"

Julio Díaz, a native of Santiago Province, had attended the Seminary in Buenos Aires as a young man, striking his professors with his potential. Bill Cooper paved the way for him to go to college in Mississippi, where he saw a very attractive redhead on campus and told his friend, "You see that girl? I am going to marry her." His friend laughed and told him he had no chance, but Julio proved him wrong. The Díaz family had first returned to Argentina as independent missionaries and started a church in Mar del Plata. Recently Julio had earned a graduate degree from Southwestern Seminary and Ben had been the grader who had evaluated his exams in the class on Revelation. Now Julio was teaching New Testament and Dorothy was the official Seminary nurse. Their daughter Gwen was one year and one day younger than David and Nelda was one year and one day younger than their son Walter. Julio's office was near Ben's and he made a point of popping out to see Nancy while she was waiting to be taken home after being dropped off by the school bus. He had a stash of *caramelos*[33] that he shared with her and called her "Nancy Francy." She fully reciprocated his affection.

Stanley Clark, a brilliant scholar and linguist whose main field was New Testament, was Ben's prayer partner, early every school day. Thirty years later, Stanley reminisced in a letter:

> *Kathleen and I remember with a great deal of joy the many happy times we have spent together. It was your initiative that got me involved in many opportunities of ministry, for example, a preaching mission and the organization of the church in Río Grande back in 1965.*
>
> *One of the delights which you and I enjoyed, Ben, was praying together when we had adjoining offices here in the Seminary and both of us served on the faculty. When I meet now with faculty*

---

33 Hard candies

members to pray, my thoughts go back to those times when we prayed together for the ministry of the institution.

At last there was a full-time music professor, Kent Balyeat. He and his wife Lloydene were so beloved by the students that many called them *Mami* and *Papi*. Kent made countless trips to churches and mission points with student groups and a ride in his *Estanciera*[34] was an unforgettable experience. He was a wild and erratic chauffeur who hailed the mad drivers of Buenos Aires as long-lost brothers. Lloydene was a legendary hostess and made beautiful handcrafted candles for every occasion.

Besides his duties as professor, John Cave was Seminary Librarian. One of his great successes was developing contacts in England that resulted in substantial donations and a huge shipment of used books at amazingly reduced prices that greatly enriched both the school stacks and the individual professors' collections. His wife Laura was a talented musician and delighted congregations with her solos and many duets with Kent Balyeat. John was pastor at Florencio Varela, a South Zone congregation, and had worked with Ben by lending not only young people from his church but his own time to help with the mission point in Solano.

Ann Margrett, a veritable institution in herself, headed the Women's Department until her retirement. She was quintessentially feminine and, in addition to academic courses, had taught deportment, etiquette and kindred subjects for years, so that it was with considerable astonishment that Ben witnessed her unexpected performing abilities during a Seminary social hour, in the course of which she crawled up onto the piano. From his very first year in Argentina Ben had often been teamed up with Ann in what the Mission liked to call "oiling committees," special task forces set up to defuse and solve conflicts. In addition to the spiritual side, she was able to understand the cultural aspects of any given situation as both missionary and missionary kid.[35]

---

34 Argentine version of the Wyllis Jeep Station Wagon
35 Her parents were the Sowells.

There was also an impressive group of part-time professors, including psychiatrist Daniel Tinao; physician, pastor and Renaissance man Carlos de la Torre; pastor, Old Testament scholar, journalist and editor Daniel Daglio; and social work champion Sarah Wilson, among others.

Santiago Canclini, beloved elder statesman of Argentine Baptists, fondly known as "Mr. Baptist," was now Chaplain. He had taught, pastored, preached, written and led for decades. David and Nelda remembered his inimitable mop of snow-white hair flapping in the wind during a visit to Comodoro and how he had told jokes and made them laugh (in her case, painfully since she had the mumps).

Juan Ciéslar, a very able and successful pastor, was Seminary Administrator for several years. He was followed by Alberto Pizzicatti, chairman of the deacons at the Bedfords' first church in Argentina, who applied all his brilliance and experience as former General Manager of Rosario's electric utility company to help the Seminary run smoothly. Other good friends from Rosario were there, too: Ananías and Nelly González, Ignacio and María Teresa Loredo, Alberto and Rosa Cáceres, Marcelo and Leonor Rodríguez, just to name a few, now students preparing for full-time Christian service. Ananías and Ignacio were working for the Convention's Publication Board and on literature for Training Union and Sunday School, respectively. Their ties to Christian Education had them collaborating closely with La Nell as well.

One of Ben's most valuable colleagues outside the Seminary was Pastor Miguel Bollatti, secretary of the Convention's Mission Board. He was instrumental in placing students and working out which churches needed help with supporting student helpers. He and Ben spent hours poring over lists and crunching the numbers.

This group of pastors, professors and students yielded an amazing crop of leaders for many years to come. They became pastors, missionaries, educators, musicians and social workers who made lasting contributions not only in Argentina but throughout the world.

Don't Cry for Me, Argentina

"Mom, can you do me a favor?" asked David.

"What is it?"

"Please don't cry when you see me off at the airport. I don't want my last image to be of you in tears."

"Well, I'll try, but I'm not sure I can promise," hesitated La Nell.

David was graduating from high school. The caption under his picture in the school yearbook said, "He walks, he talks, he eats, but mostly he talks!" He was planning to develop that gift by majoring in French. He would be attending Texas Technological College (soon to become Texas Tech University) which, in spite of its name, had a strong School of Arts and Sciences and offered an excellent degree in French, and its location in Lubbock, Texas had the advantage of being near some of the extended family in New Mexico.

His parents and sisters cheered as he spoke at graduation. Traditionally, the salutatorian's speech was the only part of the ceremony in Spanish and it fell to David. The other orator they were interested in was the guest speaker who, astoundingly, was world-renown writer Jorge Luis Borges. Of course, they were just a small part of the proceedings: procession, speeches, diplomas, awards and recession. The whole thing seemed to last forever, especially to five-year-old Nancy. Just when it looked like it was finally over, a woman took the stage to give a long and mournful rendition of *Climb Every Mountain*. For months afterwards, humming the opening bars of that song was enough to send the little girl into a frenzy of irritation.

David turned eighteen in July and dutifully registered with the U.S. Selective Service, which gave him a student deferment. This was important because the Viet Nam War was in full swing. In December of 1969 the order of call for military service for all men born between 1944 and 1950 was determined by a draft lottery. Three hundred sixty-six blue capsules, one for each birthdate of the year, were placed in a water-cooler sized jar and then removed, one by one, and listed in order of appearance, from 001 to 366. The first third corresponded to the draftees, who were sent off to war; the middle group, with numbers 120-240, had a 50/50 chance of being drafted the next year, while the last group was not drafted at all. David's birthday drew number 023, which meant that he would surely have had to go to war when his deferment ended had it not been for his leg, for which he sought and received a IV-F classification, that is, not eligible for military service. As the doctor put it, "The military will not want to bother with you." The slight case of polio in his early childhood kept him from having to make a terrible choice between duty and conscience, a luxury denied to so many young men. Remembering the life-long effect that serving as a medic in World War II had on Ben's brother Ira, the Bedfords were profoundly grateful.

All too soon, the family was gathered at the airport to see David off to college. True to his wish, La Nell made it through the last hug, the last backward look and the last wave without shedding a tear. Afterwards, it was another story.

From Hero to Villain

Braced between forked branches, Ben hugged the trunk with one arm while he reached for a twig with several leaves on it with the other. Through the foliage, he could see cars zoom by beneath him on the General Paz beltway. He climbed down and got into the car, which he had perched rather precariously on the steep embankment. Nelda received the vegetable offering gratefully and jotted down the time and place of collection.

This was the latest addition to her herbarium, the Botany class project which required each student to make a book with some fifty specimens, neatly labeled with specific characteristics. They learned that leaves have an astounding number of features. Their arrangement on the stem (phyllotaxis) can be alternate, basal, cauline, opposite, whorled or verticillate, rosulate or row. Their blades (laminae) can be simple or compound and, in the latter case, palmately compound, pinnately compound (odd or even), bipinnately compound, trifoliate or pinnatifid. Their edges can be entire, ciliate, crenate, dentate, denticulate, double serrate, serrate, serrulate, sinuate, lobate, undulate or spiny/pungent, and there are just as many types of tip, base, surface, hairiness, timing, vein patterning and size.

The catch was that no more than two specimens could be collected at the same place or time. This was unfortunate because the Bedfords' huge back yard probably would have yielded every type of leaf required. As it was, the entire family was on the lookout whenever they went out and Ben's intrepid forays into the urban jungle made him a veritable hero to his eldest daughter.

The pedestal on which she usually placed her daddy crumbled to dust when he and La Nell imparted the plans for the upcoming year. The family would be moving again in January, since the house in Ramos Mejía was needed for the Garners, the new West Zone area missionaries. After a decade of heading the Publication Board, Billy Graves was turning over its reins to a national director, Aldo Broda, and he and Chris were vacating the Mission apartment in the heart of Buenos Aires to do field work in Misiones, so the Bedfords would go there.

That wasn't so bad, but the next item was a bombshell: they would be enrolling Nelda at Lincoln. Neither pleading, nor tears, nor rage were to any avail. Not only would she have to leave her beloved Colegio Ward, which she had considered the perfect stepping stone to university in Buenos Aires, but she would be going into the belly of the beast, thrust into the environment she most wanted to avoid. To add insult to injury, Nancy would be allowed to remain at Ward.

For their part, Ben and La Nell reasoned that at the end of the next year they would be going on furlough and, judging from past experience, it would be easier for Nelda to make the transition if she was prepared for the new system. Besides, they suspected that she would never give the U.S. a chance unless she was forced to do so, and they wanted her to be acquainted with and appreciate their native culture. Then she would be able to make an informed decision about her future.

So Nelda sought solace in her books and records, reading mystery novels and listening to the Beatles, the Mamas and the Papas, the Byrds, and Simon & Garfunkel, courtesy of her big brother who had left her his record collection.

Apartment 3C

Apartment 3C was reached by an elderly elevator with classic double manually-operated scissor-type doors. The ground floor had no number, European-style, so it was actually on the fourth level. Although the building was rather nondescript, with nothing much to distinguish it from hundreds and thousands of others, the apartment itself was roomy and beautiful, boasting a small entrance hall, study, living room, dining room, kitchen, three bedrooms, two bathrooms and a balcony. There were parquet floors, a hatch connecting the kitchen and the dining room, and a small metal door to the incinerator chute in the kitchen.

It was located in the barrio of Balvanera, in the section known as Once, only a block and a half from the Pasteur subway stop of the B Line that runs underneath Avenida Corrientes, so that it was quite easy to get almost anywhere from there on public transportation. Now it was Nelda's turn to learn the stops on which to make connections with other subway lines, trains or buses. On weekdays, she rode the subway for three stops, caught a bus one street over, and got off two blocks from school after a forty-five-minute ride.

Meanwhile, every morning La Nell got Nancy ready for her school day. Having their third child had been pure joy. She was a bright spot in every family member's day and kept them all entertained with her precocious vocabulary and insightful opinions. They told people she was their *yapa*, the extra loaf in the "baker's dozen." But now it suddenly dawned on La Nell that they would have to do first grade all over again! She wasn't sure she could handle it. However, she had already taught Nancy to read in English, which she did beautifully, and they asked the *kiosquero*[36] to save them a copy of *Anteojito* and *Billiken*, weekly children's magazines that contained stories, games and, most importantly from a parent's point of view, articles and illustrations that followed the school curriculum.

It was a rare and precious time for Ben, because he got to share quality one-on-one time with his little daughter while they drove to and from school. Besides lively general conversation, he would tell her Bible stories and she would grill him on the whys and wherefores. He also sang to her. Although he had a beautiful voice, carrying a tune was not his strong point, probably because of his lack of musical education as a child. As La Nell put it, "Never mind, if you were a great singer on top of everything else, it would just be too much," and, anyway, Nancy assured him that she liked his version of many of the hymns and choruses better than the originals.

---

[36] Newsstand attendant

Murals, Clock Chains and Soccer Scores

As always, the Bedfords entertained frequently, both for business and pleasure, and there were many memorable occasions. One of these took place on the Sunday that the Plunks—a missionary family serving in La Plata, the capital city of Buenos Aires Province—visited them for lunch after Mel preached at the morning service in Solano. The two oldest boys, Jamie and Danny, rode back with the Bedfords. The children played while La Nell put the finishing touches on the meal and they waited for the rest of the guests to arrive.

On one of her trips between the kitchen and the dining room, La Nell's eye was caught by a perfect reproduction of a page from a first grade *cuaderno*,[37] complete with name and date, prominently drawn in bright colors on the wall. She summoned Nancy and Jamie.

"Who drew this?" she asked, offering a chance for confession.

Guilty silence.

"Actually, I *know* who it was. You see, Nancy does not know how to spell *Jamie*."

Jamie turned red and hung his head. La Nell dismissed the matter and sent them off to play. This was hardly the first event of its kind with which she had been forced to deal. When Nelda was three she had written on the front wall of the house with black crayon. Lucía, who helped with the housework, was horrified when La Nell set the

---

37 Notebook

little girl to scrub with a brush and a pail of soapy water while tears streamed down her face.

"Don't worry, Lucía. I know she can't get it off, but I'll let her work on it just long enough so that she won't want to repeat the experience."

Nancy, on the other hand, had recently chosen a medium that was much easier to clean for her mural—the glass panels of the balcony doors, so that she had actually been able to scrub it off herself.

Meanwhile, a fascinated four-year-old Danny had yanked on one of the tantalizing weights dangling from the wall clock, snapping the chain. La Nell put the pieces away and hoped no one would be the wiser.

When Susie and Mel walked through the door, practically the first thing they saw was their eldest son's artwork. They were naturally mortified and, although La Nell made light of it, they kept casting reproachful glances at Jamie throughout the meal, until he could bear it no longer and, undoing the Bedfords' tactful silence, he blurted out:

"Well, what about Danny, then? He broke the clock!"

If his parents could have sunk through the floor, they would have.

Because of its convenient central location, meetings were often held at the apartment. One evening La Nell was hosting fellow members of the Education Board. After the third or fourth time she had excused herself for several minutes, her guests exchanged worried glances.

"Poor thing, she must have an upset stomach!"

Little did they realize that the meeting was taking place at the same time that La Nell's beloved Racing Club was battling Estudiantes in the semifinals of the *Copa Libertadores de América*, the most important soccer championship of the Americas. The suspense was killing her, so she was making quick checks on the score on her bedroom radio.

Musical Houses

Lady, the Collie, was telling them all about it. She extended a paw, looking at them with mournful liquid eyes while she uttered a heart-rending series of throaty sounds that clearly asked, "Who *are* you and *where* is my family?"

The Caves had left on furlough and the Bedfords had gone to their house, six months after moving to the apartment and six months before their own furlough. The latest change of abode affected the various family members in different ways.

As far as La Nell was concerned, the main point in favor of the move had been to get away from the neighbors in the apartment immediately above them. The family's son must have been in a band for he practiced his drums assiduously. The mother apparently wore high heels day and night and rearranged furniture as a hobby, judging from the clacking of her stilettos and the scraping and dragging that could be heard at all hours. La Nell adjusted home logistics and continued to juggle her responsibilities as Sunday School teacher and pastor's wife; chair of the Stewardship Committee and member of the Youth Organizations Committee of the South Zone's W.M.U.[38] and corresponding secretary and Executive Committee member of the National W.M.U.; secretary of the Mission's Administration Committee; and chair of the Social Committee of the Seminary.

The Foreign Mission Board paid for one round trip for college M.K.s to visit their parents, so David was back for three months between his freshman and sophomore years, and was in on the transition. He had loved the apartment and its location, but he was just glad to be home and game for anything. Nevertheless, all the

---

38 Women's Missionary Union

excitement must have affected him at some level because one night Ben was startled out of sleep by banging noises. Tracking them down to their source, he discovered a sleepwalking David muttering in French as he purposefully attempted to climb into the closet.

Nancy began riding to school in a van that took her and several other students to Ward. She enjoyed the yard and the dog (once Lady had been taught not to jump, as she was taller than Nancy when she leapt up and put her paws on the little girl's shoulders).

Nelda withdrew into a private world. Her comfortable cultural balance had been upset: English was supposed to be the private language of home and reading for pleasure; Spanish was for everything else. An occasional American (or even a group) was acceptable and at times even delightful. Now, not only did she have to go to an American school, she had to ride there in a vehicle full of American kids and live in "the compound," an area that went through the heart of the block and contained five houses occupied by missionary professors and their families. Although she liked almost everyone at school and in the compound individually and got along perfectly with them all, put together they were overwhelming. Church provided both spiritual and cultural refuge.

On the other hand, for Ben the move meant huge savings in terms of time and wear and tear, since the house was on the same block as the buildings in which he had his office and carried out most of his work. As Director of In-Service Training, he coordinated the placement of 102 students in 58 churches in the first semester and 86 students in 45 churches in the second semester. In addition, he taught Pastoral Ministry, Old Testament Prophecy and Practical Work.

Apart from his Seminary activities, Ben served as chairman of a subcommittee of the Mission's Fraternal Relations Committee. He was the Coordinator of the evangelistic emphasis for 1968 of the five associations of the Greater Buenos Aires area,[39] which would reach its high point with simultaneous campaigns in October. There were numerous planning meetings, crowned by a dinner for the pastors

---

[39] Until recently, there had been only one Association, but as the number of churches grew, it separated into five: Federal Capital, North, West, South and La Plata.

and their wives with 125 attending, representing ninety percent of the churches. Ben also served on the Executive Committee of the Federal Capital Association and on its New Works Commission, together with Santiago Canclini, Víctor Sedaca and Samuel Martínez. A new personal challenge grew out of this.

In their 1968 Annual Report to the Argentine Baptist Mission, the Bedfords wrote:

> *The greatest privilege of every Christian is to be a member of a local church. Until recently, Ben served as pastor of the Solano church and each member of the family had his respective responsibilities. Mr. Raúl Duarte began serving as pastor on March 1. We are grateful that the Lord continues to bless it in a wonderful way. Since April our family has enjoyed working with the Andersons, Caves, Carrolls, Díaz and others in the new work which meets in the Seminary chapel. This work started with 21 decisions in the first revival in which Santiago Garabaya preached. Many of these decisions are the direct result of years of faithful witness by Seminary personnel, in particular that of Kitty Cooper. The work in this community will be slow and hard and we desire your prayers as we seek to make this a true testimony.*

Initially, the new work was led by Ben. When it was time for the Bedfords to leave at the end of the year, Juan Ciéslar took over, and the Thompsons felt called to work with him, lending invaluable aid. Eventually this group and the small congregation of Floresta decided to join in forming a new church they named Betel ("House of God" in Hebrew).

The Hub of the South Plains

Their first furlough without school! For the adults at any rate, since the children, each born in a different decade, were in elementary, high school and college, respectively. Up to now, their time in the U.S. had been spent in Fort Worth, Texas so that the parents could study at Southwestern Baptist Seminary. Ben had earned his Master of Missions on the first furlough, while La Nell had been forced to drop out of her classes toward a Master of Christian Education to spend a month at the hospital in Dallas with seven-year-old David and his badly broken arm. On the second furlough, Ben graduated as Doctor of Theology, while La Nell had to withdraw from two different semesters, first due to her husband's broken hand and then because she came down with double pneumonia.

This time they could choose their destination and they opted for Lubbock, where David was in his sophomore year at Texas Technological College, which became Texas Tech University as he started his junior year. The Hub City, as it was known, also had the advantage of being only 100 miles from Clovis and Portales, New Mexico, where Grandmothers Bedford and Watson lived. After spending Christmas with them and getting a 1969 Buick Skylark from their friend the car dealer in Clovis, La Nell looked for a house to rent while Ben nursed a nasty flu.

The challenge was to find the nicest house possible within their budget. In the field, housing and vehicle were provided by the Mission, but on furlough missionaries had to stretch their meager dollars to cover these costs. However, they got a helping hand from the congregation of the First Baptist Church, which rounded up some furniture, and even lent them a washer and dryer.

The house was at 2824 65th Street, only a couple of blocks away from the elementary school where Nancy entered the middle of first grade. No one there had the least idea where or what Argentina was, and she was frequently asked things like, "Do you eat monkeys there?" and they considered her pierced ears barbaric.

The teacher soon put Nancy in charge of the advanced reading group so she could devote her own time to those pupils who were struggling. One day the class read a story about a Hispanic girl.

"Muh-ree-ah," ventured the teacher. "Is that right, Nancy?"

"No, it's *Ma-rí-a*," said Nancy distinctly, tapping her tongue on the ridge behind her front teeth, just about where the hard English "d" is pronounced.

"Muh-ree-ah."

"No, no. *Ma-rí-a.*"

After several failed attempts, Nancy sighed, "You just have too much 'r'."

At home, she got to ride her new bicycle around the block and made friends with the six children next door, who were being raised by their grandparents and had a bus, converted into a travel trailer. During a visit from his mother, Ben found Nancy and her friends gathered around Mrs. Bedford's chair, breathlessly hanging on to every word, for she was a renowned story teller. Nancy was amazed at the sheer number of things that people had in their houses, as well as the abundance of Formica and carpet. Along with her mother and sister, she was an assiduous patron of the public library.

Nelda was enrolled in Honors classes at Coronado High School, and she got there and back in a student car pool. Since West Texans are nothing if not friendly, she soon became part of a very nice group that quickly overcame her initial cultural aversion. In fact, Bilbo Baggins could hardly have felt more dismay when he viewed the Desolation of Smaug than Nelda did upon surveying the flat, arid expanse that was Lubbock, complete with its own noxious fumes when the wind blew in from the feedlots, somehow failing to see the many parallels with her beloved Comodoro Rivadavia. Used to solid brick and concrete construction, the low ceilings and sheetrock walls appeared flimsy in the extreme, like cardboard boxes that might collapse at any moment. Many things did not make sense to her, for example, the school dress code. On the one hand, the authorities obsessed over the length of the boys' hair and sternly sent girls home to change after literally measuring their skirts (pants were not allowed) if they were more than two inches above the knee, but had no problem with cheerleaders attending their classes all day every Friday in skimpy skirts that did not begin to cover their tiny shorts when they sat down.

There was one run-in with the Math teacher, who was puzzled by the new student's method of division, to say nothing of her crossed sevens and two-stroke ones.

"You should really make your numbers like we do. 'When in Rome,' you know."

"By that reasoning, everyone in the U.S. should cross their sevens: it's in the world and the rest of the world does it like that."

However, she had only one truly unpleasant experience. This was in the History class, where on her very first day she was assigned to the team arguing against the use of marihuana in a debate. She prepared herself and delivered her arguments as forcefully as possible. A girl took exception and considered them a personal attack on her lifestyle. She began shadowing Nelda in the classroom and the hallways, insulting her and even threatening to kill her. Ignoring her did not work and Nelda finally confided in the teacher, who was in turn showered with insults and shoved when he intervened. Not long afterward, the girl was expelled after an unrelated incident led to a locker check that yielded drugs and a knife.

At home Nelda had to rely on the radio for her music, and did her homework to a varied background of the Fifth Dimension's *Aquarius/ Let the Sunshine In*, Credence Clearwater Revival's *Proud Mary*, Elvis Presley's *In the Ghetto*, the Beatles' *Let It Be*, Diana Ross and the Supremes' *Someday We'll Be Together*, and The Archies' *Sugar, Sugar*. That year Led Zeppelin, Chicago and the Jackson Five all brought out their debut albums, but the song that was played over and over in the school cafeteria was Paul McCartney's *Hey Jude*.

The family attended the First Baptist church of Lubbock, where David was already a member. David Ray was its young, energetic pastor and he was an excellent preacher. However, even the best orators are not immune to slips of the tongue, as they witnessed when he described a girl's skirt as being "four inches above the nude." The church was very large and had three well-attended morning services. Ben and La Nell's Sunday School Department had around 150 members, and it was just for people in their forties. David and Nelda were in the college and high school choirs, which sang at the 9:30 and 8:00 Sunday morning worship services, respectively. For the first month or so Ben was the supply preacher for the First Baptist Church of Clovis. He had frequent invitations to speak in different congregations and at revivals, so he explained to the church in Lubbock that he and sometimes the whole family might miss quite a few Sundays. Nevertheless, the church made it clear that they were not mere numbers in a crowd. Whenever they were absent on Sunday, they received a call or a visit the very next day to make sure they were all right.

Ben's far-flung engagements included a conference on evangelism and new works that took place in Guatemala and a variety of Schools of Mission (later called World Mission Conferences), to which missionaries were invited by associations for an initial joint meeting followed by activities with individual churches. One of the most memorable of these took place in a small town in Oklahoma. He spent that Sunday with a Black congregation that met in a small white building. A few minutes after he had arrived and shaken hands all around, the pastor's wife reached up and vigorously shook a bell hanging near the front door of the chapel. The congregation dutifully filed in for Sunday School and the visitor went to the adult class. He was taken by surprise when the pastor announced, "And now Brother Bedford will teach the lesson." Ben pulled his wits together and did the best he could with the allotted text.

As they were winding up the Sunday School class, the bell rang out again, this time summoning everyone to the chapel. After the usual prayers, announcements and singing, the pastor told the congregation,

"And now Brother Bedford will speak to us on Missions." So Ben gave the presentation he had prepared and sat down.

Then the bell clamored for a third time. After the offering and more singing, the pastor graciously announced, "And now Brother Bedford is going to preach for us." A stunned Ben quickly flipped through his Bible and stood up once again to deliver an impromptu sermon.

Besides catching up with the changes that had taken place in West Texas and Eastern New Mexico, where Ben and La Nell had grown up, the family took in the wide variety of events that occurred in the United States in 1969: President Johnson was succeeded by Richard Nixon; a huge oil slick closed down the harbor in Santa Barbara, California; the Boeing 747 had its maiden flight; former President Eisenhower died; Sirhan Sirhan admitted to killing presidential candidate Robert F. Kennedy and James Earl Ray pled guilty to the assassination of civil rights leader Martin Luther King, Jr., although he later retracted; Harvard University was seized by 300 students; the 500, 1,000, 5,000 and 10,000 dollar bills were removed from circulation; Apollo 11 made the first manned landing on the moon; Charles Manson and the Manson Family cult committed gruesome murders; the Woodstock Festival took place in upstate New York; category five Hurricane Camille, the most powerful tropical cyclonic system at landfall in history, slammed into the Mississippi coast, killing 248; the last Warner Brothers cartoon of the original theater Looney Tunes series was released; Chicago had its Days of Rage; hundreds of thousands of persons protested the Vietnam War; independent investigative journalist Seymour Hersh broke the story of the My Lai Massacre; and the first automatic teller machine in the U.S. began operating in Rockville Center, New York.

Sightseeing on a Shoestring

Upon his return from the camp in Missouri, Ben cast a dubious glance at the bed, which had no footboard.

"I'm not sure that I'll be able to sleep without having something to curl my toes around!"

The main task of missionaries on furlough was to report to the churches that supported them and promote missions. There were always many more invitations than would fit in the calendar. Ben and La Nell pored over a map and accepted speaking engagements that would allow them to take the family on a tour of the Eastern and Central United States in the second half of the summer.

After spending time with the relatives in New Mexico, Ben and La Nell attended the Baptist Convention in New Orleans, where David drove his sisters through the rolling hills of East Texas and across the mighty Mississippi River. Reunited, they continued eastward. They drove under the leafy canopies of the southern roads and wound through the lush Smoky Mountains. They saw the historic sites of the East Coast and enjoyed the glassblowing exhibition in Jamestown. They visited the monuments of Washington, D.C. and went to Capitol Hill. In New York they walked around Manhattan, went up the Empire State Building and sailed to the Statue of Liberty. They saw Niagara Falls, disappointingly halved for repairs, and ventured into Canada, where they were amazed by the smooth, silent ride of the subways and the beautiful stations of Montreal. They skirted Lake Ontario and went through Toronto. They passed the skyline of Chicago and finally reached the forests of Missouri and the camp where they were to stay the next three weeks.

Although the trip had been entertaining and informative, they were all ready to stretch their legs and relax. The Skylark was a two-door sedan that had required a lot of climbing in and out. Nancy was not at all convinced by her siblings' argument that she had to sit in the middle because her legs were so much shorter than theirs—she was sure she was the victim of age discrimination. While the motels they stayed in had some creature comforts, like icemakers and swimming pools, sleeping arrangements were rather cramped with all of them in one room, the parents on one double bed, the girls on the other and David on a rollaway. Nelda tried to stay as near the edge of the mattress as she could, but she still got kicked repeatedly by her sleeping sister. And they were all tired of hearing Nelda complain that her foot hurt whenever they walked more than a few blocks—everyone's feet hurt!

The campgrounds were very attractive. There was a swimming pool as well as several nice cabins. But they would not be staying there. Wishing to give them privacy, the organizers put them up in a converted school bus. The seats had been removed and replaced with beds, but the holes where the bolts had been were still open, allowing the humidity to ooze right in. The bathrooms and showers were down the hill, reached by a squelchy mud path. An interesting feature was that the bus was parked on a slight incline, so that the would-be sleepers slipped inexorably down their beds unless they braced their feet against the metal rail at the bottom.

After one night of this, La Nell realized that her arthritis would not survive the full course, so she and the kids abandoned Ben to his fate and drove back to Lubbock. The air conditioner quit working on the way, turning the last leg of the trip into sheer torture. La Nell made an appointment with the doctor to see about Nelda's foot. It turned out that she had a Morton's neuroma which made it feel for all the world like someone was stabbing her repeatedly with a very sharp knife. Surgery was scheduled and she would have to start the new school year on crutches.

Ben returned after three fruitful weeks of camp, full of interesting and inspiring stories, but it was some time before he was able to get rid of the feeling that he would fall out of bed if he had nothing around which to curl his toes.

My Buenos Aires

For the first time ever, the Bedfords arrived in Argentina by air rather than sea and the words of Carlos Gardel's famous tango inevitably came to mind as they flew over the capital city: *Mi Buenos Aires querido, cuando yo te vuelva a ver, no habrá más pena ni olvido.*[40] They had left David behind with one more year of college to go, but had finally convinced La Nell's mother, Nora Watson, to overcome her fear of flying. She had gone with them as far as Lima, where she stopped to spend a couple of months with her missionary son Tom and his family.

Bill Ferrell once again proved that he was a one-of-a-kind friend by moving all their furniture from storage in the Seminary into their new home, the former Carroll house, whose occupants had been reassigned to Jamaica. As soon as was humanly possible, the Bedfords headed to the mountains of Córdoba—to AWOL and the Ferrells—in their latest Mission vehicle, a Chevrolet whose greatest virtue was being new. It was a white, bare-bones, three-on-the-tree standard-drive, four-door sedan with no radio and practically no suspension.

"Why does that sign say 'taller'?" asked Nancy, gazing through the window. "Taller than what?"

"What? Where? Oh, ha, ha! It isn't 'taller.' It's pronounced *tah-sher* and means 'shop,' as in a car repair shop."

Nancy was mortified. Her pride was hurt at losing her Spanish over furlough and her initial strategy was to resist having anything

---

40 My beloved Buenos Aires, the day I see you again, there will be no more sorrow or forgetfulness. (Translation by Joseph Del Genio)

to do with it. A steady stream of visitors stopped by to see them at AWOL, as it was only a ten-minute drive away from Villa Bautista, also known as "Thea," the Baptist camp where Mission meetings and the Argentine Convention's summer camps were held. Several of them, old friends like Alberto and Rosa Cáceres, and Ananías and Nelly González from their Rosario days, but particularly Daniel and Dolores Gaydou, whose church Nancy had attended as a two-year-old, took time to pay special attention to the little girl and talk to her. They broke down the language barrier with love and in just a few weeks her Spanish was back.

Upon their return to Buenos Aires, the Bedfords settled into their new home. Although it was technically in the compound, since its back yard gave onto the space between the other Mission houses, the front door opened onto Laguna, a typical Buenos Aires neighborhood street. Everyone was happy: Ben and La Nell were around the block from the Seminary and Nelda could walk down Laguna to Avenida Rivadavia and catch a bus anywhere.

One of the first routes she used went to Ramos Mejía, where she took her little sister to a tutor every day for a month in preparation for the testing that would allow her to enter the third grade when school started. On the way they practiced multiplication tables, through the fives. Nancy passed with flying colors. She soon got to know the children in the neighborhood and eventually became the only girl allowed on their soccer team. It was commonplace for her to breeze in, looking feminine and delicate with her golden hair floating around her, while she announced brightly, "I made two goals today!"

The family had returned from Córdoba with an important addition to their family—a two-month-old puppy. She was the fifth dog in their lives. The first, a half-Dachshund named Henry Wadsworth Longfellow or "Fella" for short, had gone with them from Rosario to Patagonia, but they had been forced to leave him with another family when they went on their second furlough. While they were in the U.S., Nelda went into a pet store and fell in love with a Beagle puppy, and they proved to be inseparable. When they returned to the field, B.B. (Beagle Bedford) remained with a fellow Seminary student of Ben's, eventually ending up in Virginia, where they had recently visited her on their marathonic summer trip. In Adrogué they had taken in Dusty, an adorable little half-Pomeranian, half-Spitz with a very sweet nature. When La Nell was down with arthritis, Dusty would curl up on the floor beside the bed, quietly dispensing love and companionship. She moved to Ramos Mejía with them but was not allowed in the apartment, so she went to live with Nelda's great friend Silvia Kölln from the Solano church, and they were able to see her from time to time. Finally, there was Lady, the Caves' beautiful Collie, whom they had looked after for six months.

The new puppy was Nancy's. About the size of a Chihuahua, she was actually a miniature Doberman, with the typical broad chest and small hips, perfect in every respect except for her lower incisors, which tended to stick out over her upper lip. Like her full-size counterparts, she was fierce and loyal. In fact, she was a character. Her size earned her the name of *Cosita* ("Little Thing"). She slept in a basket by Nancy's bed, complete with a custom cushion and terrycloth cover and blanket designed and made by La Nell. Cosita considered dog food pellets a joke, fit only to bat around the floor, and preferred dining on fresh beef. The only thing that made her lose her dignity was home-made yeast rolls, for a bite of which she could be cajoled into doing practically anything. She had the run of the house except for the living room/dining room, although she asserted her personality by sitting in the doorway and putting one paw on the parquet of the forbidden room. She was to be Nancy's faithful companion from third grade to college.

A pattern developed on Sunday afternoon. While Nancy was out playing, Ben and La Nell would stretch out on their bed and listen to Racing's game on the radio. La Nell had gotten into soccer by watching it on television as a way to spend time with her son before he went off to college. David had been a fan of Rosario Central since he was tiny, but La Nell started following the game at a time when Racing was televised often on its way to winning the national championship, the South American Libertadores Cup and the World Championship of Clubs. Her heart succumbed as goalkeeper Cejas dissolved into tears when his record ended at 586 scoreless minutes. Ben even watched the second- and third-string games when he had the chance and recognized the players unerringly through the changes of teams and the passing of time.

Meanwhile, Nelda listened to Boca on another radio in the living room. She had been a loyal supporter since she was six years old, when that team had visited Comodoro Rivadavia and she had seen them play in person. It was not only lip service, either, for she bought the Boca magazine out of her allowance money every week and kept up with every detail. Her little sister followed in her footsteps.

Ben scouted out the area for the best stores and soon became a regular at the fresh food market. On one of his first visits, the greengrocer had asked rather condescendingly, "*Norteamericano, ¿no?*"[41]

Ben flashed back, "*Sí. Italiano, ¿no?*"[42]

"*¡Sí, sí!*" he ruefully admitted.

After that, as soon as he saw Ben, he'd call him over: "Look, Mr. Bedford, I've saved you the best!"

Ben often returned from downtown trips delectably laden with fruit—peaches, plums, strawberries or cherries—purchased from sidewalk stalls.

In February Grandmother Watson arrived after her stay in Peru, and lived with them until October, a delightful visit. She finally got to see for herself why her daughter and family were so crazy about this country. She was interested in everything. After a lifetime of farms and small towns, Buenos Aires seemed gigantic and the traffic hair-raising. Although La Nell took her to visit the English-language church on the North side, Nora decided that she preferred going to church with them. She recognized the music of the hymns and recalled their words in English. She was fascinated by the courteous elderly Italian gentlemen in the congregation who always looked impeccable in their Sunday suits. On weekdays, she loved to watch the boys walk to school in their uniforms with blazers and ties. On the way to visit the mountains, she was amazed by the lush land of the Pampas and declared, "If I was younger, I would get me a farm here!" While they

---

41 "North American, right?"
42 "Yes. Italian, right?"

were in Córdoba City, she developed a bad cold and sore throat, and wished to prepare a home remedy. Missionary Rayella Johnson and La Nell were forced to pluck up the courage to go into a store and ask for a bottle of whisky. For their part, the Bedfords' Argentine friends thought Nora was marvelous and adored her.

She would have stayed longer, but she developed a health problem that required an operation and, despite assurances that the medical care there was excellent, she felt that she would be better off at home. So they booked her a flight that would allow her to travel with their good friend Chris Graves, and reluctantly saw her off. Two months later, upon graduating, David came home for nine months as a break before graduate school.

Moving in the Right Direction

Not only were they just around the corner from the Seminary, the Bedfords' new congregation met only ten blocks away, on Directorio Street. This was the Vélez Sarsfield Baptist Church, which had called Ben as its interim pastor to help restore unity and create a forward-looking vision. It had lost a pastor and several members to what was called the "Spiritual Restoration Movement" or just the "Movement" for short.

Church History Professor Dr. Justice Anderson summed it up as follows in *The Argentine Baptist Mission—100 Years of Ministry in Argentina*:

> *Exported to Brazil and Argentina by Pentecostal missionaries from the United States, it was an attempt to attract evangelical churches in Argentina to a renewal of spiritual life through charismatic, Pentecostal worship patterns and doctrine. Its leaders assumed that most of the evangelical churches were spiritually dead (and some were!) and that they were to call out the small numbers of really spiritual people in the churches into "city-wide churches" which met weekly in large theatres to practice charismatic worship emphasizing the "gift of tongues" and the "second blessing." There is not time here to discuss its other manifestations, but suffice it to say that it brought controversy and division to Baptist churches for several years in the 1970s.[43]*

---

[43] p. 219 (2003)

The congregation had enormous potential. There were some wise and delightful elderly couples, mostly Italian. When called upon to pray, they started off in Spanish but soon lapsed into their native language. Then there were the García brothers. Ismael, the eldest, was a successful businessman whose endeavors included a small clothing factory and retail store, where he gave Seminary students sizable discounts. His knowledge of Argentine labor laws helped the Mission through complex red tape to obtain very helpful tax exemptions. Roberto, an accountant, was to become increasingly committed to Christian service and do sterling work as the Convention's Stewardship Promotor and later as Director of the Spanish Baptist Publishing House in El Paso, Texas. The Executive Director of the Convention, Esteban Elías, was another member. Although he was frequently absent on work-related trips, his wife Amalia was a veritable pillar of the church. Missionary Sarah Wilson also belonged to the congregation, which was closely involved in her social work at a nearby Goodwill Center. Ben arranged for a talented couple of newlywed Seminary students, Raúl and Mirta Vázquez, to be assigned to work at the Vélez Sarsfield church and live in the parsonage behind the temple building. There was a small but promising handful of young people and a healthy group of children.

The Foreign Mission Board's new Area Associate Don Kammerdiener and his family joined the congregation. His first experience with church visitation in Argentina took place when he went with Ben to see Carlos Meretta, a young medical student who of late had been somewhat irregular in attendance and participation. Carlos went on to earn his medical degree and marry Seminary graduate Mónica Knopf, with whom he had a wonderful ministry for many years in Pampa del Indio, Chaco, serving an indigenous people, the Tobas.[44]

The Kammerdieners had a large and delightful family. Dennis the Menace had nothing on their small son Donnie. Even the police were involved in what was perhaps his most memorable exploit, when he was about three years old. Legend has it that one night the doorbell rang at around 3:00 a.m. There stood a policeman, holding

---

[44] The Spanish word derives from the Guaraní toway (large face or forehead) but they call themselves and their language Qom (navel).

the little boy in one arm and a tricycle in the other. Evidently Donnie had grown bored in the wee hours and decided to go for a ride. After silently dragging a chair to the door and climbing up to free the bolts and latches, he had crossed at least one street when he was spotted wheeling down the sidewalk of Avenida Rivadavia. The neighbors deduced from his ultra-blond hair that he might belong to one of those North American families on Bolaños Street, and the policeman had tracked them down following this clue.

Of course La Nell devoted herself to teaching Sunday School. Nelda began assisting with the Juniors and was soon put in charge of the Beginners, a tiny but adorable class of two- and three-year-olds who reciprocated her affection. Two of the little girls actually talked their mothers into buying them boots *como la señorita*.[45]

Ben proposed an informal planning meeting, for which the members were to prepare by praying about what God was expecting of the congregation. Roberto García Bordoli, the Church Secretary, prominently displayed five large posters with the names of the various areas of ministry: Worship, Evangelism, Education, Service and Fellowship. The members were asked what the congregation could do in each one of them and, as ideas and suggestions were mentioned, Roberto wrote them down. When they had finished making the lists, Ben asked,

"Do you think we can do all these things next year?"

Heads shook.

"Let's go back over the items and number them by priority."

Once that was done, he asked which of them they felt could be incorporated into the church during the following year.

"Would you like for the pastor, the deacons, the leaders of each area and the treasurer to take these lists and come back with a proposal for next year's calendar of activities?"

The members agreed and soon were able to vote not only on the calendar but also on a budget. The system worked so well that both Ben and Roberto were to use it many times in the future in different places and congregations to help focus their vision and set into practice a concrete plan that reflected it.

---

[45] Like the teacher

Open Hearts

The fragrant and bountiful lemon tree by the Bedfords' front door was a harbinger of things to come.

By the time classes started at the Seminary in March, Ben and La Nell were already in full swing. Besides the church and the plethora of national, associational and Mission committees and subcommittees into which they had once again been drafted, Ben had coordinated the placement of around 100 students. A successful experiment was now launched with five groups of students in as many churches or mission points, to such good effect that the concept grew and developed offshoots with each passing year:

> *One group of 8 students worked with the Association of the Federal Capital in a new work in Villa Lugano. As they did not have a meeting place, they began with visitation. They went from house to house in a 25-block area offering New Testaments. Where there was interest they returned with a New Testament and followed through on the contact. They have been actively working with 65 families. Sixty people attended the first service in the new building. There has been an average attendance of 40 since beginning regular services. Three from the area have been baptized and 4 more are awaiting baptism. The other was an evangelistic group composed of five students. They visited 24 churches where they helped by preaching, giving testimonies, singing and doing personal work.*[46]

---

[46] Annual Report of Ben and La Nell Bedford, 1971

Ben taught four classes and wrote a chapter on church administration for a book on pastoral ministry to be published by the South American Association of Theological Institutes (ASIT). Now La Nell joined him on the Faculty, for she had been appointed Seminary Librarian. A new wing was being added to the Library building and she was in charge of moving the 28,700 books to their new stacks. Generous donations of books were being added constantly, and La Nell saw to their processing, from mending broken spines, to classifying them by the Dewey Decimal System, to typing out cards for the ever-growing drawers of the Catalogue and, while doing all these things herself, training others.

Some twenty-five years later, on the occasion of the Bedfords' Golden Wedding Anniversary, Noemí "Mimí" Zuliani, one of La Nell's assistants who later served as Seminary Librarian for many years, wrote the following in her letter of congratulation:

> *La Nell, I had the opportunity of working with you in the Library. You always made room for me and allowed me to develop.*
>
> *I remember that you always treated me as if we were equal, and there was a big difference! At that time I didn't realize it (I think I was somewhat conceited back then), but years later, thinking about relationships, I recognize that attitude of yours towards me.*
>
> *You had a way of directing and organizing with authority but without authoritarianism.*
>
> *You were at the Library until the last moment, practically with one foot in the car, when you were leaving Buenos Aires. You had so much enthusiasm (not to mention ability) in that task.*

Moreover, it was La Nell who came up with the idea that probably yielded their best teaching opportunities. The students worked very hard on Saturday and Sunday at their church responsibilities, so Monday was their day off. She suggested an open invitation to the single students to go to their home for a time of fellowship and refreshment every Monday night. She called it *Corazón Abierto* (Open Hearts).

There was no set program, and people came and went as they could. Knowing that most of them were far away from their mothers' home cooking, La Nell baked delicious treats and Ben squeezed lemons from their very own tree to make fresh lemonade. Some nights the young people would open up the piano to play and sing. Sometimes they wanted to talk about their experiences over the weekend. At times, they felt like praying or asking questions. At others, they just wanted to relax and have a good time together. The gathering quickly became an institution and was continued for many years, even after the Bedfords left.

Ben and La Nell were also the counselors for the married students. As word of *Corazón Abierto* got around, they wanted something along those lines as well. So they organized regular meetings in the afternoon while the children were at school, for fellowship, prayer and practical solutions of the problems in the apartment building that was the married students' housing. It was fortunate that the lemon tree was so productive and gave fruit all year round, for the married students also wanted fresh lemonade.

Because of Ben's role as coordinator between students and churches and his and La Nell's position as student counselors, they were the natural choice for receiving and distributing donations of clothing from church and faculty members. These were a great help, as most of the students were pursuing their training at great financial sacrifice.

All these activities allowed Ben and La Nell to get to know the students very well and love them deeply.

Showers of Blessings

The Seminary graduation banquet was going beautifully. Everyone and everything looked wonderful. Students, professors, trustees and their families were resplendent in their Sunday best. The dining-room tables gleamed with spotless tablecloths and elegant settings. Gently teasing skits had been performed and touching speeches had been given.

La Nell had a brainwave and engineered a fully functional water fountain in the middle of the room. The canvas swimming pool lent by the Plunk family was invisible beneath its strategic draping and fresh greenery.

The full impact came at the climax of the program, as they sang *There Shall Be Showers of Blessing*. They had gone through the first stanza and were belting out the chorus:

> *Showers of blessing,*
> *Showers of blessing we need:*
> *Mercy drops round us are falling,*
> *But for the showers we plead,*[47]

when the singers became aware that water was in fact becoming more abundant—indeed, it was rapidly spreading across the floor from a leak in the "fountain."

As they exchanged startled glances, two men sprang into action: Trustee William Ferrell and Professor Benjamin Bedford. They flung

---

[47] Showers of Blessing in Baptist Hymnal, Nashville, Tennessee: Convention Press 1956: 264.

off their jackets, rolled up their sleeves, and began mopping while the others finished the remaining verses of the hymn.

The centerpiece had not worked out quite as expected, but there is no doubt that it was a scene the students would never forget as well as a powerful illustration of the ups and downs of their chosen path in Christian ministry.

On the Way to School

The peanut butter sandwich the boys had tossed out the window landed squarely on the windshield of an approaching car. The bewildered driver instinctively turned on his wipers to get rid of the unidentified flying object but merely succeeded in spreading a band of goo across his field of vision. David pressed down on the accelerator and barked at the boys to cut it out.

During the summer, he had pored over city maps and traffic regulations. He took and passed the harrowing test to obtain a professional driver's license in Buenos Aires, and now he had the job of driving the MKs[48] who lived in the compound and along the way to and from Lincoln in the Mission van. Nelda was the only high schooler left and she helped her brother keep the children in check. This was not always easy, mainly because of the constant bickering between Stanley Clark, Jr. and Thomas Lineberger. There was no doubt that Stan, a fiery redhead, was gifted with great intellectual powers that allowed him to run mental circles around most of his peers, but Tom was a wily master at getting his goat, so scarcely a day went by without provocation and retaliation.

On one occasion, they had been separated and were sitting in opposite corners of the back row. Nelda was looking back for some reason just as the van ran over a bump at high speed, so she was able to see the boys being thrust upward with perfect synchronization, smashing their heads into the light fixtures in their respective corners with loud crunches that proclaimed the cracking of the plastic

---

[48] Missionary Kids

housings. They grabbed their heads simultaneously while the rest of the passengers rolled around in helpless laughter.

Of course, Tom and Stan were not the cause of all the awkward situations. One morning, as they were battling the heavy traffic of General Paz, the western beltway of the Federal Capital, one of the tires suddenly came off and went bouncing down the road, while the van careened down the steep bank to the right. Miraculously, no other vehicles were involved, the van did not flip and no one was injured. David stayed behind to deal with the mess while Nelda shepherded the children to school on public transportation and explained their tardiness at the principal's office.

Comparing their experiences, Nelda could not help but feel that her peer group was not nearly as cool as her brother's. They had been all about social awareness, civil rights and protesting the Viet Nam War, but many young people were growing tired of the constant drama and were beginning to turn inward, to focus on themselves. It was the beginning of the "Me Generation." Of the top students of her class, she was the only one planning on studying Humanities in college. The others were set on business or science. Only a handful of her classmates had gone all the way through high school at the same establishment. Most of them were the children of business executives or diplomats and had been shuttled from country to country and continent to continent every two or three years. For them the school was an oasis of continuity in their kaleidoscopic lives.

What they all undeniably got out of their time at Lincoln was a first-rate education. At least four of the high school teachers held doctorates. One of these was a world-renowned scientist, Naum Mittleman, affectionately known as "Doc." In spite of having taught chemistry for decades in high school and college, he never lost his sense of wonder and his eyes would invariably sparkle as he mixed various substances and exclaimed, "Look! Look at the beautiful colors!" Lincoln students read the classics and wrote so many essays and research papers that they could practically organize any project in their sleep. Although foreign language teacher Madame Ruegg was justly feared for her short temper, she used the *Voix et images*[49] method to such good effect that by their third year her students were reading and discussing literature and writing essays in very fluent French.

In no time at all it was the second Bedford child's turn to graduate. Like her brother, Nelda was salutatorian and gave the only speech in Spanish at the commencement ceremony. The siblings travelled to the U.S. together, David bound for a Master's degree at Texas Tech and Nelda to study English Literature at Baylor University. On the way, they made a stop to visit their Uncle Tom in Lima, where they took in the Colonial architecture of that beautiful city and visited the fascinating Gold Museum.

Although Ben had charmed the airline personnel in Buenos Aires into not charging for overweight baggage, in Lima they were sticklers. Nelda was forced to hand over the meager savings she had earmarked to buy some special items before starting college. Her father's maxim, repeated so often that his family had threatened to engrave it on his tombstone, finally hit home: "If you spend it in one place, you can't spend it in another!"

---

[49] Voice and Images

Wait a Minute, Mr. Postman

After three long weeks, there was finally a sky blue-and-white edged airmail envelope in the mailbox, but it was in Ben's handwriting. Much as she loved receiving a letter from her father, Nelda was beginning to have withdrawal symptoms, for she had received at least one letter from her mother every week that she was away from home.

La Nell was a prolific letter writer. Besides typing up all her husband's numerous work-related missives, she was the one who kept up with their large extended family. It had all started two years after she married Ben, when they moved to Fort Worth in 1948 to attend the Seminary. Telephone calls to New Mexico were too expensive, so they had begun writing. For a quarter of a century she and Nora had exchanged weekly letters. La Nell also wrote her siblings and in-laws regularly. In recent years, as David and Nelda had left for college, they had been added to the weekly correspondence list.

When Nora returned to the U.S. after a six-month stay in Buenos Aires, she underwent abdominal surgery. For years, she had been fiercely independent, working to maintain her children and then herself. After she retired, she had continued teaching Sunday School, made weekly rounds to visit the elderly bearing home-cooked goodies, kept a beautiful home flower and vegetable garden, and supplemented her Social Security income by ironing for college students. Now she was not well enough to live on her own and was forced to move into a nursing home. For her part, Ben's mother had been living with his sister Billie for many years, but now she had experienced a fall that broke her hip, which required nursing home care for her as well. Faced with the failing health of both of their mothers, the Bedfords requested permission to visit them at their own expense in December 1971, at the end of Nancy's school year.

The eldest Watson sibling, Kenneth, met them at the airport in Lubbock, but instead of going on together to Clovis, La Nell immediately booked a flight on to Los Angeles on her brother's advice: "Mother is not doing well at all. If you want to spend some time with her, you should get out there right now."

Ben and Nancy stayed at Billie's house in Clovis for several days, spending all available visiting hours with Grandmother Bedford at the nursing home. They were soon joined by David and Nelda. Now they needed to find an affordable way to get to La Nell in California.

Once again, the First Baptist Church of Clovis, Ben's home congregation, came to the rescue. One of the deacons owned an auto repair shop with an adjoining salvage yard. He rather hesitatingly told Ben, "If you don't mind driving it, I have a car in the yard that might just do the trick. It still runs. All you would have to do is make sure the lights and brakes pass inspection."

So they literally plucked a car out of the junkyard and drove it over 2,000 miles at no cost other than insurance and gasoline. While they visited Grandmother Watson they stayed with La Nell's brother W.L., who also took them to his mountain cabin in nearby Arrowhead for a day of sledding after an unusually abundant snowfall. Cold weather dogged them throughout the trip and they were thankful for Ben's expertise at navigating frozen roads on the way back to New Mexico. Through it all, the junkyard car never let them down.

It proved to be their last farewell to Nora, for she passed away two months after they returned to Argentina. She had been La Nell's first and constant correspondent. She was the one with whom La Nell had shared her joys and sorrows, trials and triumphs, challenges and daily doings. Nora's daughter had always been sure of her interest, prayers and sound advice. Now there was a gaping hole in La Nell's life. Every time she took up a pen she was flooded by the realization that their precious long-distance connection was permanently broken. It was two months before she could write anyone again and for a very long time indeed she could not help waiting for the letters that would no longer come.

Career Suicide?

"You're crazy! You are committing career suicide."

That was what many thought, but only one had the nerve to say out loud. In their eyes, Ben had finally "arrived." He had the prestige of being a Seminary professor and occupied key positions on many of the Convention's Boards from where he could be very influential in most areas of Baptist work in Argentina. They simply could not imagine him throwing all that away to bury himself in a tiny church in a small town in the mountains of Córdoba, far away from the centers of power.

To Ben and La Nell, though, it sounded like a slice of heaven. They were not sure how long their nerves and their bodies could keep up the hectic pace of the last few years. One night they had quite a scare when Ben showed symptoms of a heart attack. They raced him to the hospital in a cab, but it turned out to be a classic case of exhaustion. To be sure, it had been a wonderful and challenging time during which they felt the satisfaction of being useful. However, they believed that an important aspect of their work was not to become indispensable, but to train others to perform their tasks. The church where Ben had been interim pastor had been ready to call a full-time national minister again in November. He had been at the Seminary long enough to organize the In-Service Training program and set up a network of connections with the churches and the Convention. It had now been running smoothly for several years and could be competently run by someone else. La Nell had supervised the library's move, organizing all areas, and it was operating beautifully. Capable trainees were ready to take over. Even their beloved *Corazón Abierto* had become an institution and would continue, hosted in turns by other professors.

After returning from visiting their mothers in the U.S., the Bedfords went to Mendoza, in the foothills of the Andes, to lead a Christian Education workshop. On the way home, they spent the weekend at AWOL and Ben preached at the church in Villa Giardino. In the last week of February 1972, they received a letter from that congregation, which met in the Baptist camp facilities, inviting them to pastor the church and help them extend the Gospel in the surrounding towns. By mid-April they were ready to say yes.

When Ben told Jack Glaze that they were praying about this invitation, the Seminary President had said rather wistfully, "When God asked Abraham to sacrifice his son, it was a test. Maybe this is like that: you just have to be willing—you don't actually have to do it!" But he bowed to the inevitable, and the Bedfords were sent off at the end of the semester with the following blessing expressed by the Chairman of the Board of Trustees:

> *Our Lord Jesus Christ always had words of acknowledgment for his servants who showed faithfulness, loyalty and diligence in carrying out their tasks. We believe that attitude should be imitated by all those who claim to be followers of the Master.*
>
> *The Board of Trustees of the International Baptist Theological Seminary, in considering your resignation to the position of Director of Practical Work, at its last meeting unanimously resolved to send you these lines of acknowledgment and gratitude for your efficient, dedicated and heartwarming work at the head of that department.*
>
> *It is the sincere desire of the Board that your passion and spirit of service be richly blessed by the Lord of the Harvest in the new field He has assigned to you.*

Ben and La Nell felt extremely fortunate. They were closing a fruitful chapter of their service and were about to embark on a new adventure in the fields closest to their hearts: evangelism and teaching. Not only that—they would be in one of the most beautiful places on Earth.

Horse Trading

How would the kids react to leaving Buenos Aires? Ben and La Nell were pleasantly surprised when their elder children both expressed warm approval, but of course it would not affect them nearly as much as Nancy, who was now half way through the fifth grade. Except for the year in Lubbock, she had attended the same school since kindergarten and had lived in the same neighborhood since she was six years old. Would she be very upset?

Unlikely as it might seem, it was just the right time for a move. Things were changing in every area of Nancy's life, starting with family dynamics. Although they had weekly news and received visits from her siblings, for practical everyday purposes Nancy was now an only child. The family had just closed a chapter at the Vélez Sarsfield church. School routines had been disrupted when her English teacher had to leave suddenly owing to illness. Neighborhood patterns were shifting as her playmates, most of whom were two or three years older, began attending secondary school and their usual meeting ground in the field behind the married students' housing was closed to non-Seminary related children.

What clinched the deal and made Nancy positively look forward to the move was the promise of her very own horse, a book-inspired dream she had cherished as long as she could remember. One of the first items on the agenda was getting *Canario* ("Canary"), a sweet older bay named for the light-colored body that contrasted strikingly with his dark mane and tail. Since he was not a show horse, the transaction did not make a very big dent in the family finances.

Nelda was home for three months after her first year in college and joined in finding a house, packing their belongings and setting up again, a process the family had perfected to a fine art. The real estate agent showed them several places for rent in La Falda, where the church had asked them to live. The coolest by far was an old place with a cylindrical library, but they chose a nice two-bedroom house on Boulevard Santa Fe (unpaved despite its grand name) that was located only a couple of blocks away from the main street and whose sunroom would be perfect for holding cozy Bible studies. Meanwhile, Nancy was enrolled in school in nearby La Cumbre: English in the morning at St. Mary's and Spanish in the afternoon at Colegio Nuestra Señora de Lourdes, a Catholic school on the village square.

In Glorious Technicolor

Goldilocks would have loved the Punilla mountains: they are just right. The peaks are high, but not too high: 6,400 feet at their tallest and 3,064 at mid-valley in La Falda. There are four well-defined seasons and the weather is dry, but not too dry: practically no rain during fall and winter but plenty of spring and summer showers. Summers are hot, but not too hot: warm enough to swim by day and cool enough to snuggle under a blanket most nights. Winters are cold, but not too cold: light freezes most nights and snow every year in the higher altitudes and occasionally in the lower ones. Nature is benign, but not boring: small tremors may occur at any time, strong winds whip things up in spring, and spectacular electrical and hail storms unleash their brief fury toward the end of the year.

How to explain the allure of this sixty-two-mile long stretch of land and why it is preferred by many over other more imposing, majestic or spectacular sites? Perhaps it is the crumpled folds of the mountains pushing against the smooth sky. Perhaps it is the endless variety of stone, poking out of the hills like bare bones or lying in the streambeds like slumbering giants or crumbled into pebbles, in every hue of gray from silver to charcoal. Maybe it is the range of color in the vegetation, from the ochres of the scrubby bushes and native grasses swaying in the breeze to the vivid reds, purples and yellows of the tiny wildflowers, and the green palettes of the trees that sprang up in the wake of the settlers: dreamy willows, majestic cottonwoods and elms, tall pines and cedars, cloudy eucalyptuses and pointed cypresses. Maybe it is the clean smell of the air and the sudden aromatic bursts of mint, basil, lemon verbena and peperina. Perhaps it is the hypnotic patter of the leaves in the breeze, the soothing gurgle of water dancing down the streams, the crunching of the earth on the footpaths, or the competing bird songs. Perhaps it is the star-studded night sky and the spectacular moonrises. Or maybe it is the combination of all these and, most of all, the amazing quality of the light that alternately brightens and softens the landscape with never-ending variety. The overall effect is paradisiacal—a beauty so deep that it pierces and so peaceful that it heals.

When the Spaniards arrived in the late 1500s, the area was inhabited by scattered indigenous peoples who called themselves *Hênîa* or *Kâmîare* according to their location but came to be known collectively as *Comechingones*.[50] They were sedentary and grouped into independent chieftaincies, living on subsistence farming, llama-pastoring, poultry-raising[51] and hunting-gathering, according to the terrain. As occurred throughout the Americas, the Europeans brought along diseases against which the original inhabitants had no defenses, and most of the Comechingones succumbed to smallpox, measles and certain types of influenza. Nearly all the remaining native population was absorbed by the immigrants, all the more readily because of their Caucasoid features.[52] But the Comechingones left a mark that endures to this day: they are credited with giving rise to the distinctive Cordoban sing-song accent or tone curve that consists of prolonging the pre-tonic syllable, thus *cor-do-o-bés* rather than *cor-do-bés*.

While Córdoba City grew and prospered, establishing the first university in Argentina, developing a thriving industrial and commercial economy, and eventually becoming the second largest city in the nation, the Sierras remained largely unpopulated until the advent of the railroad in the late nineteenth century. The beauty of the place and the healthy climate attracted investors and developers. A string of towns[53] grew up northwest from the capital alongside the river,[54] the railroad tracks and National Highway 38 (unpaved until the 1960s). Most of the year they were sleepy little towns but swelled

---

50 The Spanish approximation of the war cry *Kom-chingón* ("Death to them")
51 *Pava de monte*, literally "mountain turkey," dusky-legged guan
52 Interestingly, around ten percent of them had green eyes
53 Villa Carlos Paz, Bialet Massé, Santa María de Punilla, Cosquín, Casa Grande, Valle Hermoso, La Falda, Huerta Grande, Villa Giardino, La Cumbre, Los Cocos, San Esteban and Capilla del Monte
54 Known both as Río Grande de Punilla and Río San Francisco

to several times their size during the tourist season, for the Sierras became the second most popular national vacation destination after the beaches of Mar del Plata.

Each place had an interesting and colorful history. A German army officer named Robert Bahlcke inspected the Sierras on horseback and bought a 900-hectare[55] property on which he built a luxury hotel. He also bought property beside the railroad tracks for a station and a long strip between the two holdings. The hotel attracted national and foreign aristocrats, politicians and celebrities, reaching its heyday between the two world wars. The greater part of the property was eventually subdivided and sold, initially to wealthy families for vacation homes. In the 1920s the owners were a German couple, the Eichhorns, who met Adolf Hitler at the beginning of his career in Austria and became fervent admirers and supporters. By 1934 La Falda had its own municipality, public institutions and thriving businesses. The Eden Hotel went along adding chalets, a golf course, theater, skating rink, ballroom, swimming pool and stables. Shortly before World War II came to an end, Argentina declared war on the Axis and the hotel was confiscated to serve as a luxury prison for the members of the Japanese diplomatic corps. Two years later it was returned to the owners, who sold it to a private national company. It struggled financially for years and finally closed its doors in 1965. It was left to decay for two long decades, until it was declared a Municipal Historical Monument in 1988 and eventually became a museum.

Meanwhile, under Perón's populist government, trade unions built hotels in the country's main tourist destinations. Part of the workers' benefits was to stay there free of charge and receive discounts on transportation. The Sierras had the greatest concentration of these vacation colonies, which numbered around twenty-three by mid-century.

For its part, Villa Giardino did not receive its definitive name until 1964. Toward the end of the nineteenth century an Italian engineer named Miguel Thea bought a large tract of land there that was used for limestone exploitation. It had an old windmill for which

---

[55] 2,225 acres

the property was named[56] and that became the town symbol. He donated land for the railroad line and the station bore his name. To this day, the Baptist Camp is referred to as both *Thea* and *Villa Bautista*. Around 1938 Ugolino and Juana Micono Giardino bought the Altos San Pedro landholding and began subdividing it the next year. Mrs. Giardino built and donated a school that was named after her. Despite the town's small size, by 1947 it had inaugurated a Catholic church, the municipality, a theater house, the post office, a maternity ward and a police station. In a play on the Giardinos' name and the storybook prettiness of the town, it has become known as the "Garden of Punilla."

The congregation of the Villa Giardino church was every bit as colorful and varied as the place itself. Amadeo Marconi, the Baptist Camp's first caretaker, was retired but still lived there and was the church secretary. He and the first national administrator, former Cosquín pastor Raúl Bolsani, had begun a Bible study in the early 1960s with their families and some Camp employees and neighbors. The group had grown and attained church status but had never called a pastor, the various leaders taking turns to preach and lead the services. Rubén Simari had now been Administrator for several years and was the church's *encargado,*[57] as lay leaders were often called at that time.

Rubén and his wife Sarita were old friends. They had been part of the young people's group at Distrito Sud in Rosario, the Bedfords' first church in Argentina. Rubén's father had been a hard-working and successful businessman who had passed his skills on to the next generation. Sarita's parents Mario and Margarita Ávalos lived nearby. She attended services regularly, but he was a cantankerous character who only appeared now and then. However, he was the only one with whom Cosita, a kindred spirit, was content to stay when the Bedfords were out of town. The first time, they told him that if the dog gave him any trouble he had could just say "Go to bed" and she would get in her basket. La Nell had to repeat the phrase several times, since he didn't speak English. By the time he needed it, he couldn't quite remember

---

56 El Molino (The Windmill)
57 In-charge

how it went, but his approximation worked well enough: when Don Mario rapped out "Gutenberg!" Cosita hopped smartly into bed.

Sarita's sister Ana lived in La Falda. The Bedfords had met her husband in an unusual manner several years before. While Ben and La Nell were driving through heavy traffic on Avenida del Libertador in Buenos Aires, they became aware of a pick-up truck beside them and when they stopped at a light the woman on the passenger side waved madly. It was Anita Ávalos, whom they had not seen in years! At the next stop, the windows were rolled down in both vehicles and Ana shouted, "I want you to meet my husband Demetrio!"

Demetrio Miciu had paid for his studies toward a degree in Civil Engineering by painting. He came by his talent naturally, for he was the son of an artist. His parents were Constantino[58] and Alejandra Miciu, he a talented painter and she a gifted musician from Romania. They had been forced to flee their native country and leave everything behind except their small son. First, they went to Austria where their second child Georg was born. Eventually they made their way to Argentina and were now in the Sierras. They were low-profile, unassuming, deeply spiritual people with a very simple lifestyle. Georg, known as Jorge, had a United Nations passport as he had no nationality: due to each nation's citizenship laws, he was not Romanian because he had not been born in Romania and he was not Austrian because his parents were foreigners. This suited his bohemian tendencies perfectly. He travelled all over Europe and the U.S., earning his keep with his art. He was to become a very well-known and critically acclaimed painter as well as the unintentional founder of an artist colony in Villa Giardino, commonly referred to as "the hippies."

Carlos and Elsa Balistreri and their daughters Silvia and Patricia were another active family. Carlos was an enthusiastic lay preacher and drove around everywhere in a vintage green Estanciera. There was also a trio of older ladies from La Higuerita, the mainly working-class neighborhood across the highway from the Camp: Doña Justa, Doña Rivadera and Doña Carmen. Mrs. Rivadera was a housewife and her husband a gardener. Their oldest son had moved to Buenos Aires,

---

58 Latinized version of Konstantin

where he worked as a reporter, but they still had two girls at home. Doña Carmen, a widow, was the matriarch of a large family and had spent her working life traveling in the family circus as a trapeze artist.

The challenge was to bring all this rich diversity together as a coordinated and complementary unit. So Ben and La Nell set about making sure that the foundations were strong and stable. Ben began preaching a series of sermons on basic doctrine and teaching a baptismal class for six candidates. La Nell taught the adult women's Sunday School class, chaired the program committee of the Women's Missionary Union, played the piano for the services and produced a weekly bulletin called *La luz del Valle*[59] on the mimeograph.

The congregation worked on preparing a program for the next year and voted its first budget ever. To their surprise, the pledges exceeded the budget by nearly fifty percent and the next year they boldly doubled it. The church owned a lot in town and plans were made to begin construction of a church building. The increased offerings allowed them to purchase a sixteen-millimeter movie projector, a slide projector, a cassette recorder and even a venerable old 1942 Chevrolet bus to use in their education and extension programs.

On Saturday afternoons Ben would pick up a busload of boys from Barrio San Jorge in La Falda and take them to Thea to play soccer. During the break between the first and second halves they would have refreshments and watch a slide show or a film, usually the dramatization of a Bible story or one of the Moody nature series.

Twenty-one years later, during a visit to La Falda, Ben was filling up the tank of his borrowed car at the gas station. The attendant did a double take.

"Aren't you Pastor Bedford?"

Ben nodded.

"I'm one of the boys you used to take to play soccer!"

---

[59] The Light of the Valley

An Awkward Question

"But what exactly *is* circumcision?" asked Nancy.

The others held their breath, eyes wide, but all that happened was that Ben explained it in simple and natural terms, and the conversation flowed on. It became more dynamic than ever as the participants realized that no questions were off limits.

In the spirit of the Decade of Advance, the Villa Giardino church had commissioned its new pastor to work in evangelism and extension in the area. The two other churches in the Valley were currently pastorless. Ben led a mid-week service in Bialet Massé and the laymen from Villa Giardino took turns preaching at the Sunday morning services. He also served as interim pastor of the church in Cosquín, where he went on Wednesdays for visitation and a Bible study on Sunday afternoons. Twelve of the young people enrolled in Seminary extension courses. A committee of four members worked with Ben to carry on the church program while the laymen from Villa Giardino again cooperated with the preaching until the local members worked up the courage to take charge of the services. They doubled their budget and began looking outward for service opportunities. Ben was named Christian Education Promotor for the Córdoba Association and La Nell was immediately coopted to serve in the Associational WMU.

The main focus, however, was on establishing a new work in La Falda. Accordingly, they bought an initial batch of 100 Bibles in a modern language version and began visiting their neighbors and giving away Bibles. By September they were ready to start a Bible study that met in their home, in the sunroom. Quite a few of the neighbors came, as well as Constantino and Alejandra Miciu, who lived nearby. Attendance was sometimes as high as twenty-three, but the average was around fourteen, most of whom had never had any previous exposure to Protestants.

They began by studying the Gospel of John. When they finished, they were curious about how the early Church had developed after Christ's death and resurrection, so they read Acts. Then they asked for something on doctrine, so they went on to Romans and from there to Hebrews.

Almost everyone loved reading out loud, but none more than the retired policeman. He read the Bible with exactly the same intonation he must have used for thousands of police reports and applied the corresponding jargon. Thus "Chapter 3, Verse 1" became "Section 3, Article 1" and so on. His wife hung on his every word and supported him by unfailingly repeating the end of his sentence:

"It was beautiful yesterday, so we went for a walk," he would say.

"Yes, we went for a walk," she would echo.

A few meetings into the study, several of the attendees asked to be taught some of those prayers and were surprised to learn that they could just speak to God freely about whatever was on their minds.

In December, the group was invited to a service of the Villa Giardino church, in which Nancy would be baptized. She had made a public profession of faith at their previous church, Vélez Sarsfield, in Buenos Aires after much soul searching and analytical thinking. She later told her parents that when she got home that day she had rushed to weigh herself on the bathroom scales because she felt so much lighter. Ben loved this and it became a favorite illustration about guilt along with his own "Vinegar, Vinegar!" childhood story.[60]

The baptisms took place in the icy waters of the spring-fed Camp swimming pool. A group from the Baptist Children's Home in Esperanza, Santa Fe was there for a retreat and sang at the service. To everyone's delight, one of the guests from La Falda made a profession of faith and the visitors were so struck by the music that they asked

---

[60] The full story is told in To the Ends of the Earth: High Plains to Patagonia

if they could learn some of those songs. So hymns and choruses were added to the program.

Here, There and Everywhere

On Nancy's first trip alone with her parents she saw the Atlantic Ocean, the Petrified Forest, her birthplace and the Andes. As usual, these amazing sights were simply incidental bonuses. The real reason for the trip to Patagonia was to mediate between the pastor and the congregation in Comodoro Rivadavia. Ben had received letters from both sides that made him understand and sympathize with St. Paul and his efforts of loving but firm admonishment to unite the Corinthians. Thankfully, things worked out and the church reached a new level of understanding and cooperation from which to move forward.

On the way down, they had taken the coastal route and stopped in Puerto Madryn, in the Province of Chubut. Golfo Nuevo[61] is the breeding site for southern right whales from May to December. Across the bay, the Valdés Peninsula is home to penguins and elephant seals. Nancy became acquainted with her siblings' childhood home and her birthplace, Comodoro, which she had left when she was just one month old. On the way back, they took the Western roads, to the lake-and-mountain country. As they went, Ben and Nancy feasted on delectable local grapes, cherries, peaches, plums and pears, while La Nell looked on longingly and drank glasses of milk to soothe her upset stomach, sadly unaware that dairy products were the actual culprits. They made a stop in Bariloche, where they took in the majesty of the Andes, tallest mountains of the Western Hemisphere. They sailed across beautiful Lake Nahuel Huapi to the famous Arrayán Forest now protected in a recently created national park. There were over twelve hectares[62] of

---

61 New Gulf
62 30 acres

giant myrtaceous bushes fifteen meters[63] high and 400 years old, with individuals up to 200 years more ancient than that. Their cinnamon-colored bark and unusual shapes were the inspiration for Walt Disney's forest in the beloved children's film *Bambi*. They spent the night in the very comfortable electric utility workers' hotel—a quid pro quo from one of Rubén Simari's friends.

Accommodations were slightly different when Ben took a bus full of mostly young people from Villa Giardino on an eight-hour trip west to the National Baptist Convention in San Juan, home of vineyards and olive groves. The best that could be said for their sleeping quarters is that they were free. Their hosts had obtained permission for them to camp out in an unfinished high-rise building. There were floors and ceilings (and, thankfully, a bathroom) but no walls or furniture. A local company had graciously lent mattresses for them to sleep on, provided they were kept in their original plastic wrapping. Unfortunately, they were one short, so Ben slept on the cement floor, on top of a blanket. The meetings were a great success and Ben saw many old friends. One of them, missionary Kitty Cooper, had an unusual experience on the way to a session when she fell into a sewer ditch. She emerged messy but unscathed. The Pippins lent their kitchen to prepare sandwiches for the return trip. About an hour away from home, the bus broke down on a bumpy stretch of unpaved road. Most of the travelers got rides but Ben was forced to stay until the vehicle was repaired.

In the U.S., the Bedfords' two eldest children had planned to spend all summer together in Lubbock. David had been translating a proposal that a local feedlot company submitted to the Algerian government. Meetings were set up to hammer out the details in person and the company asked David to go with them to Algiers as interpreter since he already had a firm grasp of the terminology. He would be paid enough for him to spend a week in Paris before returning. It was a golden opportunity and he gratefully accepted, with only a slight twinge of remorse for ditching his sister in mid summer.

---

[63] 50 feet

When their parents heard of it, La Nell said, "Let's see if we can bring Nelda home." So they called the Hulen dorm at Texas Tech and got put through to her room at 5:00 a.m. Central Time.

"Have you registered for the second summer session yet?"

"No," she replied groggily, "that's next week. I'm in the middle of finals."

"How would you like to come home for the rest of the summer?"

Superman had nothing on Nelda: faster than a speeding bullet, she wound up things in Lubbock and two days later was on her way. Her parents picked her up at the Pajas Blancas airport in Córdoba, and when Nancy opened the front door of the house, Nelda was stunned to discover that she was no longer her "little" sister but rather her younger sister, for they were now at eye level.

They were able to afford this trip because the Bedfords and the Ferrells had just sold AWOL to the Simaris. It made no sense to keep a house in the city where they lived and, when the Ferrells visited, they wanted to be together. Financially they pretty much broke even, but the memories were priceless.

A family trip to Buenos Aires was in order. As of May 1973, for the first time in his missionary career Ben had no official responsibilities in the Convention. La Nell, on the other hand, was a member of the Finance Committee of the national WMU and had been put in charge of preparing a program to launch the women's missionary offering. It exceeded the goal by one-and-a-half times, and she was asked to prepare and produce a thanksgiving program at the next WMU Convention in Rosario. Accordingly, on the way home they stopped by Rosario so that La Nell could confer with Daniel Gaydou, now pastor of the First Baptist Church, which was to host the Convention. She asked him to rig up a system for suspending a large cornucopia from the ceiling of the auditorium. She also broke with tradition by choosing a theme song from lay music—*La montaña*[64] by Roberto Carlos, a popular Brazilian singer and composer who also recorded his songs in Spanish. Not only that but, daringly, she chose

---

[64] The Mountain

guitar accompaniment, an unprecedented break from piano and organ in this type of event.

By the time they got home that night, Nelda had lost her appetite and was not feeling quite up to par. Left to her own devices, she would not have dreamed of seeing a doctor for such mild symptoms, but her mother insisted. On the first house visit, the doctor said they might be due to almost anything. When she was informed the next morning that the nausea had disappeared and been replaced by a strong headache, the physician took the patient's temperature, diagnosed appendicitis and ordered immediate extirpation. The surgeon came out of the operating room dangling a grossly swollen and deformed appendix. Although none of the typical symptoms had been present, there was no doubt that in a few more hours it would have ruptured. The worst part of the process for the patient was the IV line, which had taken repeated stabbings to establish and which she had ripped out of her arm before coming out of anesthesia, leaving impressive bruises. On the other hand, the return to the U.S. was her best international flight ever: she was not allowed to carry or lift anything heavier than a small purse.

Building Blocks

Ben soon became quite popular with the construction material providers. He was forever ordering cement, sand, gravel, bricks, wire, steel rods and pipes for three separate building projects.

The first was for the Villa Giardino church. They already had a lot in an excellent location, only half a block from the charming new bus station and one block off the main street. Plans were drawn up, permits obtained and the foundations laid.

The second project was for the Camp. Improvements and additions had been an ongoing process since the beautiful grounds had been purchased by the Mission in the late 1950s. The first new structure had been the *Comedor*,[65] a large two-story building with a hotel-sized kitchen and dining area downstairs, and an auditorium and group meeting rooms (used as bedrooms when necessary) upstairs. It was quite dramatic when the slab between the two floors gave way during construction but, amazingly, no one was injured. *Ruinas*[66] had risen from the rubble and now housed about a dozen rooms of various sizes, several bathrooms, a kitchen and a living area. The house where the administrator lived had been enlarged from one to three bedrooms and from one to two bathrooms, and had added an office. Now two more buildings were in the works, for the Camp was bursting at the seams in the summer: *Casa Nueva*[67] with eight rooms and two bathrooms in the middle, and a kitchen and common area on each end; and *Coqueta*[68] with four bedrooms and two bathrooms on each side,

---

[65] Diner
[66] Ruins
[67] New House
[68] In Argentina it means well-groomed, pretty or stylish

and a kitchen and common area in the middle. Ben was in the thick of this as Chairman of the Camp Board.

The third project was a house in La Falda. In keeping with Mission policy, it would be used by the area missionaries and eventually become the parsonage of the future church. Theoretically it was a loan, but every year that a missionary lived in it the rental cost was subtracted from the construction total. In this case, as in many others, by the time the church was ready for a national pastor the house had paid for itself and cost the congregation nothing.

The first step was to find a lot. When they began putting out feelers, one of the men who attended the Bedfords' home Bible study told them of a friend with property on the main street. He owned and ran a parking structure in Córdoba and could use the money from the sale to improve and expand his business. This sounded promising, so they checked it out. The property turned out to consist of two contiguous lots on the 700 block of Edén. "Downtown" La Falda petered out after about four blocks and then the street became more residential, dotted with inns and vacant lots as it climbed up toward the decaying yet majestic Hotel Edén. So far there was only one building on the main street's side of the block, a house on the corner going uphill. Negotiations began and a hitch developed: the available funds would cover only one of the lots but the owner insisted on selling both. Rubén Simari did some scrambling and came up with Don Domingo Margiotta, a local pharmacist who was willing to buy the other lot as an investment and give them first dibs on a future sale.

Demetrio Miciu drew up the plans for all the projects, but La Nell was the real brains behind this one and he translated her design into architectural terms. The parsonage was to be built at the back of the lot to leave room for a chapel in front. La Nell made scale models of their furniture and planned the rooms to be just large enough to accommodate it. The "public" area would be downstairs and the "private" area upstairs, as pastors' homes see an endless parade of visitors. There would be built ins everywhere: generous pantries, cabinets and drawers in the kitchen; a wall full of shelves, cabinets and drawers in the dining area; roomy closets, drawers and mirrors in the bedrooms; and shelves and filing cabinets in the study. The idea was for a pastor and family to live there comfortably without having to bring much more than a table, chairs and beds. The garage could double as a meeting room. It turned out to be a gem of a house, both charming and practical.

Parenthesis

As usual, furlough seemed to fall at an awkward time. There were quite a number of irons in the fire. Fortunately, they were in a collective endeavor, so they handed off the various concerns to their church members. The Bedfords would be gone for a year and the Villa Giardino church was now able to support a national pastor. They called Esteban Elías, a gifted speaker who had been the Convention's Executive Secretary for many years. He and his wife Amalia and youngest child Adriana would move into the house in La Falda as soon as it was finished to keep things going there until the Bedfords returned and they found a house of their own.

The last furlough had been spent in Lubbock so the family could be with David. Now they would be in Waco, Texas where Nelda was attending Baylor University. They rented a townhouse-style apartment where the girls shared a room and David, now a couple of hours away in Austin, slept on the sofa when he visited. The best feature was the location—at the edge of a golf course, on which the parents were able to play often. Many churches gave financial assistance to missionaries on furlough to help with housing or car payments. A church in Houston sent $50.00 every month toward car rental.

The year went by in a blur. Ben, La Nell and Nancy attended Northside Baptist Church, where Ben helped organize a Deacon Ministry emphasizing service rather than governance. Ben and La Nell participated in World Missions Conferences, camps, Conventions, a Literature Conference in El Paso, Foreign Missions Week at the camp in Glorieta, New Mexico, revivals and other speaking engagements.

Nancy attended a public junior high school, which she found academically easy and culturally fascinating. It was racially integrated and gave her a whole new insight into life in the United States. During a visit from La Nell's missionary brother Tom, his daughter Elizabeth spent a day at school with her cousin. Because there was no room, she had to sit out one of the classes in the reception area. An African-American girl asked if she could sit beside her and soon they were deep into a lively conversation. Suddenly the girl said, "You act just like a girl I know—Nancy Bedford."

"She's my cousin!"

"Where do *you* live?"

"Peru."

"What a family!"

Nelda was in her last year at Baylor. At her parents' insistence, she tacked on a minor in Secondary Education to her double major in English and History, taking four Education courses in summer school and student teaching five junior English classes at Midway High School in the fall. She discovered that she really *was* a teacher. She also got to be present at the football game in which Baylor beat the University of Texas at Austin, winning the Southwest Conference championship for the first time in fifty years.

Their brother was working on a multidisciplinary doctorate in Foreign Language Education at U.T. and giving Spanish classes as a Teaching Assistant. He had learned sign language in Lubbock and spent a summer on B.S.U. missions in a church in Worcester, Massachusetts, where he made friends with a charming deaf family. Now he was teaching a Sunday School class in sign language at University Baptist Church.

The family managed to fit in another of their hop-skip-and-jump trips during the summer. After visiting Ben's mother and sister in Clovis, New Mexico, he and La Nell flew to California and Oregon for Schools of Missions. He stayed on in Oregon and she went to visit her brother W.L. in Los Angeles. The kids drove there, picked her up and headed north along the Pacific coast. They drove through the breathtaking Sequoia National Forest. They visited Ben's brother Ira in Fresno, and enjoyed eating strawberries from his garden and seeing his big standard poodle François jump several feet straight up into the air as if powered by giant springs.

114

Ben was to be picked up in Oregon, from where they would be going to Yellowstone National Park and the Dinosaur Park in Utah on the way back to Texas. His directions had been both confusing and amusing, for they were to recognize the turnoff by a "pile of sawdust." They could not imagine that such a thing could last very long. What if it had blown away?

As the odometer reading indicated that they were getting near, they kept their eyes peeled. Sure enough, it was still there, only the "pile" was actually a gigantic mountain of sawdust: they really were in logging territory!

A Rough Start

Although they were eager to get back to La Falda, it had been very hard to say goodbye to their loved ones, in particular Ben's ninety-year-old mother. She told him:

"Son, I hate for you to leave. At the same time, I'm glad that you are going because I know that is where the Lord wants you. I'll be praying for you. Some of us may not be here next time around. If not, we'll be waiting on the other side."

Taking advantage of the fact that she had graduated early, Nelda went home with them for nine months. At the check-in counter one of her bags was found to be overweight. To avoid the extra charge, she opened them both up right then and there, rearranged a few things and put on her suede boots instead of her shoes. That did the trick.

The Glazes picked the Bedfords up at the airport in Buenos Aires. Jean had prepared a fabulous meal of homemade cannelloni. As they stared at each other across the table, it was hard to say who felt the most dismay: Ben could not eat the dish because the onions would make him violently ill; La Nell because the white sauce and cheese were off limits from her lactose intolerance; Nancy because tomatoes were temporarily forbidden for dermatological reasons. Only Nelda could eat it, and she had never been a fan of white sauce!

Ben had suffered through many awkward meals over the years. In language school in Costa Rica in the early 1950s, he had begun experiencing increasingly frequent and worsening stomach pains. By the time they were living in Rosario, they had identified onions and garlic as the culprits. While they were serving in Comodoro, he had been in Buenos Aires giving a message on First John when he had felt so bad that he had been forced to leave and rush to the British Hospital where he was diagnosed with a bleeding ulcer. He was on a restricted diet for quite some time and La Nell grew very weary of preparing fish. Eating out was always hazardous, as no one seemed able to grasp that "just a little" was too much; in fact, if a knife that had come into contact with onions or garlic touched anything Ben ate, it meant three days of throwing up.

It had been a relief to discover that La Nell's severe gastric problems were due, after all, to lactose intolerance, but it was amazing how difficult it was to avoid food that contained it. The easiest solution was to pop a little steak on the skillet or grill and throw together a salad. Unfortunately, her uric acid shot up and she had to be abstain from red meat until it returned to normal limits. By that time, her system could no longer tolerate it, so red meat was another item stricken from her diet. Eventually lactase pills became available and solved the main issue, but until then she had to make sure nothing she ate contained dairy products. Their most treasured memory of that time was the day that they had pizza at a little joint in Fort Worth, Texas. La Nell of course had to order hers without cheese. Their teenage waiter was appalled:

"But ma'am, it ain't no good without cheese!"

The Simaris lent them AWOL for their first night back in the Sierras. The Elías family had moved out of the house and Bill—the amazing, long-suffering Bill Ferrell—had once again moved their furniture for them when the lease on the rented house was up. The only available vehicle large enough for the purpose was a dump truck; therefore, he used that. By now he knew his friends so well that he was even able to place the items in their intended places. They just had to clear off the dust and unpack their dishes and clothes.

The next morning, they were greeted by a bright, hot late spring day. They had just parked the car in the garage when a sudden pounding began overhead. It was hailing stones the size of golf balls! They were forced to crouch behind the car as glass began flying in every direction from broken windows. But where was Nancy? As soon as the glass settled, the others dashed out, calling her name. She had gone upstairs looking for Cosita and had narrowly missed being speared by a giant wedge of glass that flew across her room.

It took them forever to get rid of all the broken glass, which had even gotten into the washing machine, whose lid had unfortunately been open. The damage in broken roof tiles, smashed windows and dented cars in the area was colossal. It took some time to get everything repaired. Hotels and businesses had priority, as the tourist season was less than a month away, but the biggest jolt was discovering the status of the work. They found that the Bible studies in La Falda had been suspended, progress on the church building in Villa Giardino was at a standstill, Associational activity was at a low ebb, and the pastor at Villa Giardino was planning to leave the Valley. It looked like they had their work cut out for them.

Jumpstart

Summer was intense. The Bedfords threw themselves into bolstering up the somewhat deflated Villa Giardino Church. La Nell and Nelda taught the young people and intermediate girls in Sunday School, for which they enjoyed trading ideas and motivational activities. Ben presided over a children's service during the sermon at the morning worship service. Nelda lent a hand with the thirty or so young people on Saturday evenings.

They were not alone in their efforts. Several new families had moved to the area and were contributing to revitalizing the congregation. The Arrojos were one of these: Andrés and Irma, with their two youngest children, Elisabet and David. Don Andrés was a hardworking immigrant from Spain who had built up a very successful grocery retail and wholesale business in Buenos Aires, which he now left in his elder sons' hands. He put even more work and dedication into his Christian service, giving unstintingly of his time, energy and resources. Among other things, he was soon teaching a Bible study in Capilla del Monte on Friday afternoons and to all intents and purposes became the lay pastor of the budding congregation.

Nevertheless, the Bedfords had originally been called by the Villa Giardino church to start a new work in La Falda and they felt that it was time to get on with it. Pastor Elías, who had decided to stay after all, was loath to see them go and felt the congregation could not spare any families to assist them, except for Constantino and Alejandra Miciu, who had worked with them since the initial Bible study in the rented house. However, wonderful help came in the shape of one of Rubén Simari's brothers, Osvaldo (better known as "Cacho"), his wife Azucena and their two youngest sons, David and Rubén. They were old friends from the early Distrito Sud days in Rosario. Cacho had completed a very successful career handling accounts in Acindar, the largest steel factory in Argentina. Now he was ready for a break from his hectic pace and set up a small business selling doors and windows. He was faithful, committed and versatile, for he could preach, teach and sing. In fact, he was later to go into full-time Christian ministry.[69] In a short time there were morning and evening worship services meeting in the Bedfords' garage and five Sunday School classes in various rooms all over the house.

A little later down the line, the need for a local association was brought home to them when the Córdoba Association forgot all about an event and failed to show up. The Punilla Valley Association of Baptist Churches was organized on September 8, 1976 with the dream of opening new works in eight more towns in the Valley.

---

[69] He was to run the Argentine Baptist Publishing House and pastor several congregations, including his own home church of Distrito Sud in Rosario, and the Villa Mora church in Asunción, Paraguay, while his son Ernesto eventually became Administrator of the Baptist Hospital in Asunción

Ghost Student

March 1975 was an important milestone in the Bedford family—Nancy was starting high school! There had been several options. Sending her off to Buenos Aires to board and attend Lincoln was not one of them. A ten-hour drive was much too far away. One possibility was returning to St. Mary's and Lourdes in La Cumbre. It had been interesting for her to get to know British and Anglo-Argentine culture at St. Mary's and Catholic culture at Lourdes. There were other bilingual girls at St. Mary's but her special friend had been Gillian, newly arrived from Liverpool for her paraplegic father to recover from his accident in the peace of the mountains. There had been Anglican and Waldensian students and teachers. At Lourdes, she had been to mass and Catholic Religion classes, where she quizzed the nuns. The future theologian posed so many awkward questions that they finally asked her to take a free period instead of attending class. Some of the teachers at Lourdes resented what they considered to be the spoiled and privileged kids from the English private schools (St. Paul's, St. Mary's and Reydon) and purposefully piled on the homework. On the other hand, the principal had been incredibly helpful. When her parents had asked for materials for their daughter to study so that she could take the seventh-grade tests upon returning from the U.S. (where she would be taking classes that would not be credited), the principal had decided to keep her on as a "ghost student" with fictitious attendance and grades, handing over her elementary school certificate so that she wouldn't have to be tested on work she had already done.

That whole scene sounded exhausting to Nancy. She was tired of going to school in another town with so many hours of class and homework that she had no life in the town where she actually lived. So, she was enrolled in one of the public high schools in La Falda: Escuela Normal Superior "Arturo Capdevila," better known as the "Nacional," which she was to attend through graduation. She had classes in the afternoon except for the mornings that she had Physical Education, to which she sometimes rode on her new horse Indio.[70]

Nancy was soon part of a close group that often gathered at her house for projects and snacks. Her best friend at that time was Virginia, who like her had recently come to live in the Sierras and had spent her childhood vacations there. They traded stories, Nancy about a German lady who had a motorcycle and a little girl her age, and Virginia about some *ingleses*[71] with a little blonde girl with whom she had played and whose big sister had been kind to her when she was stung by a scary insect. They discovered that those little girls had been neither German nor English: they were them!

The Bedfords did not abandon St. Mary's altogether, however. Nelda had an interview with Mrs. Place, owner and principal, who hired her as the fourth and fifth form English mistress for a semester, two hours per day in which she was able to put into practice her recently acquired educational theories and teaching methods. Classes were held in a large old house on the edge of the golf course that provided classrooms and boarding quarters during the school year and operated as a hostel for tourists during the summer months.

Nelda was scheduled to go to the University of Pennsylvania in late August to begin work on a doctorate, but these months gave her time to reflect that, much as she loved English literature, her current plans would essentially narrow her career path to U.S. academia, far from the culture she loved. In a mad scramble, she got accepted at the University of Texas at Austin to pursue a Master of Arts in Spanish Literature. David, now ABD[72] in his doctoral studies, helped her get set up in the apartment he was vacating before leaving to take up his new position as Associate Director at the Foreign Mission Board's Missionary Orientation Center ("MOC") in Pine Mountain, Georgia, where he would be in charge of cultural and linguistic orientation.

---

[70] Sadly, Canario had passed away while she was in the U.S.
[71] English people
[72] All But Dissertation

"Urches"

The pace heated up with a vengeance. Both Ben and La Nell had their fair share of Mission and Convention responsibilities. La Nell was recording secretary, member of the Executive Board and of the Personnel and Mixed Loan Committees of the Mission, while she served in the Department of Christian Education and the Executive Committee of the Convention. Ben was Press Representative, Mass Media Coordinator, President of the Seminary Trustees, Advisor to the Administrator of Thea Camp, member of the Finance Committee and the Committee for the Recording Studio, area representative for the Loan Board, and member of the Evangelism and Missions Department of the Convention.

The Punilla Valley Association was beginning to promote fellowship, training and outreach. It put its main efforts into helping Mina Clavero in an evangelistic thrust, Bialet Massé in its preaching ministry (mainly through laymen) and Cosquín to recover from a profound crisis. Ben became interim pastor there for the second time, using laymen to help preach, until the arrival of the new pastor, Raúl Ramos.

The Bedfords continued as members of the Villa Giardino church, where Ben served as deacon and chairman of Evangelism and Extension. Its new building was finally finished and inaugurated in December of 1975.

But, of course, their main task was the work in La Falda. In their annual report to the Mission and their newsletter for 1976, they wrote:

We have moved at least 96 times this year as it was necessary to rearrange the furniture in four rooms twice each Sunday.

Sunday School has an attendance of between 50 and 60 meeting in six classes all over the house. It is difficult and trying at times but great to see God working in the lives of people and forming a church. We bring about 30 children on a bus from another "barrio". Ben calls them the "urches", derived at a tired moment from "urchins". They were wild, man, wild a year ago, but it has been amazing the change that God has wrought. To illustrate, a four-year-old that had been attending for a year was in the hospital recently and gave a real testimony—as they gave him glucose, with tears running down his cheeks, he sang "Dios está aquí, qué precioso es," which translated freely means "God is with me, how precious He is." From 12 to 15 such Beginners meet each Sunday in a small room (8 X 9'). An intermediate girl, Marta Farías, was converted in La Nell's Sunday School class not long ago. Her parents had been converted earlier when we visited them in their home. We have been working with the family since being in La Falda. The mother worked for us before our last furlough. Recently she said to La Nell, "Jesus has made such a difference in our home. I wish I had known Him before." Pray for them as they prepare for baptism.

It was clearly time to go for that second lot.

More Mortar!

Pharmacist Margiotta was willing to sell the contiguous lot on one condition: that they help him open a bank account in the U.S. Ben and Rubén applied for and were granted a joint loan to take advantage of the opportunity while it was available. The cost of the lot and the building was eventually covered by a combination of local offerings, the Strategic Property Fund, the Small Chapel program and a contribution from the Bedfords' best friends and colleagues Bill and Opal. The Ferrells had served their first two terms as missionaries in Córdoba—first in the provincial capital and then in Alta Gracia—and it always held a special place in their hearts. Theoretically it was a loan, but they asked for the money to be paid back not to them but to the church in Alta Gracia to help that congregation with its own building project.[73]

The lot was soon cleared and the foundations laid for what was projected as the educational building. The ground floor would have a large meeting area, three classrooms, bathroom and kitchen, plus a multi-information center. In addition to the regular meetings, the congregation planned community service there, including tutoring for secondary students, information for tourists, a lending library, a book store, and an adult literacy program.

Missionary Glenn Johnson cleared ten days from his busy schedule to lend them a hand. Besides being a hard-working pastor

---

[73] Later, their daughter Lynn and son-in-law Bob Naughton were to give the La Falda church part of the tithe of Bob's inheritance from his father to help in building the second floor. Missionary David Ford was pastor at that time and hid the cash behind a loose brick under the stairs for safekeeping until it was needed, as depositing dollars in local banks was not an option.

and passionate evangelist, he was a skilled mason and generously donated time to lay bricks in countless projects all over the country. On the Sunday he was there he rested from physical work to preach at the worship services. That meant that he raised all the walls from ground to ceiling level in nine days.

Although several of the men and young people, including Nancy, came to help after their own full days at work or school and on the weekend, most of the time Ben was the only helper. While Glenn started bright and early and laid an astounding average of 1000 bricks per day, Ben had an even earlier start to take the bags of cement from the garage to the construction site and prepare the first batch of mortar (sand, cement, gravel and water, mixed manually with a shovel because there was no mixer available). He spent all day moving bricks within reaching distance and preparing and carting pails of mortar. However fast he worked, Glenn was constantly bellowing, "*¡Más mezcla!*"[74]

Glenn quit laying bricks at 5:00 p.m. and returned to Villa Bautista to finish off the day with several games of tennis, while Ben stayed behind to clean and put away the tools and materials, and to use a small board with a nail driven through it to scrape the mortar between the bricks in order to achieve a uniform joint profile. Passersby stopped to stare and marvel at the amazing transformation.

It would take about a year to add the other things the building needed to be in working condition: ceiling, doors and windows, electrical wiring, plumbing, floors, plastering and painting. It was an exciting and rewarding time of cooperative effort by the congregation that brought them even closer together.

---

[74] "More mortar!"

126

A Surfeit of Celebration

La Nell stared in dismay at the two patterns that she was somehow supposed to combine into an approximation of the dress illustrated in the glossy page torn out of a bridal magazine. Her daughter had absolute trust in her ability to meet any sewing challenge for La Nell had kept her in the latest fashions throughout her teens and into her twenties: minis, midis, maxis, hot pants, suits, coats—she had coped with them all.

Now Nelda wanted most of the top from one pattern and the bottom from the other so she could have a seamless skirt. La Nell experimented with an old sheet before cutting the material that had been brought from the States. The dress called for lace on cuffs, neck, and bodice as well as around the bottom of the skirt. They combed the stores in Buenos Aires before settling on some beautiful heavy stuff that was actually meant for curtains. Unfortunately, it did not quite match the off-white tone of the dress material but a little staining with tea did the trick. The lace flowers had to be cut out one by one and sewn onto tulle in the desired pattern, and each flower had to have seven small pearl beads sewn onto it, over 3000 pearls in all. That would be a job for the bride: La Nell handed her daughter a shoe box in which to put flowers and beads until it was time to use them.

That was not all the sewing required, however, not by a long shot. The bride needed a dress for the civil ceremony and a going-away dress. There was a dress each for the civil and religious ceremonies for La Nell. Ditto for Nancy. And a dress for Nelda's future mother-in-law.

The amazing thing was that Nelda was actually getting married. La Nell and Ben had met and married in college, but David had gone through a B.A., an M.A. and a Ph.D., and Nelda had earned a B.A. and was well into her M.A., and nothing! Nelda had soon opted out of the whole American dating scene: she saw no point in wasting the money and potentially losing the friendship of men in whom she would never be romantically interested.

The previous year the Bedfords had all been together in Argentina for the first time since 1971, five years before. Nelda had renewed her acquaintance with Alberto Gaydou at the annual National Baptist Convention and plunged into a whirlwind romance. Here was the man she had always dreamed of: charming, intelligent, funny, hard-working *and* a practicing Christian. They were the same age and shared the same background as pastor's kids and, to top it all off, he was extremely handsome.

When they picked David up at the airport in Buenos Aires, he found his sister literally glowing with happiness. Perhaps this motivated him. Be that as it may, during the family's visit to their old church in Solano he came across Patricia Roberto, now grown into a beautiful young woman with enormous slightly slanted brown eyes that gave her an exotic and almost Oriental look. They entered into a correspondence that soon turned into their own love story.

Through logistics that would have made any general proud, the two weddings were planned for the following year. Nelda took a semester off from graduate school and David applied for an extended one-month vacation. Alberto and Nelda's religious ceremony would take place on May 14 at the Villa Giardino church, and David and Patricia's on June 11 in the Seminary Chapel in Buenos Aires, while the respective civil ceremonies (which were what counted legally) would precede them by several weeks rather than the customary one day in order to get through the red tape required to obtain the future spouses' permanent U.S. resident visas.

The Consulate did not exactly lay out the red carpet for them. In fact, it attempted to get rid of the whole mess by suggesting that it would be much simpler for them to marry in the States. The officials seemed to view their desire to share the moment with family and friends as an unreasonable whim. Although she was a U.S. citizen, because she was born abroad Nelda needed a "Certificate of Citizenship" from the

State Department. The office in Washington never replied and, after Ben read the fine print on his daughter's Record of Birth Abroad, it was a very kind officer in the San Antonio Immigration Office who came to the rescue the week before Nelda traveled by processing her application on the spot and typing out an official letter with the certificate number. The original (signed by Henry Kissinger) arrived over a year later. The knowledge of how to obtain this document proved to be very helpful to other MKs in the future.[75]

After months of building up an impressive folder of birth, marriage and health certificates, police reports, letters of recommendation and fingerprints, and swearing to be good in a final interview, Nelda and Alberto left the Consulate triumphantly clutching the precious visa, headed for a celebratory lunch, when they were forced to return upon discovering that Alberto's occupation had been listed as "housewife." On the other hand, when David turned up at the Consulate a couple of weeks later, the Vice-Consul exclaimed, "Bedford? But we already *did* Bedford!"

The weddings created quite a stir in the Argentine Baptist world. The last marriage between an MK and a national had taken place a generation before, between Josie Hawkins and Freddy Smith. When Nancy tied the knot years later, the Bedfords became the only missionary family all of whose children married Argentines.

Some 200 friends descended upon the Sierras, many from Buenos Aires and Rosario. Ben and La Nell put them up at the Camp, where Rubén Simari gave them a special discount and also lent the facilities for the reception. Francisco Pons, an old friend now working for the Convention's Media Department, recorded Bach's *Brandenburg Concerti* and Handel's *Water Music* on reel-to-reel tape and Alberto's brother Daniel worked the equipment. The local blacksmith tapped into his artistic side and made a beautiful set of candelabra and rose-shaped holders for the pew ends that were filled with custom candles made by Lloydene Balyeat and lit by Nelda's sister and sisters-in-

---

[75] The Bedfords were also able to pass on a couple of other red-tape gems. One was how to establish a permanent U.S. residence despite living abroad, which allowed MKs to study without paying out-of-state tuition fees. The other was exemption from certain Argentine taxes.

law. The bride and bridegroom's mothers were the matrons of honor, Daniel Gaydou spoke on Christian marriage, and Ben walked his daughter down the aisle and then performed the ceremony.

Less than a month later he presided at his son's wedding before many of the same people, now crowded into the Seminary Chapel. The mothers stood up front and Patricia walked in on her father's arm, so her mischievous five-year-old brother was kept in check by Nelda and Alberto, who held him up high in order for him to see the bride march in. The intricate ties of friend- and kinship were a bit hard to explain, so that Daniel Gaydou once introduced David's parents-in-law at his church as "relatives on the Bedford side of the family."

Still, the Bedfords had not been idle during that intervening month, for a very important date fell between the two weddings: Nancy's fifteenth birthday, an occasion which is traditionally celebrated in Argentina with a large formal party. Her parents explained that another big event was simply out of their reach. However, that did not keep them from hosting an unforgettable *quinceañera*.[76] The unfinished meeting hall of the new building in La Falda was temporarily turned into a barn with bales of hay, saddles and blankets. The guests attended in jeans and roasted marshmallows brought from the U.S. especially for the occasion by the birthday girl's brother. The guests unanimously declared it the best fifteenth birthday party ever.

The two pairs of newlyweds had barely made their goodbye rounds and departed to their new homes when it was time for another big milestone. The Evangelical Baptist Church of La Falda was formally organized on August 17 with twenty-four members and its new building was dedicated by the congregation before the neighbors and city authorities on August 20, 1977.

---

[76] Fifteenth Birthday

Turn, Turn, Turn

Judging by the times they played it, the Byrd's version of "Turn, Turn, Turn" was one of their children's favorite songs. The lyrics were taken from Ecclesiastes 3:1-8:

There is a time for everything,
and a season for every activity under heaven:
a time to be born and a time to die,
a time to plant and a time to uproot,
a time to kill and a time to heal,
a time to tear down and a time to build,
a time to weep and a time to laugh,
a time to mourn and a time to dance,
a time to scatter stones and a time to refrain,
a time to search and a time to give up,
a time to keep and a time to throw away,
a time to tear and a time to mend,
a time to be silent and a time to speak,
a time to love and a time to hate,
a time for war and a time for peace.

While their lives had an abundance of love and laughter, they were not exempt from other kinds of experiences.

They had been expecting it, but the news of the death of Ben's mother, Nancy "Tennie" Bedford, a couple of months after their farewell hit them hard. She had been a shining example of faith and comfort throughout her long life. La Nell lamented, "We have lost the last person we know who prayed for us every day."

There were some health issues. Ben now carried around an epinephrine injection kit after being stung by an ant while he was working in the yard. Alarmed by the rapid swelling, La Nell had called the La Falda Clinic. The owner himself, Dr. Germán Sestopal, dashed to their home, syringe in hand, just in time to prevent Ben from suffocating. For her part, La Nell had to undergo surgery to remove a breast tumor and the family endured some tense weeks until the results of the biopsy confirmed that it was benign.

A real blow was the Ferrells' decision to resign as missionaries and move to Mississippi. Although there were many lovely people in their lives, no one could fill the gap left by the absence of their best friends.

Of course, they were affected by strange or disturbing experiences of others. One day they were participating in a home Bible study in nearby La Cumbre, when a woman from Buenos Aires arrived looking for the "seer" to help contact her son and solve some serious problems. Ben explained that he was no prophet but a simple preacher and that she was welcome to stay and hear the Word of God, where she could find the solution for her real need. So she stayed and asked to buy a Bible, invited them to visit her at her vacation house in Capilla del Monte and later made a profession of faith in their home. On her next visit, she took them a basket of fruit and promised she would attend the services and continue seeking help and guidance.

Although they did not personally come across it very often, they were aware that superstition and the occult were far from absent. In fact, Capilla del Monte, also known as the City of Energy, was and still is a paranormal hotspot. Much like Roswell, New Mexico, it is a center for UFO sightings, and teems with healers, pyramids, New Agers and Gnostics. There had been a recent upsurge of this kind of thing as the President's closest advisor, a follower of esotericism and the occult nicknamed *El Brujo*,[77] rose to power.

---

[77] The Sorcerer

After seven years of military rule, elections had finally taken place again in March 1973. Héctor Cámpora, running for the Peronists since their leader was still banned, received 49.5% of the vote, half a percentage point from preventing a run-off election. However, the runner-up, Ricardo Balbín, conceded rather than cause another political crisis. In July, after several months of unrest, protests and strikes, Cámpora resigned to make way for a new election in which Juan Domingo Perón returned to the presidency with his wife "Isabelita"[78] as his running mate. He died the next year and she became Argentina's first female president.

During their last stint in the U.S., the Bedfords had witnessed the aftermath of the withdrawal from the Vietnam War and President Richard Nixon's resignation to avoid impeachment in the wake of the Watergate scandal. They had also followed the story of newspaper heiress Patty Hearst's kidnapping by the Symbionese Liberation Army, her participation in a bank robbery, and her subsequent capture and imprisonment.

Terrorist and guerrilla groups flourished throughout the Western world in the 1970s, from Black September, which carried out the Munich Massacre in 1972,[79] to the Red Brigades, responsible for violent incidents, kidnappings and assassinations all over Europe into the early '80s. Argentina was no exception to this international trend. It had the leftist Peronist Montoneros, whose initial objectives had been the destabilization of the Argentine Revolution[80] and the return of Perón. Later they fought for socialism as the natural evolution of the Peronist movement, but not all Peronists agreed. In fact, since the party covered a broad ideological spectrum held together only by the General's magnetic personality, a diametrically opposed ultra-right-wing terrorist group arose, the Argentine Anticommunist Alliance, better known as the "Triple A," a paramilitary organization dedicated to exterminating militant leftists both in and out of the Peronist party. One of the organizers and prime movers of the AAA was José López

---

[78] María Estela Martínez
[79] They kidnapped and killed eleven Israeli athletes during the Olympics
[80] The military regime from 1966 to 1973

Rega, who became Isabelita's right-hand man and de facto prime minister.

The entire South Cone had swung to the right, and every other country—Bolivia, Brazil, Chile, Paraguay and Uruguay—was ruled by military regimes, backed by the U.S. under its National Safety Doctrine. Many felt that things could hardly get worse and were secretly relieved when the military deposed Isabelita in 1976. But they were wrong. The so-called National Reorganization Process, which lasted until 1983, took political repression to a whole new level.

Because a tight lid was kept on the news, most people were unaware of much that was happening until years later, although rumors abounded. Movies, books and songs were censored or banned, and many persons fled the country in an unprecedented "brain drain." The general feeling was that it was safest to mind your own business and not get involved in anything beyond family and friends.

This was the time of the "disappeared," persons who were carted off and never heard from again. Estimates vary from several thousand to tens of thousands of victims. Clandestine detention centers were set up where mostly young people were tortured and often killed. Babies were taken from their parents and given up for adoption. The bravest persons to speak up during these years were the Mothers and Grandmothers of Plaza de Mayo, who demanded information about their children and grandchildren, and protested the lack of answers before the main government buildings, identifying themselves by wearing white scarves and marching around the square two by two to circumvent the laws against public groups of three or more.

The journalist son and daughter-in-law of the Rivaderas, from the Villa Giardino church, were among those who disappeared in Buenos Aires. A couple from the Gaydous' church in Rosario had their apartment broken into and trashed by the military before they realized that they were on the wrong floor. Alberto's parents held their breath every night as they heard machine-gun fire in the distance and waited for their son to return from work safely.

While La Falda and its surroundings were an apparent oasis of peace, it was later known that one of the most infamous detention centers, La Perla, was located not many miles away, just outside of

Córdoba, and the stories of bodies being dumped in the San Roque Lake at night from helicopters were given credence by the discovery of human remains after a particularly long draught. Nonetheless, the Sierras were an ideal place in which to hide.

The Bedfords' first-hand experiences were mercifully quite mild. One day La Nell heard a crash outside. Peering from her second-floor bedroom window, she saw that a pick-up truck had lost control and run into a light post across the street. Several failed attempts were made to start the motor. Suddenly, two young men jumped out and ran up the street until they were out of sight. The abandoned vehicle proved to hold a small arsenal.

During a trip to return their visiting future daughter-in-law to Buenos Aires, they were stopped at a road check and made to get out of the vehicle. Ben was frisked and forced to stand with his arms on the roof of the car and his legs wide apart while the women were grilled, for all young people were viewed as potential terrorists. Nelda was considered suspicious for not looking enough like her mother and Patricia for not having memorized her recently acquired eight-digit ID. The explanation of her relationship as David's fiancée was received with open skepticism. But all the paperwork was in order, so they were reluctantly allowed to go on their way.

The '70s also witnessed some tremendous natural disasters, including the 1976 Tangshan earthquake in China, which was the largest in the twentieth century by the death toll, from 250,000 to 650,000 depending on the source consulted. Closer to home, on November 23, 1976 an earthquake levelled the town of Caucete in San Juan Province, claiming around 100 fatal victims and producing a terrifying liquefaction of the soil, opening up craters and sand volcanoes, and shooting out violent streams of water ten feet up into the air. The only thing left standing in the Baptist church building there was the pulpit, with an open Bible still resting on it. The tremors reached far and wide, even breaking the upstairs windows of the main building at the Baptist Camp in Villa Giardino, 300 miles away. Baptists all over Argentina, including those in the Punilla Valley, joined in the relief effort.

Outreach

The exciting and exhausting year of 1977 ended with the Bedfords trading the Argentine summer for the U.S. winter, taking advantage of the Foreign Mission Board's new furlough policy. Until recently, it had been five years on the field and one year in the States. Now, however, there were options, from four months to one year stateside with proportionally more or less time on the field. Ben and La Nell decided that four months would be ideal: they would have time to visit loved ones and speak at churches, but Nancy would not miss school and they would not be away from the church for too long. Nancy's friend Virginia went with them.

The First Baptist Church of Cleburne, Texas, thirty miles south of Fort Worth, offered its missionary residence, which was gratefully accepted. As had now become a tradition, the Grogans met them at DFW (the Dallas-Fort Worth airport). After a delightful visit and getting a car, they set up house in their new home away from home. They were out and about for much of the time, although the entire family did get together there at Christmas. Between them, they had 100 formal speaking engagements at 38 churches, two associational meetings, two World Missions Conferences and a visit to the Missionary Orientation Center. Ben, La Nell, Nancy and Virginia drove all the way to California. They went to Disneyland, took the girls skiing and stopped at several national parks in between visiting relatives: two of La Nell's brothers in California, and two of Ben's brothers, in California and Arizona. For the first time, they had Schools of Missions in New Mexico, and the girls stayed with Ben's sister Billie in Clovis while he and La Nell went to Albuquerque and Hobbs. While they were in Albuquerque, Hoffmantown Baptist Church threw them a special dinner. Unfortunately, between onions and cheese, the peas were the only item on the menu they were able to eat.

School and work were waiting for them after this brief interlude. The congregation in La Falda was growing steadily, both from local people and families moving into the area. The Leanza family (José, Susana and their three children Ángel, Marcela and Liliana) had spent some time commuting from Buenos Aires but finally settled down in time to become founding members of the church. José worked with glass, creating crystal glasses, vases, bowls and figurines.

Raúl and Pierina Peirano added quite a bit of spice to their lives. Although business sense was not their strong point, they were extremely intelligent, talented, well-educated and capable people. Their daughter Andrea became a close friend of Nancy's. One of the family undertakings was a tea shop called *Aquel Lugar* ("That Place"), whose name was dreamed up by La Nell. Raúl, brought up as a Methodist, was bighearted and versatile. He told Ben, "I want to give until it hurts." And he did. He volunteered his truck to pick up building materials in Villa Carlos Paz, during one of which trips it broke down.

Pierina was quite the character, a unique mixture of down-to-earth practicality and mysticism. She gave generously of her time to tutor underprivileged children in Barrio San Jorge. At first the church rented a ramshackle house that had no windows but whose roof at least afforded protection against the sun and rain. Ben also held Bible studies there. One day, as they were studying the Gospel of John, one of the women came up to him afterwards, lowered her voice and said, "Can I ask you something?"

"Of course!"

Her voice dropped even lower, to a whisper: "What does *unigénito*[81] mean?"

The Mission came up trumps for funds to purchase a good-size lot in the neighborhood with an old house and room to build a chapel for the mission point.

Pastor Elías had resigned from the Villa Giardino church and for a while, except for Raúl Ramos in Cosquín, Ben was the only pastor in

---

[81] The only begotten son

the Valley. However, in a short time Hugo Moreira was called to Villa Carlos Paz, David Ureta (now married to Graciela Ragni)[82] to Cruz del Eje and Daniel Gaydou to Villa Giardino, and the Association could once more think of expanding. A lovely property became available on the main street of Capilla del Monte and Daniel Gaydou lent his carpentering skills to repair the house that would be used as a temporary meeting place now and the parsonage later when the chapel could be built.

The Dmytriws, of Brethren background, began attending the La Falda church after their adorable little girls Gabriela and Silvina's first Vacation Bible School there. Miguel, a metalworker of Ukrainian descent who owned his own business, was a man of few words but deep convictions and soon became an invaluable help.

Then there were the Bongiovannis. Ben saw the father quite often, for he had worked at the La Falda Automotive Club for decades. The senior Bongiovanni never did visit the church, but he said, "I have a son who should go!" This was Daniel, born and bred in Valle Hermoso. He had studied kinesiology in Córdoba City, where he met and married Graciela, a lifelong churchgoer, and now they had a small son, Esteban. Both of them had fiery temperaments but were incredibly charming and charismatic people with an amazing gift of evangelism. They knew everybody in the Valley, and countless persons heard of the Lord and came to know Him through them. On one occasion Daniel and Ben made a trip together to the Baptist Children's Home in Esperanza, Santa Fe. They were so engrossed in their conversation that they missed a turn and had gone some fifty miles out of their way before they realized their mistake and doubled back.

The church reached out to the community in many ways, including special events. Mel Plunk, now pastor of the Mendoza Oeste Church, brought his choir to sing in La Falda and at two other churches in the area. Bruce and Nancy Muskrat, recently appointed missionaries who had just joined the Seminary faculty, were both gifted musicians

---

82 David was the son of Floreal Ureta, a pastor and professor from Rosario whom the Bedfords had known since the early 1950s and Graciela was the daughter of the Ragnis, also from Rosario, with whom they had shared so many construction and educational projects.

and accepted an invitation to perform in La Falda. The church asked Pharmacist Margiotta, President of the Italian Club, if they could rent the facilities for the concerts. Margiotta answered, "I can do better than that! Why don't we co-host the event? If you rent the piano, we will pay to have it moved in here."

So, besides two evenings of performances at the church, the Muskrats gave two concerts at the Dante Alighieri, playing classical and Christian music on the piano and the violin, as well as singing. They gave their testimonies of how they had become first musicians and later missionaries. It was a roaring success.

Dr. Daniel Tinao, renowned psychiatrist, pastor and Seminary President, preached on three nights of a revival. Afterwards he gave workshops and counseling for different groups of people: the first night for parents of small children, the second for parents of adolescents and the third for couples.

Of course, most of their community involvement grew naturally out of their daily activities, many related to Nancy and her school. Ben sometimes took the church's old 16mm projector and showed films from the Moody nature series. Not too long after the military took over, the new "president," General Videla, and his entourage attended an event at IOSE,[83] the army's vacation complex in La Falda. Nancy and her friends asked Ben to take them there to deliver a petition, since the General claimed the military had taken over in order to help the people. Although they had no official standing or connection of any kind, the group, dressed in school uniform, made it all the way to a top aide. The petition requested funds from the government for the construction of a building for the school, which belonged to the national rather than the provincial system, and had long been functioning in a decrepit former inn. They never knew whether their gesture made any difference, but it is a fact that things finally got moving and the school inaugurated its new building a few years later.

However, it was La Nell who was most involved in regular town life. She took private French lessons in a class taught by a teacher from the Alliance Française. She participated in the parents' school

---

[83] Instituto de Obra Social del Ejército [Army Social Welfare Institute]

coop, the Argentine version of the PTA, volunteered time to repair the books in the school's meager library and baked countless cakes for fundraisers. She made her home a place where kids were always welcome, and even bought a set of glasses especially for their late afternoon refreshments. Although her classmates were puzzled by the different standards of strictness compared to their own parents (Nancy was not allowed to go dancing, the typical Saturday night activity for most Argentine teenagers, but she was allowed to go to Buenos Aires alone on the bus), they loved the warm atmosphere hers created.

Another thing that puzzled Nancy's middle-class school friends was her extended social circle that included people from every class, with many of whom she would not ordinarily have come into contact. Some of her church-learned attitudes and skills rubbed off on her classmates. The military government was far from encouraging most of the civil rights and responsibilities of a democracy, but growing up in a congregational church taught people to think analytically, participate in group activities, prepare presentations, speak in public, serve people in need and accept the notion that all persons are valuable. Nancy and her friends were considered troublemakers at school, not because they misbehaved but because of their questioning minds and activism.

SOS

More than a letter, it was a cry from the heart. Daniel Tinao had brought up the subject several times over the past few months and now sent a formal invitation for Ben to return to the Seminary as professor of Evangelism, Missiology and Church Administration with a view to organizing and directing a Department of Practical Theology, and for La Nell to take over the direction of the Library.

> *I would like to confirm in writing what we have talked about repeatedly regarding the invitation for you to return to serve here at our Seminary. As I told you in person, this is not simply an idea of mine, but one that has grown in the heart of several of us here and has also gone through a stage of testing and prayer. I have shared it with the Academic Dean, Dr. Stanley Clark, and others here, who agree completely with my opinion that at this time your ministry here at the Seminary would be providential. For reasons you know, we are working with a greatly reduced faculty and very few possibilities of increasing the national staff for now.*
>
> ....
>
> *Dear Ben and La Nell, may the Lord bless you richly in your work there in La Falda. We always remember you with great affection and even at a distance we appreciate the great support that you still give our Seminary.*

With a few brief exceptions, throughout his entire missionary career Ben had either been on the Board of Trustees or the Faculty of the International Baptist Theological Seminary of Buenos Aires and its ministry was very dear to his heart.

When Ben and La Nell resigned from the faculty to accept the invitation to serve in the Punilla Valley, there was been a full complement of capable professors. In 1975 Ben had the privilege, as President of the Board of Trustees, of installing the first national president, Dr. Daniel Tinao, but circumstances change with time, and the Seminary was no exception.

The past few years had witnessed the departure of most of the missionary professors. Now the Andersons, Glazes, Thompsons and Díazes had all moved on to different places of service. Only the Clarks, the Balyeats and Sarah Wilson remained, and just one new couple had been appointed, the Muskrats. Although the Music Department was now stronger than ever, Clark alone taught Bible and Theology. To be sure, there were capable nationals, but the Seminary did not have the funds to hire new full-time professors. Now the pressure was on for Ben and La Nell to help fill in the gaps.

The Bedfords prayed long and hard about the matter and, although they increasingly felt that this would be the next step for them, they were convinced that they could not leave La Falda yet, and they worked out a provisional arrangement. For now, the Seminary would schedule classes so that Ben could teach a double load one semester and only commute half the year. In practice, it meant catching a long-distance bus on Monday evening, getting off at Liniers, on the western edge of the Capital, and taking a city bus on into the Seminary in time for the first class on Tuesday morning. He taught all week and spent the nights in a Seminary guest room. On Friday evening, he took a bus back, to spend Saturday through Monday in visitation and church-related activities, while La Nell kept everything going the rest of the week.

The first semester with this onerous schedule was in the second half of 1978, on the heels of the excitement over Argentina hosting and winning soccer's World Cup for the first time. Only a month into the new arrangement, La Nell had to go to Texas for four weeks, and Nancy spent the weekdays with her friend Virginia during her absence. The occasion was the birth of the Bedfords' first grandchild: Andrea Beatriz Gaydou. The morning after La Nell arrived in Austin Nelda went into labor and Andrea made her appearance shortly after

4:00 a.m. the next day. La Nell cooked, sewed, pampered and soaked up every minute of the experience. Her verdict of "*¡Divina!*"[84] and her accounts of the extraordinary liveliness and intelligence of the little one were received with amused indulgence by the other set of grandparents, for whom this was the fifth grandchild.

There was only one jarring note. They had just brought the baby home when La Nell was alarmed by a pungent smell.

"Have you been painting something?" she asked Alberto.

He had not. Still, throughout the remainder of her stay, at intervals La Nell would insist that she smelled paint and that it was giving her terrible headaches. Mystified, Nelda and Alberto, who couldn't smell anything of the kind, combed the entire house over and over without finding the source of the problem.

When La Nell returned home and stepped into the driveway at the house in La Falda, she stopped in her tracks and exclaimed, "*Here* is that smell!"

Ben had taken advantage of her absence to surprise her by sprucing up the house with a coating of spar varnish on the brick exterior. Every weekend, the smell had given him sick headaches. Ben asked his friend Tinao, who was a psychiatrist, if it was possible for La Nell to have sensed what he did thousands of miles away.

"Yes! When people are very close they can experience the same things even if they are not physically together."

---

[84] "Adorable!"

Girls' Day Out

Ben wondered how much longer it would be before the girls returned from their hike. This was his first babysitting stint as a grandfather and he had just about shot his bolt. Nelda and Andrea had come for a full month and would soon be joined by Alberto. The Bedfords and the Gaydous (now running the Baptist Camp) had been having a great time getting to know and showing off the baby.

Light as a feather and quick as lightning, Andrea was beginning to walk and talk. She would cruise around the coffee table, its sharp edges softened by a blanket, and earnestly repeat the adults' frequent admonishment: "Be careful—don't fall!" But there were just so many games and conversations to be had with a nine-month-old. What would happen when she got hungry and sleepy? Would she turn cranky?

Mother and grandmother were having a rare time alone. They had chosen to climb Cerro La Banderita, where there was a path of sorts and fabulous views, but they decided to return by a short cut, crossing over to Cerro El Cuadrado so they could go the rest of the way down its broad dirt road. At least that was the theory. In fact, it was a dry creek bed they followed, and it soon got steeper and rougher than they had anticipated. Unfortunately, it was much too dangerous to try to climb back up and they were forced to carry on. Often they had to sit and scoot down and across rocks, hanging on as best they could to the slender branches of bushes and small trees. There were frequent stops to strategize the next descent.

On one such occasion Nelda was astounded to see her mother grasp a long branch, swing out and glide down to the next level in a graceful and feminine version of Tarzan.

"I don't think I can do that!" she exclaimed.

"I didn't mean to—I was just hanging on and slipped!"

They eventually made it down in one piece each, with the seat of their pants scraped thin. But there was no rest for the weary: there was a baby eager for her mamma and a grandfather eager to be relieved.

Empty Nest

"I think 'There's a Ford in your future'!" quipped Miguel Bollatti at the Convention. He was referring to David and Janene Ford, the newly appointed missionary couple. Ben and La Nell had talked to the church in La Falda explaining that, as difficult as it would be to leave their beloved Sierras, they felt called to return to the Seminary, which had been so eager to get them that they had requested their assignment directly from the Mission. Through the Convention, the congregation put in their own request for a missionary pastor.

Although their family was increasing in number, the Bedfords' nest was now empty. David and Patricia had presented them with William Adrian, their first grandson and so far the only male Bedford of his generation, in March of 1979 and another grandchild was on the way in Nelda and Alberto's family. But they were far away and now Nancy was off to college, covered in glory when she graduated in December, after being the school's *abanderada*[85] in her senior year, an honor bestowed to the student with the highest grades of the class. La Nell travelled with her to the U.S. to help with enrollment in the spring semester at The University of Texas at Austin, not far from Nelda, now in the Houston area.

Until the new pastor arrived, Ben and La Nell commuted, living in the apartment[86] in the Women's Dorm at the Seminary in Buenos Aires during the week and in La Falda on the weekends. Daniel and

---

85 Flag-bearer

86 This apartment was first occupied by Ann Margrett and the Bedfords got to know her father, the legendary Sydney Sowell, over chats as he sat in his favorite spot out-of-doors. Later their good friends the Díazes had lived there for a time.

Graciela Bongiovanni visited them in the Capital at the end of the summer. They shared a cookout on the Seminary grounds, prepared on the Bedfords' trusty little portable picnic grill, and went to a game between Boca and Ríver, the greatest rivals in Argentine soccer.

The move was carefully orchestrated, with the same van transporting the belongings of the incoming and outgoing tenants. The Bedfords' furniture and boxes rested on the lawn while the Fords' things were transferred into the house in La Falda, and then they were hauled to Buenos Aires—but not to the apartment. When the Thompsons left, Stanley Clark was named to replace Cecil as Dean and assigned their house. Because the Clarks preferred apartment living, they had a proposition for Ben and La Nell: would they swap living quarters? So it was that Ben and La Nell found themselves in a very comfortable house on Laguna, next door to the one they had lived in before.

Motorcycles and Bone Fragments

The motorcycle came flying out of nowhere. It crashed into the door on the driver's side and the cyclist sailed gracefully over the car. Although adrenaline prevented Ben from realizing it until he saw blood dripping into his hands, the bike had not only smashed into the door, but also into his face, catapulting his glasses into the back seat.

Shortly after the Bedfords moved to Buenos Aires, they had gone to the Sierras for the weekend as usual and were on their way to a speaking engagement in Capilla del Monte. At the town square, they stopped and looked both ways. They had nearly made it through the intersection when they were struck.

The cyclist was uninjured except for scraped knees. Since there were several witnesses, he had to give up the tempting idea of pressing charges and asking for damages. The trusty little automatic Dodge they had been driving for the past three years had a broken window and a crumpled door. In La Falda, the Bedfords' friend Miguel Dmytriw hammered it enough to open and shut until they could have it repaired in Buenos Aires.

La Nell's back did not take kindly to the jarring it received and it took her some time to recover. The doctor who examined Ben's upper jaw gave him a sobering assessment: "You have been incredibly fortunate. Two inches up and you would have lost your eye; two inches to the side and you would have been struck in the temple and probably died."

At the very time the accident took place, Nancy was out with a college group in Austin. Suddenly she burst into tears. Her concerned friends asked what was wrong.

"Something terrible has happened to Daddy!"

Five years later Ben felt a stabbing pain in his mouth. Upon examination, the dentist discovered that the upper jaw had actually been fractured in the accident and now a bone fragment had broken off and was on the move.

"That will have to go. There's no telling where it might end up."

Unfortunately, Ben was allergic to one of the ingredients of dental anesthesia: lidocaine. This had become apparent when he had quit breathing and lost consciousness shortly after receiving an injection for some routine work several years earlier, to the extreme alarm of the dentist who then worked frantically to get his patient to come back around.

An appointment was scheduled immediately after a trip Ben had to make to Uruguay. The prospect of being cut into with no anesthesia was rather daunting. When the day arrived, he sat in the chair, opened his mouth and resigned himself to his fate. The dentist made a preliminary check and poked around a bit while he planned his strategy. The suspense built up as the silence extended. Suddenly the dentist pulled his hand out of his patient's mouth, triumphantly holding aloft the bone splinter in his tweezers. It had almost worked its way completely free on its own and required only a slight tug for full extraction.

Stopgaps

By the late 1970s, a sizeable Korean community had grown up in Buenos Aires and one of its churches became the largest Baptist congregation in Argentina. As a result, there was a large influx of Korean students at the Seminary. Many of them had been waiting for qualified professors to be available so they could complete their required credits. La Nell was received with open arms and given a huge load of Christian Education classes. For his part, Ben was the wild card that the Dean shuffled into whatever course was missing a professor. He spent hours with Stanley piecing together the pedagogical puzzle and planning how to divide up the courses until reinforcements began arriving the next year. In addition to Practical Theology and Evangelism, they would both teach Bible, with Ben on the Gospels and Stanley on Pauline literature, and while the Clarks were on furlough Ben would have to spread himself even more thinly.

The Bedfords had new church responsibilities, too, since the Clarks' absence left the Flores church without a pastor and Ben was called as interim. Two Seminary students were assigned to serve there and one of their tasks was to help prepare the candidates for baptism. In the middle of a deacons' meeting, Ben was called out.

"Pastor, there's a situation here that you'd better deal with. We don't know what to do."

It so happened that one of the candidates was a very nice middle-aged woman who was eager and willing to follow Christ. The snag was that she was in an informal relationship. Her husband had abandoned her many years before but they were not divorced. In those days regularizing this kind of situation was far from a simple matter. Until the Civil Code of 1871 was passed, marriage and divorce had been regulated exclusively by the Catholic Church, which meant no divorce without proven fault and no remarriage. From that time forward, such matters remained under church control, but civil judges now had the authority to determine the consequences, for example, child custody and division of property. In 1888, the regulation of marriage and divorce passed to the State, but remarriage was still not authorized. No-fault divorce and remarriage were introduced in 1954 and rescinded the next year when Perón was ousted from power. In 1968 divorce by mutual agreement was authorized, with no remarriage. It was not until 1987, still several years away, that divorce could be requested by one spouse without the consent of the other following a de facto separation, and remarriage allowed after at least three years. So, at this time, those who wished to remarry had the following choices: obtain an annulment or get divorced and remarried in another country, usually nearby Uruguay, so that it would be legal, although not in Argentina. Both options were complicated and expensive, and most people were forced to do without the benefit of the law.

In this case, after much thought and prayer, it was decided to accept the person as she was when she became a Christian, reasoning that it was not the church's business to punish and penalize people for things done to them by others or done by them and forgiven by Christ. When the laws changed, most people in the churches set about the business of straightening out their legal marital status.

Led by Rodolfo "Fito" and Irene Cappello, the church opened a new work that first met in a house (lent by missionaries Robert and Annette Crockett). It eventually became the Villa General Mitre Baptist Church, where Bruce and Nancy Muskrat served for many years.

An Unexpected Turn of Events

Things were finally settling into a groove and the Bedfords were looking forward to a regular semester and spending the last decade of their missionary career at the Seminary. Don Kammerdiener had recently resigned as Associate Area Director in order to become the Director for the Caribbean. He had told Ben that he would like to have him as his own Associate, and he and La Nell had tried to imagine what it would be like to make such a drastic change, but nothing came of it as Don had come across an ideal candidate with years of experience in that field. The Bedfords took it as confirmation that they were in the right place. Classes had barely gotten under way in February when Ben received a call from Dr. Thurmon Bryant, the Foreign Mission Board's Area Director for Eastern South America. Now that Don was gone, Dr. Bryant needed a replacement and Ben was his first choice.

"I'll need some time to consider it," stammered Ben.

"Fine—I'll call you back in a week."

Ben and La Nell stared at each other. Could this possibly be right? By great good fortune, their friend Billy Graves was in town for a visit. He had recently lost his wife Chris to cancer and was soaking up love and friendship. He was able to share first-hand knowledge of the lifestyle and work involved in being an Area Associate, since that was the position he now occupied in Central America.

Administratively, the Foreign Mission Board divided the world into congenial geographical regions, each with its own Richmond-based Area Director, who in turn had one or more Associates in the field depending on the size of the Area. In this case, Eastern South America was divided into two: Portuguese-speaking Brazil in the north, so large that it had three separate missions, and Spanish-speaking Argentina, Uruguay and Paraguay in the south. Ben was being offered the latter.

The basic job description of an Area Associate was to be the liaison between Richmond and the field, representing the Foreign Mission Board to the missionaries, and the missionaries to the Board. He was responsible for projecting the overall vision and program of the FMB and for pastoring the missionaries, combining spiritual guidance and administrative acumen.

By the end of the week they had felt led to accept as a team, for La Nell had been formally offered the position of Secretary to the Associate. Thurmon was overjoyed.

"Great! Pack your bags and come to Richmond, Ben. We'll set you up and get you going."

Ben scrambled to meet his flight. Fortunately, he had a very able teaching assistant, Carlos Villanueva (who would one day become President) ready to cover for him while he was away. He wasn't the only one struggling to keep up with things. Before leaving, Ben made a quick call to Jimmy Spann, President of the Uruguayan Mission, to ask them to name a liaison for an upcoming partnership program.

"Okay, but why are *you* calling about it?"

"Haven't you heard? I'm the new Associate to the Area Director."

"Oh!"

In Richmond, Ben was given orientation as well as some equipment he would need for setting up his office. Technically, he and La Nell no longer belonged to the Argentine Mission but to the Foreign Mission Board staff. While he was in the U.S. he stopped in Mississippi to help coordinate the new partnership program between the churches of that state and his Area missions.

The trip allowed Ben a brief stopover in Houston, where he saw his daughters and met his newest grandchild, Veronica Gaydou, now nine months old. She had been born in late May of the previous year, with no grandparents, aunts, uncles or cousins within traveling distance. It had been a bit traumatic because mother and child had incompatible blood types, causing the baby's bilirubin level to shoot up and requiring several days in the Children's Hospital's intensive care unit. The church family had stepped up to help care for twenty-one-month-old Andrea until everyone was home, but by the time a month had gone by, Nelda could no longer bear not being able to show off her beautiful new baby to her loved ones, so the little family threw together a few things and drove ten hours to the Ferrell's new home in Sylvarena, Mississippi for the Fourth of July weekend. They were all there, including Lynn and her family, who had travelled all the way from Idaho for the occasion. Ben was also able to share Veronica's first birthday in person after a lightning trip to the Spanish Baptist Publishing House in El Paso. La Nell had to wait a little longer.

Jugglers

The new assignment made fulfilling their current obligations with the Seminary and the church rather challenging. Somehow, they had to make it to the end of the semester, when they were already committed to a year-long furlough in Fort Worth, Texas. Former colleague Justice Anderson had been to the January Mission Meeting bearing an invitation from Southwestern Seminary for Ben to be the visiting professor of Missions. They would go ahead with that plus the Associate duties.

In between teaching, preaching and pastoring, they had to attend all the mission meetings in the three countries in the area and carry out an assessment of each missionary who was about to go on furlough in order to analyze the latest term. This included a personal interview, sending out evaluation forms to other missionaries and nationals, and preparing a report. They were in charge of the missionary language proficiency evaluations and either had to carry them out themselves or find qualified people to do so, in order to determine whether further training was necessary. They were responsible for enforcing the Foreign Mission Board's strict new housing policy, which involved personally measuring the houses to be sure they did not exceed the allowed square footage. And they had to get a handle on the work at the Spanish Baptist Publishing House, the Mississippi Partnership and MasterLife. These duties would continue during their time in the U.S.

Two new missionary couples arrived to bolster up the Seminary faculty—Randal and Janet Pannell, and Bill and Patricia Stancil. Randal and Bill helped Ben move box upon box of books from his office to the garage of the Bedfords' house. Ben told the Dean he should make a quick grab for the office while he could, and Stanley did just that.

Gauchos and Giraffes

All the booths were colorful and attractive, displaying maps, posters, typical objects and traditional costumes of the countries they represented. But the one for Argentina stole the show because the models for the *gaucho* and *paisana* costumes were the Bedfords' two-year-old grandchildren William and Andrea.

They were at the Glorieta Baptist Encampment for Foreign Missions Week, their first engagement after arriving in the U.S. The Gaydous had met them at the airport in Houston, with Nelda torn between anticipation and apprehension. It had been astounding to watch her level-headed, down-to-earth mother transform into the ultimate doting grandmother. Could she possibly be just as crazy about another granddaughter? For her part, Veronica, though adorable, definitely had a mind of her own and did not dispense charm indiscriminately. She had been known to counter friendly overtures from strangers with a cold up-and-down stare.

She needn't have worried. Veronica took one look at her grandmother, reached out her arms and melted onto her shoulder. Although she didn't know it, this was a stroke of genius because, while La Nell was great with babies, Ben was a positive magnet for the little ones, who invariably chose him out of all adults present. And when the fourteen-month-old made a supreme effort to pronounce her name and came up with "Grandmer," the conquest was complete.

On the way back to Texas, the Bedfords stopped in Clovis to see Ben's sister Billie and buy a brand new bare-bones little Honda Civic for Nancy for $5,000. It proved to be an amazing vehicle that served the entire family nobly at one time or another for over two decades.

Ben and La Nell settled into an apartment in Fort Worth that had just been vacated by their friends the Bartleys, and Ben began preparing his classes. He would be team-teaching two courses on Missions each semester, one for regular degree students and one for diploma students, with former professors and present-day colleagues Dr. Guy (in the fall) and Dr. Gray (in the spring). Years later, after the Bedfords had retired, they attended a service in the Baptist church of Evanston, Illinois when its founding pastor, Dr. Mark T. Coppenger, was visiting. He beamed at the congregation as he told them that his very first class at the Seminary had been one of those Missions courses with Ben. Dr. Coppenger had gone on to become President of Midwestern Baptist Theological Seminary and then Director of Extension for Southern Baptist Theological Seminary.

Although La Nell lacked only two classes to finish her Master's degree, which had been interrupted at various points in time by different family emergencies, she decided not to go back to school so that she could be free to enjoy family. Nancy was close enough to spend many weekends and Nelda was only a few hours away. They even managed to see David several times.

Right away they received a visit from Nelda and Alberto, their girls and his parents. The senior Gaydous had come to the U.S. for a month and were now on a mini-tour of Texas. Ben thrilled his students by inviting Daniel to teach a class with him as interpreter, but perhaps the most memorable moment was the whole group's outing to the legendary Fort Worth Zoo. While Veronica spent most of her time in Lola's arms, Andrea stuck with Ben, chattering non-stop. When they reached the giraffes, the little girl's eyes widened in amazement as she followed the line of the neck higher and higher, and was hit by the revelation that those images she had seen in her books represented real things in the world. Her grandparents missed the sequel to this experience when, a few weeks later at the supermarket, Andrea joyfully pointed to one of the shoppers and sang out in a clear, ringing voice, "Look, Mommy—Miss Piggy!" Her mother could not really fault her: face and hair were definitely those of the famous Muppet diva.

The Bedfords did a lot of traveling that year between the usual speaking engagements, family, and Associate duties. There were at least two trips per year to El Paso, as all the Area Associates in Latin America automatically became permanent members of the Board of Trustees of Casa Bautista, the Spanish Baptist Publishing House. The rest of the Board consisted of rotating elected representatives from the various national conventions. Casa Bautista published Bibles, Bible commentaries, Bible study materials, theological works, magazines, devotionals and inspirational books, both original and translated, for the entire Spanish-speaking world, a large undertaking since Spanish is the second most widely spoken language in the world, surpassed only by Chinese.

Very good people worked there over the years, many of them old friends from Argentina whose service coincided with Ben's at different points in time: former missionaries Thompson, Carroll, Campbell and Stanton, and talented nationals Aldo Broda, Ananías González, Rubén Zorzoli and Roberto García Bordoli. The year before Ananías had unsuccessfully tried to persuade Ben to become the full-time head of the recently created Evangelism Department when Dr. Lyon left. During his ten years on the Board, Ben pushed especially hard for two projects. The first was an original series of Sunday School materials designed to cover the entire Bible in nine years, with books for students and teachers of adolescents, young people and adults. The second was an original series of Bible commentaries for both pastors and laymen, the last of whose twenty-four volumes was published shortly after Ben's retirement. These series are still being used today.[87]

While they were on furlough Ben and La Nell underwent training in language proficiency evaluation at the Language School in Costa Rica, led by their own son David and Harry Rosser from Boston College. Although they both received the training and carried out countless evaluations, La Nell had by far the lion's share of this work. She was universally recognized as one of the most linguistically outstanding missionaries ever on the field. In fact, quite a few of their Argentine friends would ask La Nell to proofread and edit important letters or papers. All missionaries had to be evaluated and this usually took place during the Mission Meetings.

---

[87] See Joe T. Poe's fascinating book, A House for All Nations: A Centennial History of the Baptist Spanish Publishing House, 2004).

Starting now Ben took advantage of his twice-yearly trips to El Paso to visit and encourage new missionaries appointed to his Area, alternating between the Missionary Orientation Center in Pine Mountain, Georgia (which also allowed him to see David, its Associate Director) and the Language School in Costa Rica.

Ben and La Nell also received training in MasterLife at this time. In spite of Ben's kidney infection, they attended the workshop with La Nell's missionary brother Tom and his wife Iris at Camp Copass, the same camp where David had broken his arm in 1956. The training was led by the creator of the program, Avery Willis, who had been a classmate of Ben's in the Seminary. Willis had begun developing MasterLife in Indonesia, where he served as missionary. Three men from the Sunday School Board had approached him and asked if he would be willing to move to the U.S. and develop it into a world-wide discipleship program. When they returned to Argentina, Ben and La Nell taught a MasterLife workshop at Thea for representatives from Argentina, Uruguay, Paraguay and Chile. Later they led workshops for leaders in each country and taught the course to church members in their own home. Once again, La Nell was the principal, with Ben as her co-leader. He suggested teaching the course as an Evangelism class in the Seminary. This was put into practice and soon Stanley and Kathleen Clark became experts, teaching and training many workers over the years.

There were also several trips to Mississippi. The Foreign Mission Board was promoting partnerships between state associations and various countries. Tennessee, for example, entered into one with Chile, but Mississippi established a partnership with all three countries in Ben's Area, and he coordinated the representatives from that state and from the three missions: Mark Alexander and then Don Mines in Argentina, Jason Carlisle in Uruguay and Gilbert Nichols in Paraguay. The idea was to set up trips to the field with teams of church people from Mississippi. Over the years, they did a bit of everything, according to what was needed, from evangelism to construction, to music (including a hand-bell choir), to radio and television programs. Originally envisioned as a three-year program, it was extended to five and was amazingly fruitful.

159

Equator Party (Courtesy Roger Garner) 1964

David, Nancy and Nelda in Rio, 1964

Nancy, Dusty and Nelda in Adrogué, 1965

La Nell, Buenos Aires ca. 1965

Church building in Solano, 1966

Ben preaching in Solano, 1966

Ferrell and Bedford girls at AWOL in La Falda 1966

Family portrait, Ramos Mejía 1967

Ben and Seminary colleagues, Buenos Aires,1968

Two Nancies and Ben, Lubbock, TX, 1969

Nancy, Nelda and La Nell, Buenos Aires, 1972

Nelda, Ben and Nancy, La Falda, 1973

Ben at Daniel Tinao's inauguration, Buenos Aires, 1975

Ben working on La Falda church building, 1976

Nelda and Alberto, La Falda, 1976

Newlyweds Patricia and David, Buenos Aires, 1977

La Nell and Ben with grandchildren William and Andrea, Glorieta, NM 1981

Thurmon Bryant and Ben, new hospital wing, Asunción, Paraguay, 1985

168

Ben, Alejandro, Andrea, William, Veronica and La Nell, Villa Giardino, 1985

Nancy and Daniel, Germany, 1991

La Nell sewing a quilt, Albuquerque, 1992

Ben with grandchildren Sergio and Sabrina on their baptismal day, Fort Worth, TX, 2001

Ben with great-grandsons Joshua and Thomas, Austin, TX, 2004

Ben at top left, Albuquerque, NM, 2006

La Nell and Ben, 61st wedding anniversary, Nicaragua, 2007

Ben at medical clinic, Nicaragua, 2007

Ben baptizing in the Pecos River, NM, 2009

Grandson Alejandro's family (Cintia, Evangelina and Nicolás), Capilla del Monte, Argentina, 2011

Grandson William and family (Sofia, Dorrie and Ellie), England, 2012

Family portrait, Evanston, Illinois, 2013

Singing Christmas hymns with granddaughters Valeria, Sofia and Carolina, Evanston, 2013

Ben turning over the pastorate to Yessenia and Chrisitan Castro, Evanston, 2016

Ben and La Nell at the church where they were married, Portales NM, 2017

Cycle of Life

While La Nell had been the only extended Bedford family member present when Andrea was born and none had been present when William and Veronica arrived, there was a full albeit fleeting contingent for Alejandro Daniel Gaydou. For a change, Ben and La Nell had been nearby during the entire pregnancy and had been able to care for their daughter and granddaughters when Nelda was ordered a month of bed rest and Alberto could not take time off from work.

This happy event kept them all from brooding obsessively over the Malvinas[88] War between Argentina and Great Britain. In fact, Alejandro was born the day the war ended. David and his family were there because Patricia, who turned out to be a magnificent soprano, was recording several songs at a studio in Houston (the video sessions were taped later in Georgia and aired all over the Spanish-speaking world on thirteen episodes of *Círculo Tres*,[89] an evangelistic program produced by John Magyar in the Media Center in Cali, Colombia). Nancy had only to hop in her car and drive down from Austin. It was at the very end of the Bedfords' furlough and, while La Nell had scheduled some extra time to lend a hand, Ben had to hope that the baby would arrive between his trip to El Paso and his return to Argentina.

They had just finished loading up the car and were about to lock up and turn in the key to the apartment that had been their temporary home in Fort Worth. Ben would be catching a flight to El Paso while La Nell drove to Houston, but the phone rang and changed their plans in an instant. Missionary Bob Burtis had suddenly suffered a massive

88 Falkland Islands
89 Circle Three

heart attack and passed away in Argentina, and the family and his body were being flown back to the U.S. The funeral and burial were to take place near Houston, so Ben and La Nell drove down there together to be with Betty and the children. They not only offered spiritual and emotional support, but they made sure that all the paperwork surrounding the traumatic event was in order to help pave the way for the future.

After his Board meeting in El Paso, Ben arrived in Houston to discover that his daughter was in labor and postponed his return to Argentina by one day so that he could hold his little grandson in his arms at the hospital. Then he was off. He barely had time to pull the dustcovers off the furniture before he had houseguests—Dr. and Mrs. Skinner, missionaries from Paraguay on a visit to Buenos Aires. Meanwhile, the rest of the family had a little excitement apart from the baby: a tornado ripped through town uprooting trees and tearing off roofs on the other side of their block, but they were unscathed.

Shell-Shocked

The entire nation was in shock after losing the two-and-a-half month Malvinas War. Argentines felt not only grief, pain and anger but, above all, betrayal. They had been betrayed by their own government, which had unleashed a war it thought no one else would care about in order to distract the people from mounting internal problems, lying at every turn; betrayed by the British government, which had also used the conflict to replace domestic dissatisfaction with patriotic fanaticism, having until then largely ignored the islanders; betrayed by the U.S. government which could have remained neutral in a conflict between allies but had given the British aid without which they would not have been able to win; betrayed by a world which washed its hands of the whole affair; betrayed by neighboring Chile which had helped the enemy. Only Peru had been a true friend.

Although most people's anger with the U.S. was intense, personal ties and friendship outweighed politics, and the Bedfords were welcomed back with open arms. Over thirty years later the Bedrossians, a couple from the Flores church, recalled those days:

> .... *The Flores Church was greatly blessed by your pastorate which, although interim, enriched and strengthened it. The young people never forgot the brigade to La Pampa, recalling the enthusiasm that experience generated.*
>
> *La Nell: for you my gratitude and remembrance are enduring: I will never forget that during the Malvinas War I was in very great anguish; it made me ill and one Sunday after the service you called me aside and comforted me with wise words; I even remember the place where we sat...... Those marks remain.*

In the event, this disastrous war proved to be the final downfall of military dictatorships in Argentina. Popular feeling was so strong that the generals were forced to step down. Elections took place the next year and the ugly truths hidden for so long began working their way out into the open.

The message of peace, reconciliation and renewal proclaimed by the church was more important than ever.

Getting to Know You

Thurmon and Ben went a long way back, in fact, long before they actually met, back to the first summer after Ben and La Nell married, in 1946. Ben was riding a tractor, mowing the grass on the college campus to earn some extra cash, when he was waved down by a young man who introduced himself as Ben's cousin Dolores' brother-in-law. Her wedding had been the first one that Ben had ever performed and now he was being asked to officiate at another. The bride-to-be was none other than Thurmon's sister.

Dr. Bryant was a wonderful boss. He shared a deep love and understanding of the work from his own missionary career in Brazil, where he had been president of the seminary in São Paulo. He had an able and delightful wife, Doris, and the two couples got along famously. Although they conferred frequently, Thurmon believed in giving his Associates plenty of scope for getting things done in the way that worked best for them, offering help and support when needed.

Ben and La Nell prayed and planned. They considered their substantial administrative duties tools to be used in their most important job: pastoring the missionaries and making sure they had what they needed to carry out the Great Commission.[90] In order to do this, they felt that it was essential to get to know all 124 missionaries individually, in their own homes and fields of service, assuring them

---

90 "Then Jesus came to them and said, 'All authority in heaven and on earth has been given to me. Therefore go and make disciples of all nations, baptizing them in the name of the Father and of the Son and of the Holy Spirit, and teaching them to obey everything I have commanded you. And surely I am with you always, to the very end of the age.'" (Matthew 28:18-20)

that someone had their backs. So they set about visiting every one of them.

Shortly after they returned to Argentina, they were assigned a car that La Nell could actually drive. When they had accepted their new positions, they had inherited their predecessor's vehicle—an Estanciera whose stiff steering and even stiffer manual transmission were too much for her arthritis. But now they had the use of a brand-new automatic Ford Taunus that they would be driving until they retired. The first long trip they made in it was to Paraguay, to spend three months immersing themselves in the culture and work of that country and spending one-on-one time with the missionaries there.

Known as the "Heart of South America," Paraguay is the smaller of the two landlocked nations of that continent.[91] What it lacks in oceans, it makes up for in rivers. While there is no consensus on the exact meaning of its name, all interpretations are variations on the same theme: "river which originates sea," "river-crowned," "river of the Payaguás," "river that flows through the sea," "river of the habitants of the sea," or simply "born from water." The Paraguay River divides the country in two: the Eastern Region, mostly grassy plains and wooded hills, and the Western Region or Chaco, characterized by low, marshy plains. There are no high mountain ranges to break the winds, which can rush up to 100 miles per hour. Warm winds from the Amazon Basin in the north prevail between October and March, while cold winds from the Andes in the west predominate between May and August. Temperatures can drop below freezing in winter but are scorching hot in summer.

Together with the Pilcomayo, the Paraguay River forms the border with Bolivia in the northwest. Both of these and the Paraná divide Paraguay from Argentina in the southeast. The Paraná, Paraguay and Apa rivers, strung together by the Mbaracayú and Amambay hills, separate it from Brazil in the northeast. At the famous Tri-Border area, Paraguay, Argentina and Brazil share the spectacular Iguazú Falls.

In the sixteenth century, Spain colonized the area, which had been inhabited by indigenous peoples for thousands of years. The

---

91 The other one being its neighbor Bolivia

various tribes belonged to five distinct language families and even today seventeen separate ethnolinguistic areas remain, the largest by far being the Guaraní. Jesuit missionaries attempted to convert the natives and create an autonomous Christian Indian nation, protected from the virtual slavery usually imposed by the Spanish settlers. The Jesuits were expelled by the Spanish government in 1767 and the Spanish colonial administration was ousted in 1811, after which Paraguay was governed by a long succession of dictators. The first of these, Rodríguez de Francia, isolated the new nation even more and sought to create a utopian society along the lines of Jean-Jacques Rousseau's *Social Contract*. His new laws greatly reduced the power of the Catholic Church and forbade colonial citizens from marrying each other. They were to marry blacks, mulattoes or aborigines, thus creating a mixed-race or mestizo society. Later Italians, Germans, Russians, Japanese, Koreans, Chinese, Arabs, Ukrainians, Poles, Jews, Brazilian and Argentine immigrants were added to the ethnic mix, and a large community of German-speaking Mennonites was established in the Chaco, but the Spanish-Guaraní culture prevailed.

The nation endured two international wars. The first was the Paraguayan War, which ended in 1870 with sixty to seventy percent of the population lost to war and disease, and around one quarter of its territory lost to Argentina and Brazil. The second was the Chaco War in the early 1930s, in which Paraguay defeated Bolivia and established its sovereignty over most of the disputed Chaco region, albeit with heavy losses. So Paraguay had little reason to love or trust its neighbors.

Medical History

Ben counted pills and handed over the number requested by Dr. Bill Skinner. It was just about the only thing he could do other than observe the doctors and nurses in action. He had tagged along on the mobile clinic's trip to the interior. Unfortunately, he could scarcely understand anything that was happening.

One of the fascinating things about Paraguay is the fact that the vast majority of the population is bilingual in Spanish and Guaraní. Although it is estimated that today over 90% of the population is bilingual, in the 1980s about 25% still did not speak Spanish, mostly in the interior. Foreigners frequently miss out on jokes and puns, which often switch back and forth between languages or depend on word plays between the two.

The Baptist Hospital in Asunción was the center of a great deal of missionary work. Its origins lay back in the 1940s when Miriam Willis, a missionary nurse, had started a small clinic in an impoverished area of Asunción with little medical attention available. Franklin Fowler, medical doctor and Argentine MK, arrived in 1947 to help her. Eventually the clinic grew into a hospital served by many missionary doctors, nurses and administrators over the years. Most local government officials, including the President, used the services of the hospital, which was officially inaugurated in 1953 in the new facilities made possible by the Jarman Foundation.

A Vacation Bible School for children on the hospital grounds was the starting point for one of the largest and most active congregations in Paraguay, the Villa Mora Baptist Church. A nursing school was established, medical internships were made available and, starting in 1963, Clinical Pastoral Education was offered under the direction of missionary James Watson. Mobile clinics with medical and dental services began making regular trips to the out-of-the-way places in the interior.[92]

As Associate, Ben was on the Hospital Board of Trustees and scarcely a month went by in which he didn't make a trip to Asunción. It wasn't all plain sailing, either. On one occasion, when the entire staff was feeling mutinous, Ben took the time to meet with every doctor, nurse and administrator individually and mediated a working arrangement to which they could all commit.

A partnership was established with the Jacksonville Baptist Medical Center in Florida that was very fruitful in terms of training and equipment. Several years later, in 1988, Marlin Harris was named administrator and given the mission of guiding the transfer of the institution to the Paraguayan Convention. He overhauled the administration, identified and trained capable Paraguayan leaders, and hired Ernesto Simari (Cacho Simari's eldest son) as his assistant and successor. The hospital became a full medical center and, at the request of local professionals, incorporated a heart institute that was to perform the first transplant in the country. A wing with twenty private rooms was added (for which Thurmon and Ben put in countless hours rounding up the funding), as well as a campus for the Baptist Medical Center University. Thurmon spoke and Ben interpreted for him at the new wing's inauguration service, which was attended by Paraguayan President Alfredo Stroessner.

Ben's first encounters with the future administrator and his wife both occurred under somewhat unusual circumstances. He was making the long, long trek at Miami International Airport to reach the gate for his flight to Paraguay when he saw a man looking around him in a rather uncertain manner.

"You wouldn't by any chance be Marlin Harris?"

"Yes, I am!"

"I'm Ben Bedford and we're supposed to be in Asunción together."

---

92 Justice C. Anderson. An Evangelical Saga: Baptists and their Precursors in Latin America. Xulton Press: 2005, pp. 300-303.

Marlin was on a reconnaissance trip. He was appointed and went through missionary orientation but had to take several courses at the Seminary before going to the field.

Sometime later, while he was passing through Fort Worth, Ben stopped at a bookstore. He saw a young woman making purchases from which he made certain deductions. He asked her:

"Are you a missionary?"

"Yes! My husband and I are going to Paraguay."

It was Marlin's wife Jean. They had met and married at the Seminary, so she had to go through the appointment process after her husband. Marlin joked that he was the only person who had been made to repeat missionary orientation.

Politically Incorrect

Of course, the hospital was not the only institution in which Baptist missionaries were involved in Paraguay. It sponsored several schools, including one that followed the U.S. curriculum, a Bible Institute (founded in 1956) and a camp in Itacurubí de la Cordillera that became a well-equipped and much used Conference Center.

On the Bedfords' first trip to the camp, Gail and Jerry Joule took them to a nearby stand that sold an amazing array of *ñandutí*,[93] the beautiful traditional Paraguayan embroidered lace. It became the go-to item for gifts on special occasions, like Ben's sister Billie and her husband Marion's fiftieth wedding anniversary, when they received a spectacular tablecloth with matching napkins. There were other handcrafted items as well. As they drove away, La Nell mused, "I really should have gotten that carved wood Indian head—it reminded me so much of some of the men in Ben's family." Gail stood on the brakes, spun around and drove back. From then on, that Indian head occupied a place of honor among the Bedford family portraits.

During another meeting at the camp one of the missionaries invited Ben to a soccer game near his home. Thurmon overheard and decided that he would also like to go (after all, one does not live in Brazil for years without becoming a fan). Ben was afraid that Dr. Bryant's presence might prove to be unfortunate, not because he wouldn't be good company, but because he foresaw trouble over this particular missionary's living quarters.

The Foreign Mission Board had adopted a commendable policy to ensure that missionary housing was not ostentatious and did not project a paternalistic or colonialist image. Among other things,

93 Spider web

there were strict new limits on the square footage allowed. Existing overlarge houses were either sold or divided up and used for other purposes. Dwellings bought or rented for missionaries were personally measured by the Area Associates. In Argentina and Uruguay this was not much of a problem, since both countries had large middle classes and many suitable properties were available, although Ben felt that it was a bit unfair not to allow a little more space for field missionaries who, unlike their professor, doctor or administrator peers, did not have separate office space.

But in Paraguay it was much more difficult to be politically correct. There was a large poor class and a small very affluent class with not much in between. As a result, the houses offered for rent tended to be either much too small or much too large, and this was a case in point. Predictably, Thurmon was horrified.

"This is way over the allowance! It is completely unacceptable."

"But there was literally nothing else available," explained Ben.

"Then we should build them a house," replied Dr. Bryant.

"That would be very expensive and who knows how long they will live here? If we have to sell soon, we will be taking a loss."

But Thurmon was adamant. A new house was built and, sure enough, not long afterwards the missionary family was called elsewhere and it had to be sold.

Roughing It

The pastor and the baptismal candidates were carefully lowered into and raised out of the deep round water hole by a rope ladder. Jim and Jean Hausler, field missionaries in the northern Paraguayan city of Concepción, were showing the Bedfords around their area. Now they were at a mission point deep in the interior. After the moving baptismal and worship service, they shared a meal with the little congregation. It had grown quite dark and the few lamps cast a fitful light that did not reach as far as their plates, so that they were not quite sure what they were eating, which, given their respective food intolerances, made Ben and La Nell a bit nervous. There was really no choice but to go ahead on faith and, miraculously, they suffered no ill effects.

On the same trip, they went to another location where there was great interest in the MasterLife program. Ben rode in the back of the pickup with the equipment as they bounced around over increasingly rutted dirt roads until they could go no further. They climbed out and covered the last half mile on foot carrying the equipment for the presentation, which was delivered by the Paraguayan leader they had brought with them.

They not only heard missionaries and nationals hold forth, but were often asked to preach or give studies or devotionals in the churches and at the Mission Meetings. By now La Nell had been a Women's Missionary Union leader in Argentina for over three decades and the Paraguayans took advantage of the Bedfords' visits to invite her to speak. On one occasion a national WMU worker pressed La Nell to go to Pedro Juan Caballero, near the eastern border with Brazil, and arranged transportation on a small cargo plane. La Nell had one of the regular seats, but Ben was relegated to a bench that ran down the side of the aircraft. The space in the middle held cargo, including cages of chickens. Because they were flying low, they were able to get a close view of the landscape, not only through the windows but around the edges of the ill-fitting door and between the gaps in the floorboards.

They landed on a reasonably level stretch of prairie and spent a couple of days sharing with the ladies in Pedro Juan Caballero. While they were there it rained torrentially and they were unable to retrace their steps. The only option was to cross over into Brazil and catch a commercial airline flight to Asunción, which involved going through immigration and customs on both ends.

Their visits showed them that, on the whole, the missionaries worked very well with their national peers, assisting where they were most needed. Paraguayan Baptists had organized and directed the work in their country since 1956, when the Convention was created with its own boards, committees, projects and programs. At that time there were 5 churches, 13 preaching points, 3 ordained ministers and 655 members. The churches gave 10% of their offerings to the Convention's Cooperative Program and the Mission provided funds for church loans and Baptist institutions. By the mid-1980s there were 46 organized churches, 96 missions, 5000 members, 35 pastors and 49 foreign missionaries.

The Mansion

Three-year-old William, at that time a miniature blond male version of his mother, was on an extended trip to spend time with his grandparents and strengthen his Spanish. This worked so well that on one occasion that the Bedfords had him, they admonished him to speak in English.

"*No puedo*," [94]he answered sadly.

Patricia had turned her little son over to Ben in Miami when he was returning to Argentina from a trip to El Paso. William fell asleep waiting for the connecting flight and did not wake up until long after they took off.

"When are we leaving, Granddaddy?"

"We already did! We are on the way."

But it was pitch black outside and the ride was so smooth that he could not believe it.

The two sets of grandparents took turns keeping him. After a few days they would switch, sharing a meal and several hours of company to ease the transition.

"Guille,"[95] asked his Grandmother Esther, "how come you behave so beautifully here and run around wild at my house?"

William looked her in the eye, shrugged his shoulders and replied with devastating frankness, "Because you let me."

He was the one who christened the Bedfords' house "The Mansion," for the two-story house seemed huge to the little apartment dweller, and he liked nothing better than to run up and down the stairs, much to the detriment of his grandparents' nerves. William's name for the house stuck within the family circle.

---

94 "I can't."
95 Short for "Guillermo," the Spanish version of "William"

The little boy returned to the U.S. with Ben, La Nell and Ignacio Loredo, who all had business in the North. They changed planes in Rio and while they were waiting for takeoff the aircraft next to them began moving.

"I want to go on that plane, Granddaddy!"

"Ours will be taking off soon."

"No, it won't."

"We have to take turns. You'll see."

The little boy was not convinced. Echoing a popular television commercial, he shook his head and solemnly intoned, *"No va a andar; no va a andar."*[96]

The Bedfords received many guests at The Mansion, especially since the office was in the house. The previous Associate had occupied a room in the Mission Office, but when he left and it had been reorganized and expanded, the Mission took advantage of the opportunity, snapped up the room and put it to another use. So Ben and La Nell received a steady stream of visitors at home.

---

[96] "It's not going to work; it's not going to work."

A Tough Nut to Crack

The Bedfords' relationship with Uruguay had begun long before the three months they spent visiting the missionaries there in 1983. In fact, they had nearly been transferred to that field at the very beginning of their career after extending their stay in Costa Rica for language training because their visas for Argentina were delayed. The Foreign Mission Board had finally scheduled their voyage and told them that if they had not received their visas by the time they left, they were to disembark in Montevideo and serve in Uruguay. The paperwork went through at the last minute.

When they arrived in Argentina in 1953, Paraguay had already withdrawn from the River Plate Mission, but Uruguay and Argentina were still together, and Ben was elected President at the first Mission Meeting they attended. Many of the older missionaries had worked in two or more of the three countries.

La Nell's brother Tom Watson and his wife Iris served as missionaries in Uruguay and two of their three daughters were born there. The Bedfords visited them several times before they transferred to Peru. The first time they were surprised that no one received them at the airport in Montevideo. They asked around and were directed to a city bus that left them practically at the Watsons' doorstep. They had been so busy preparing that they had lost track of time.

Next, they visited them in Durazno.[97] Airline officials sought them out at the airport in Buenos Aires to congratulate Nelda on her seventh birthday and give her the red-carpet treatment. Because she had injured it roughhousing, she waited to tell her parents about the pain in her little finger until she couldn't take it any longer. As

---

97 The city's name means "Peach."

a result, they spent a good part of their vacation sitting in waiting rooms, getting x-rays and having a splint put on the fractured digit by strangers in another country.

La Nell went alone to see her brother and his family in Colonia when her niece Elizabeth was born. She travelled over on the flying boat or hydroplane, a fixed-wing aircraft that can take off and land on water. That was fun, but when she tried to return the same way it was no longer available, as that had been the very last hydroplane flight between Buenos Aires and Colonia.

The Bedfords felt quite comfortable in Uruguay, which is very similar to Argentina in many ways, including ethnic makeup, socioeconomic structure and language. They found more similarities between Montevideo and Buenos Aires than between the Argentine Capital and other cities in its own nation. A large proportion of both populations even speak with the same accent, known as *rioplatense*.[98]

Still, Uruguay has never appreciated being treated like Argentina's little sister and has managed to escape assimilation by its larger neighbors and aggressive European powers. At 68,000 square miles, it is the second smallest nation in South America. The Charrúas inhabited the area for some 4000 years, driven south by the Guaraní. The Portuguese founded Colonia del Sarmiento in 1680 and the Spanish built the military stronghold of Montevideo in the early eighteenth century. In an offshoot of the Napoleonic Wars, in 1806 and 1807 the British attempted and failed to seize both Buenos Aires and Montevideo. Between 1811 and 1828 Uruguay fought to maintain its identity as it was caught in a four-way struggle between Spain, Portugal, Argentina and Brazil. José Gervasio Artigas emerged as the national leader and championed federalism in the constituent assembly of the new government in Buenos Aires, asking for political and economic autonomy for each area, particularly for the Oriental or Eastern Band, as Uruguay was known at the time. Buenos Aires pursued unitary centralism and Artigas refused to go along. At various points in time Uruguay was part of Argentina and in 1816 the Portuguese invaded, captured Montevideo and annexed it to

---

[98] Of the River Plate

the Portuguese Kingdom of Brazil as "Cisplatine." Uruguay took advantage of regional squabbles to establish itself permanently as an individual state, and was recognized as such by Argentina and Brazil in the Treaty of Montevideo of 1828.

Known as the most progressive, liberal and middle class country of the Americas, Uruguay has 410 miles of coastline, a dense fluvial network of four river basins, rolling plains, low hill ranges and temperate weather with four marked seasons. It is strong in agriculture and tourism, and is an important commercial and banking center.

It is also the most secular country of the Americas, with no official religion and complete separation of church and state. Approximately 45% of the population calls itself Roman Catholic, 9% non-Catholic Christian, 14% atheist or agnostic, 0.6% Animist or Umbandist and 0.4% Jewish. Around 30% claims to believe in God without belonging to any religion. Uruguay has been called the most difficult mission field on earth, not from opposition but from indifference. Its missionaries felt a strange mixture of fierce love and frustration for their adopted home. On the whole, they did not require help with their work in the local churches and institutions, but rather moral and spiritual support, and personal counseling. So that was where the Bedfords concentrated their efforts.

In the first few months after he was named Associate, Ben visited Uruguay several times before his furlough, to get an initial grasp of things and get logistics going for the Mississippi partnership. He worked closely with then Mission President Jimmy Spann. He had gotten to know him when he helped him gather and send off brother-in-law Tom's belongings to their new field of service in Lima, Peru. Jimmy was very handy with tools and in fact made the boxes in which they packed the Watsons' worldly possessions. He was in charge of the Seminary while Jimmy Bartley was on furlough and invited Ben to speak both there and at Mission Meeting.

Mission Meetings in Uruguay alternated between the Seminary in Montevideo and the Christian school near Colonia. The town of Conchillas, where the school was actually located, had grown up in the late nineteenth century around the Walker Company, a British firm that kept the construction of the new port in Buenos Aires supplied with cheap sand and gravel. Besides the factory, the town had two cemeteries and an Anglican church. When the British withdrew, they gave the church building to the Baptists, and the congregation still meets there today. The furnishings included pews with reversible backs that came from Charles Spurgeon's church in England.[99]

While Ken and Mary Ann Evanston were on furlough, the Bedfords used their house in Montevideo as the home base from which to visit all the missionaries in the interior, driving a borrowed car. Sometimes, they took their own vehicle across the Río de la Plata on the ferry. On several of his solo trips Ben experienced a wide variety of sleeping arrangements, from comfortable beds to sleeping bags in tents and even church pews, for example, when he had been called on to approve a prospective rental house for Truman Chatman with Gene Dubberly.

Gene had been in Thea, the Baptist Camp in Argentina, with a group from Mississippi. Before splitting up, they had taken advantage of a perfect day to relax over ice cream and coffee at a sidewalk café on the main street of La Falda. They were having a great time swapping stories when a gnat darted straight into one of Ben's eyes. Of course, he would be slightly allergic to it, and his eye soon got red, swollen and utterly miserable. However, there was no time for coddling—they were off to Uruguay the next day.

Dubberly was quite an interesting character. One of the things he liked to do was hitchhike around the country and witness to his captive audiences. On this occasion, however, he drove Ben in the orthodox manner far up north into the interior. They had to make an overnight stop and, since there were no hotels in the area, they slept on church benches. After inspecting the house, they began the long drive to Montevideo. Unfortunately, the car began to act up and, as it was not only Sunday but a holiday, everything was closed. They managed to limp into a service station and rig up a temporary fix that allowed them to make it to the Capital.

---

[99] Charles Spurgeon, also known as the "Prince of Preachers," was a highly influential nineteenth century Particular Baptist British pastor.

Circular Migration

It eventually became apparent that the Bedford family was developing a circular migration pattern. In 1983 Nelda and Alberto were appointed as volunteer missionaries to Paraguay. After attending Missionary Orientation, selling their house and sending off a small shipment to Buenos Aires, the Gaydous spent a month in Argentina visiting relatives before beginning their adventures in Asunción, where Alberto supervised maintenance at the Baptist Hospital and Nelda taught at Asunción Christian Academy.

While they were there, Nancy graduated summa cum laude with a Bachelor's degree in Communications and French. The entire family pictured her writing insightful articles and making waves from international journals. However, she decided to go in another direction. After taking off a semester to soak up the familiar sights and sounds of home like her siblings before her, she was planning to start on a master's degree in Theology at Southwestern Seminary.

When their year of service was up, the Gaydous moved to the mountains of Córdoba, for Alberto had been hired as the new administrator of the Baptist Camp, much to the astonishment of both sets of parents. When they heard that Alberto's father had resigned from Thea to pastor the church in La Falda, the Gaydous had written the Argentine Mission expressing an interest in the position, submitting Alberto's resume and informing them that none of their parents were aware of their application. The Bedfords first heard of it when Mel Plunk asked them if they would rather have Nelda and Alberto stay at their house or at a hotel when they went to Buenos Aires for the job interview. They agreed to put them up.

Meanwhile, back in the U.S. the Foreign Mission Board had reorganized the Missionary Orientation Center, moving it to Richmond, but David and his family did not go with it. At the beginning of the same year that his sisters were in Argentina, they went north and west when David accepted the position of Language Lab Director at Southern Illinois University at Carbondale.

Fun with Dick and Jane

"One more, Grandmother—*please,* just one more!"

Andrea simply could not get enough of *Fun with Dick and Jane,* the classic reading primer. The Gaydous were half way through their year in Paraguay, and she had gone home with her grandparents at the end of her family's summer vacation in Argentina. Ben would return her when he went to Asunción in ten days' time, although a change of plans stretched it to three weeks. La Nell took advantage of the stay to teach the five-year-old to read. Andrea, who had learned the entire alphabet well before she turned two, soaked it all up at lightning speed and was so thrilled to be reading that she slave-drove her grandmother. In fact, they went through all the first-grade material and got well into the next level.

Andrea had no trouble switching languages, either. While she was with them at The Mansion, La Nell had a work session with her old friend Delia Ragni. The two of them were collaborating on a series of Sunday School lessons called *Diálogo y acción,*[100] for La Nell continued to be active in the Argentine Convention's Education Board. Delia, who had seen all sorts of children throughout her long career as an educator, was amazed and amused at Andrea's flow of verbiage that effortlessly kept up with the adults, no mean feat among Argentines, who are notorious talkers.

Before sending her granddaughter home, La Nell went on a shopping spree and got her several adorable outfits, including leather sandals in the little girl's favorite color—red. Ben and Andrea left Buenos Aires at the crack of dawn, stopping on the North Side to pick

---

[100] Dialog and Action

up Don Mines, who needed to coordinate some Mississippi Partnership planning with his Paraguayan peers.

Andrea was finally reunited with her family, just in the nick of time to prevent her mother from going into a major child withdrawal syndrome, and Ben met up with his boss Thurmon Bryant for a road trip that would include a good number of missionary homes and fields of service in their three countries, beginning with Paraguay. They crossed over into Argentina from Encarnación to Posadas, and later on into Uruguay over the bridge in the Entre Ríos Province that joins the cities of Concordia and Salto.

While they were in the Capitals, they stayed at the hospitality apartments of the respective Missions and when they were in the interior, at the missionaries' homes. They even made a quick foray into Brazil from northern Uruguay. They went through a variety of settings, from sophisticated urban to very basic rural, eating all sorts of meals in all sorts of places. Ben made it through them all with no problem, that is, until they were treated to a fine restaurant in Montevideo.

The most likely explanation is that his succulent steak had been touched by a knife previously used to chop onions or garlic. Be that as it may, he was so violently ill that he was forced to stay in bed, something practically unheard of for him, and Jason Carlisle, former MK turned missionary, stood in for him on the next leg of the trip to the interior.

When the tour was over, Dr. Bryant flew back to the U.S. from the Montevideo airport and Ben returned to Buenos Aires on the ferry over the Río de la Plata.

The Mother Lode

Nancy was to say that she hit the mother lode of travel during her break between college and seminary. On her previous visit, when she had gone with them to Uruguay, they had run into a snag at the check-in counter. Argentina has an agreement with the bordering nations that allows their respective residents to travel back and forth on national IDs with no need for passports and visas. Although they had their IDs, Nancy could not travel without her *permiso de viaje*, the parental travel permission for minors, which she had not brought with her because she was actually travelling *with* her parents. But rules are rules.

They dashed to a pay phone and called their neighbor Mary Evelyn Divers, who had a spare key to their house so that she could water plants and keep an eye on things while they were away. That gracious lady not only located the document but drove all the way to the airport at full speed just in time for them to make their flight.

Now that Ben and La Nell were entering their late 50s, they were going on their first authentic, non-work related vacation ever— to Europe! Between their accumulated miles and vacation days, they were able to get an excellent price on tickets for a month-long trip. Before leaving, they planned their general itinerary and budget. La Nell and Nancy each made lists of the places they wanted to see. Ben left the route to them, asking only to save four or five days at the end for pure rest and to limit expenses to $100 per day, covering travel, lodging and food for the three of them. In turn, La Nell and Nancy made Ben promise that he would not look up anyone—strictly no business, and that included going to cathedrals on Sunday rather than Baptist churches.

They flew by LAP (the Paraguayan airline) from Asunción to Madrid, where they rented a car. They had a marvelous time driving through Spain, France, England, Holland, Germany, Switzerland and Italy. They even managed to stay within budget, lodging in a hostel if they ate out or snacking on bread, crackers and fruit if they stayed at a hotel. The shopkeeper at a French bakery gave them a strange look when they insisted on buying three sandwiches, shrugged and handed over three loaf-long packages. They were good for several meals.

La Nell was able to try out the French she had learned in La Falda. In turn, France laid out the red carpet for her. For much of the trip Nancy was their interpreter, drawing on her stores of not only English and Spanish, but French, Italian and Portuguese as well. Changing gears between five languages can get complicated. For example, at one point they were in Italy and she needed to explain to the waiter that Ben could not eat onions. She might have been able to hold forth on art, literature and philosophy in her foreign languages, but it was the everyday things that could be tricky. The Spanish and French equivalents for "onion" floated up out of her subconscious, and she hesitated between *cipolla* and *onione*.

The waiter, with whom she had been exchanging pleasantries with no problem for several minutes, asked impatiently, "*Ma, parla o non parla!?*"[101]

When they got to England, Ben thought he would finally be able to get around on his own and give Nancy a rest. He asked for directions in Greenwich and listened to the answer with increasing bewilderment. He did not understand a single word, so he turned to his daughter:

"What language is he speaking?"

"It's English, Daddy!"

She didn't get a break from interpreting after all.

An overnight ferry took them from Harwich to the Hook of Holland, and they drove south through the Germanic countries. When they crossed the Alps into Italy, that adoptive Latin American Ben breathed a sigh of relief:

---

101 Well, do you speak or not!?

"At last—civilization!"

The Bedfords rounded off their trip with four blissful days of reading, napping and lolling on the beaches of Costa Brava in northeastern Spain. Along the way, La Nell memorialized their adventures in an amazing scrapbook diary.

Ministering to Ministers

The shrill ringing of the telephone interrupted an animated conversation between La Nell and her eldest daughter. Nelda had just arrived from Asunción with a bus full of Paraguayan ladies to attend the Women's Missionary Union Convention in Buenos Aires and to spend some precious time alone with her mother while her father was off on one of his jaunts to the U.S. and her husband dealt with their three little ones. She watched her mother's face with affection and then with growing concern as her expression changed from friendly to worried, to horrified.

"What is it?!"

There had been a freak accident in Ramos Mejía. Lloydene Balyeat had driven to the station to pick up her husband Kent, who often rode the train back and forth to teach his classes at the Seminary. She waited and waited but he did not come out. Suddenly a police car and an ambulance came roaring up and she felt a terrible foreboding. She was told a blond middle-aged man had suffered an accident. Unable to face the situation alone, she called for reinforcements, and Mission President Mel Plunk rushed over to take her to the police station. She was asked what her husband had been wearing and they verified that Kent was the victim. Evidently his poor eyesight and the roar of another train had kept him from seeing or hearing the gray engine against the gray dusk sky.

Now La Nell was being asked to relay the news to Ben and the Foreign Mission Board, and Lloydene wanted her to translate the funeral service. While she pulled herself together, Nelda wrestled with the long-distance operator until she tracked her father down in Pine Mountain, Georgia. He was staying with David while he visited the new appointees to his area at MOC (the Missionary Orientation Center).

Some months before, Kent had been visited by a strange dream that prompted him to write down the service he would like to have when he died and the songs he would like to have sung. The two women worked on the translation late into the night, typed up the program and got it ready for the service, which was held the next day in the Seminary Chapel. Argentine law requires burial or cremation within twenty-four hours as embalming is not practiced, so events move very quickly.

The Seminary was bursting at the seams, for Kent and his family were much loved. He and Lloydene were *Papi* and *Mami* to scores of Seminary students. Kent, Director of the Music Program, was a great favorite not only of students and faculty, but of the many congregations that he had blessed throughout his ministry. Everyone wanted to pay tribute to his life and express their love to Lloydene.

After the service, the burial took place in Chacarita, the largest cemetery in Argentina, founded in 1887 and covering 230 acres. Hundreds of prominent persons are buried there so that there is a constant stream of mourners and tourists. A large crowd gathered around the graveside and turned into a mighty choir as they sang the hymns that Kent had chosen—all songs of praise, joy and victory. The cemetery employees in charge of lowering the casket and filling in the tomb with earth were amazed. They saw burials day in and day out, but they had never seen anything like that outpouring of love, sweet sorrow and faith.

Meanwhile, back in the U.S., Ben left Pine Mountain immediately for the home of the Balyeats' eldest son, Michael, who happened to live in Georgia. The entire family gathered there, and Ben brought what comfort and help he could. Arrangements were made to hold a memorial service in a few days' time.

Ben was scheduled to go to the Baptist Publishing House in El Paso. On the way, he had a speaking engagement at the First Baptist Church in Austin, Nancy's congregation. Kent's memorial service was to be held that same day in Wichita Falls, but there was no time to drive and no useful airline connection. A member of FBC generously solved the problem by offering to have her pilot take him there on her private airplane. Nancy drove Ben to the airport with his luggage and the pilot took him to Wichita Falls, waited until the service was over and flew him back to the airport in Austin to catch a commercial flight to El Paso. So Ben was able to be with Lloydene and her four children on that beautiful and terrible occasion and speak on behalf of Argentine missionaries and nationals.

Missionaries are regular people, with the same challenges and problems that everyone faces. The difference is that they are expected to be the ones who dispense comfort and counsel to others. Ben and La Nell's main role was to pastor them and provide a safe setting for blowing off steam. At times their charges needed to vent about personality clashes between missionaries, conflicts between Conventions and Missions, frustration with the effects of the divisive charismatic movement in their congregations, and other stressful situations related to their ministries. At others, the missionaries were experiencing personal problems. Over the years, the Bedfords dealt with culture shock, the death of loved ones, inappropriate sexual conduct, marital problems, rebellious children, empty nest, teen pregnancies and every other type of problem imaginable that occurs wherever there are people. Their goal was always to reconcile and restore but, on very rare occasions, they had to make the difficult decision to recommend that someone should leave the mission field.

On the personal level, Ben usually counselled the men and La Nell the women. Once they were visiting Dennis and Jean McEntire in the interior of Paraguay. Jean was dealing with a seriously ill mother in the U.S. and deciding on the best approach to their children's schooling. La Nell sat cross-legged with her on the living-room floor and drew upon her own experience of losing her mother and making educational choices for her family. She told Jean about the home schooling system she had used, in her case mainly to teach reading in English. She encouraged the McEntires to enroll their children in the local public school even if they only audited, because it would be the best way for both children and adults to become a real part of the community, learn to speak Guaraní and get to know and love their new culture.

Scenes like this repeated themselves across the three countries. The Bedfords were now putting into practice several decades of experience in pastoring churches to minister to the ministers.

Steering

A letter from Dr. Thurmon Bryant arrived in late December 1984, inviting Ben to form part of a steering committee named by the Foreign Mission Board to lead a five-year emphasis on stewardship for the churches of Latin America and the Caribbean, in response to repeated requests from Baptists throughout the region. It outlined the general purposes and objectives of the plan the committee would formulate and submit for approval:

1. The preparation of culturally relevant and modern stewardship materials for publication and distribution in the major languages used throughout the region.
2. Motivation and training for leaders responsible for stewardship ministries.
3. Assistance at every level of Baptist life to make possible a major advance in giving within the churches for the cause of missions.

This was the second time Ben had been asked to become closely involved in a stewardship campaign. The first had been an invitation to serve as the promoter of an integral stewardship effort in Argentina, which he had declined although he participated actively in it at the church and associational level. It was the model from which this continent-wide effort was developed.

Now he felt led to accept. Accordingly, he attended the initial meeting of the Steering Committee in Miami, Florida that next February and was named treasurer. Aldo Broda, a valued colleague since the 1950s, was chairman and resigned from the Spanish Baptist

Publishing House to become the managing director of the Campaign. José Missena, the fiery Paraguayan leader with whom Ben had shared so many endeavors, became its promoter all over Latin America. His position as president of the Latin American Baptist Alliance helped open many doors. This campaign was originally intended to last five years but the event proved so useful that it was extended to 1992, prolonging Ben's duties until his retirement. It was instrumental in helping national churches and conventions throughout the Americas become financially self-sufficient and begin sending and supporting their own missionaries. As a natural corollary, the number of foreign missionaries needed from the U.S. eventually began to decrease.

Ben's duties as treasurer required much attention to detail, given the large amount of money involved—over half-a-million dollars. With La Nell's help, he fine-tuned every year's budget and accounted for every cent. The lion's share of the expenses went to the creation of high-quality literature in Spanish, Portuguese, French and English that would serve for many years to come. Of course, the Publishing House in El Paso, on whose Board of Directors he served, played a very important role in the development and production of that literature.

One of the planning meetings was held in the Caribbean island of Barbados. Before turning in one night, Ben stepped out with his old friend Billy Graves and nephew-in-law Al Gary (missionary to Guadeloupe) to watch an eclipse of the moon over the night ocean.

Change of Venue

Ben and his friend Roberto García Bordoli returned to Argentina after a meeting for the Stewardship Campaign in El Paso with $5,000 each stuffed into money belts. The Bedfords had emptied out their checking account and borrowed the rest from the resourceful Julio Díaz. They were buying an apartment in Buenos Aires and had to pay in cash, in dollars.

Several months earlier, the Argentine Baptist Mission had asked Ben and La Nell to consider the possibility of relocating the Associate's office to Córdoba City and acting as unofficial area missionaries. The Bedfords in turn submitted the proposal to their boss, without hinting at how much was riding on his decision. La Nell's arthritis was giving her grief again from the years in the humid weather of Buenos Aires and they had come to the conclusion that they would either have to move the office or resign as Associates and return to field work. However, Thurmon readily agreed that it was a good idea and they prepared to move.

They were instructed to look for a house to buy in Córdoba and there was only one available that was anything like what they needed: a nice little two-bedroom house with a garage in Barrio Cofico. The funds also extended to a small office on the third floor of a downtown building that shared a wall with the Provincial Legislature and was only fifteen blocks away from the house so that they could usually walk, avoiding traffic and parking problems. However, their frequent travels would have them going through Buenos Aires on a regular basis, often requiring overnight stays and a quiet meeting place, so they decided to purchase a property of their own if they could afford it. They found a one-bedroom apartment for $10,000 a block and a half from the Acoyte subway station and only fifteen minutes away by car or public transportation from the Seminary and the Mission Office. It was the first real estate they had ever owned, apart from AWOL, half of which had belonged to the Ferrells. Nancy's bed and dresser and their breakfast table-and-chair set outfitted the place. They bought a sofa bed for the tiny living room and a narrow refrigerator for the miniscule kitchen to complete the furnishings. It proved to make their lives much easier during the next few years and they often lent it to friends who needed to stay overnight in the Capital.

The Bedfords felt at home in Córdoba from the very first; in fact, it was something of a homecoming, being so close to their beloved La Falda. It had now become the second largest metropolis of the nation with nearly one-and-a-half million inhabitants, a proud city whose history goes back to 1573. It has many historical buildings, including the famous Jesuit Block that houses a group of seventeenth century buildings and has been declared a UNESCO World Heritage Site. The National University of Córdoba is the oldest university in Argentina and the second oldest in Latin America, older than any university in the U.S. Córdoba has always been strong and independent, a perpetual thorn in the flesh of the central government in Buenos Aires.

In addition to his duties as Associate, for all intents and purposes Ben was DOM (Director of Missions) for the Córdoba Association. Right away he met with its Executive Committee and worked with all the pastors. He was frequently invited to preach at their churches. While he pursued his passion for Evangelism, La Nell felt called to bolster up the program at the San Martín church where she and her husband became members, and soon she was teaching the young people in Sunday School.

An added bonus was that they were now only forty-five miles from one of their daughters and three of their grandchildren, who were at a delightful stage of their lives. They got to keep the kids overnight from time to time, spoil them with videotapes of cartoons and M&Ms from the U.S., and, last but not least, show them off to their appreciative friends. A little later down the line, La Nell was pressed into service to teach Veronica and Alejandro to read in English.

211

Of course, many of the people who passed through Villa Bautista knew of the Gaydou-Bedford family connection. One of their friends had the following conversation with their youngest grandchild:

"*¿Y cómo está tu abuelo Benjamín?*"

"*¡Él no es mi 'abuelo'!*"

"*¿No?*"

"*¡No! ¡Es 'Granddaddy'!*"[102]

It was clear that the little boy considered this person quite dense: obviously, his paternal grandfather was *Abuelo* and his maternal grandfather was *Granddaddy*.

The first family reunion in Argentina since the famed weddings of 1977 took place the next year. They had the campgrounds at Villa Bautista all to themselves and the winter weather was gorgeous. Every day a different couple prepared lunch for everyone. When it was their turn, Nelda and Alberto treated them all to a picnic by the beautiful Pintos River, serving strawberries and chocolate almond pie for dessert, while the children ran up and down the banks of the river.

Nancy and David set up their tripods and cameras and the rest of the family grouped together to memorialize the occasion. "You should stand on the end," Alberto told Nancy's boyfriend Hans. "That way, if it doesn't work out, we can just cut off the edge of the picture," but Hans ignored these prophetic words, laughed and planted himself firmly in the middle.

---

[102] "And how's your Grandfather Benjamin?"

"He's not *Abuelo*!"

"He isn't?!"

"No! He's *Granddaddy*!"

Multitasking

"Thurmon, I could really use a word processor."

"Hang on just a little longer, La Nell—I'm working on getting you a computer."

La Nell was the ultimate multitasker. Over the decades, she had not only raised three children and ably seconded her husband in all his endeavors, but had herself held many positions in the churches, associations, conventions and the Mission to which she had belonged. Her first love was Christian Education: she had taught all types of classes, trained teachers, translated and written original materials and served on the Convention's Education Board throughout her career. She had also always been extremely active in the Women's Missionary Union at every level. She had been recording secretary for the Mission several times and kept the books for multiple building projects. She had been Ben's unofficial secretary since they were in college and kept up with a constant stream of business and personal correspondence, including a strict filing system. The skills gained as Seminary Librarian had been used to order and classify Ben's considerable personal library.

Now she held the official title of Secretary to the Area Associate and it was a never ending challenge to keep on top of all the paperwork. Letters were constantly going back and forth between Ben and Richmond, the Missions, the missionaries, the Spanish Baptist Publishing House, his co-workers in the Stewardship Campaign and the Mississippi Partnership, among others. Her business degree came in handier than ever, and she used her shorthand, editing, typing, bookkeeping and organizational skills practically on a daily basis.

Over the years, she had pounded away on layers of letterhead, carbon paper and plain paper in a series of manual typewriters, prepared stencils, and churned out copies on mimeographs. An IBM Selectric typewriter had made things easier, but a technical revolution was under way around the world and La Nell was on the front line of office transformation.

She mastered the DOS operating system and a series of word-processing software programs culminating in WordPerfect and Word; added floppy disk storage containers to her filing system; went through a series of complicated email precursors; figured out how to connect printers and fax machines; and ran a photocopier.

La Nell loved the challenge of learning something new, but in one task she remained strictly old school. As a way of assuring their charges that they were constantly in their thoughts and prayers, she took it upon herself to send a card on the birthday of every missionary family member and the anniversary of every missionary couple in their Area. Each card had a loving note in La Nell's beautiful handwriting. This meant well over a thousand cards per year. Practically every time he travelled to the U.S. Ben brought back several boxes of cards, and La Nell consulted her calendar daily to make sure the greetings were mailed in time.

A Lamp unto my Feet

Avery Willis, creator of the MasterLife discipleship program, led the first workshop on the field in person. Ben had driven him from the airport in Córdoba to Thea where missionary and national leaders from the three countries had gathered to hear him. On the way, they stopped for lunch at a nice little restaurant next to the bridge over the Cosquín River. The waiter had brought them succulent steaks and a mound of crisp French fries. Avery looked around for ketchup, but this was still in the days when such a combination was unheard of in Argentina. When Ben explained to the waiter, that nice man went to a neighborhood store and bought the crazy gringo a bottle of the repellent red stuff.

The Foreign Mission Board was promoting this material worldwide. It was a fifty-two-week in-depth Bible study in which key Christian concepts were covered and ways of putting them into practice were explored. Eventually it was translated into more than fifty languages and used in more than one hundred countries. It proved to be a very useful tool for spiritual growth, discipline and commitment in the South Cone.

In his article "A History of the Argentine Baptist Mission 1982-2003" in *The Argentine Baptist Mission—One Hundred Years of Ministry in Argentina*, Mark S. Alexander wrote:

> *In 1982, the first MasterLife workshop was held with the objective of training individuals from different parts of the country. Workshops were held in different parts of the country in the following years, and throughout the rest of 1980s, MasterLife was used extensively in the International Baptist Theological*

> *Seminary, in regional institutes and in local churches to disciple*
> *believers and train leaders for ministry. In 1986 alone there were*
> *330 individuals going through the course (Statistical Report of*
> *the Argentine Mission, 1986). During Dr. Avery Willis' visit*
> *to Argentina in 1994 a meeting of thanksgiving was held in*
> *recognition of how God had used Dr. Willis'work to train hundreds*
> *of Argentine believers.*[103]

As part of this effort, the Bedfords were involved in teaching intensive workshops for leaders in each of their three countries and the full year-long study several times, with La Nell as leader and Ben as co-leader. Their first regular MasterLife group met in The Mansion, their house in Buenos Aires. The group included Pastor Roberto Modroff, his wife Sonia, whom they had known since she was a teenager in Rosario in the 1950s, and Roberto García Bordoli, who had been a member of their congregation in Vélez Sarsfield in the early 1970s. Roberto, a busy accountant, fell into the habit of taking food to his office and using his lunch hour to study and prepare. This experience was instrumental in his decision to go into full-time Christian service. He eventually became the director of the Spanish Baptist Publishing House.

After they moved to Córdoba, the Bedfords taught MasterLife both in the Sierras and in the provincial capital. Once a week they met in the La Falda parsonage with a group that included their daughter and son-in-law. Before beginning the study in Córdoba, they invited all the pastors and spouses to their home in Barrio Cofico for a get-acquainted party. The division that had arisen among them as a result of some disagreements became evident as they refrained from mingling even on this social occasion and one group drifted to the patio with Ben while the other milled around La Nell in the living room. People from both groups participated in the MasterLife study. At a pastors' retreat Ben was awkwardly placed between two pastors from opposing factions, one of whom prayed in very specific terms for the Lord to work on the sins of the other. But by the end of the program a beautiful

---

[103] p. 228

reconciliation had taken place and a new leaf was turned in the work in Córdoba, with much needed unity and cooperation. Over two decades later, Ben and La Nell were visiting Nancy's church in Buenos Aires, and one of the pastors who had been in their Córdoba group was preaching. He referred to them with affection as his "teachers." Ben racked his brains trying to figure out the reference, since they were the same age and this pastor had never taken any classes under him at the Seminary. Then he remembered that MasterLife course.

Stanley and Kathleen Clark became leading promoters of the program. Together with the Bedfords, they led a workshop in Santiago, Chile. They arrived on Saturday night and no arrangements had been made for Sunday breakfast. Unbeknownst to each other, Kathleen and Ben had gone foraging for bakeries in opposite directions. When Ben returned, he saw Stanley pacing back and forth on the sidewalk, unsure whether to go looking for his wife or stay put. She took so long that they called the nearest hospital and the police, to no avail. At long last Kathleen turned up. She had gotten thoroughly turned around and lost. But she was nothing if not resourceful: she saw some people with Bibles, followed them and found her way back.

Unscrambling Eggs

"How do you unscramble an egg?!" declaimed the visiting pastor, making a confident pause to allow his interpreter, Missionary David Glaze, to translate. David, himself an MK and native bilingual, cast a desperate glance at Nelda and Alberto, who were in the congregation and devoutly grateful not to be in his shoes. There simply was no equivalent and this particular oratorical effort fell flat. It was one of the hazards that went with the job, but it was worth it.

The wonderful partnership between the churches of Mississippi and the three countries of Spanish Eastern South America involved impressive logistics, coordinated by representatives from the Mississippi Associations and each of the Missions, in turn overseen by Ben.

Mark S. Alexander described it from the missionaries' point of view:

> Missionaries were involved in several aspects of the Mississippi partnership. At the Mississippi Baptist Convention, a number of missionaries rotated through the position of helping to coordinate and give orientation to the numerous groups of volunteers that went to Argentina. In Argentina, missionaries were involved with the logistics of transportation, housing, and food for the volunteers, but most importantly, in accompanying the different teams and serving as translators. The demands of this job implied that missionary couples were often juggling their family and ministry schedule in creative ways in order to allow one or the other to be away from home for extended periods of time to accompany volunteers. As a result of the partnership many

congregations were blessed, decisions for Christ were recorded, and volunteers were forever changed in their view of international missions. In 1985 alone, 268 volunteers participated in the partnership, serving on 52 teams that reported 3,610 professions of faith (ABM Narrative Report, 1985). In the years following this emphasis, a number of missionary families arrived for service in Argentina, whose first contact with the country had been on one of these volunteer trips.[104]

The three Missions were fortunate to have several native bilingual MKs in their ranks—David Glaze, Mark Alexander and Paul and Laura Shelton in Argentina, Jason Carlisle in Uruguay and Thomas Law in Paraguay—for whom interpreting was almost second nature, but practically everyone was pressed into this challenging service. Ben and La Nell were no exception. La Nell of course was particularly good at this. In fact, one visiting team member who understood some Spanish told his leader, "My, my, La Nell certainly did improve your sermon!"

She served as interpreter and Ben as chauffeur for a team of three women, including Mrs. Kelly, wife of the Mississippi Convention's Executive Secretary. The trip started in Asunción and hit several points in the interior of Paraguay, including Encarnación. They crossed over to Argentina and went to Posadas in the Province of Misiones, where there is a fascinating ethnic mixture, heavy on Guaraní, Germans, Russians and Poles, and on to Resistencia in the Chaco Province. They were interested in the work with the Toba Indians and were taken to an all-day gathering at a Toba settlement by a missionary supported by German Baptists. They arrived in the middle of the service but the hosts graciously stopped to welcome them. They had the visitors sit on a bench along one wall and everyone in the substantial gathering greeted each newcomer individually. The women from the team spoke and La Nell interpreted. They were participating in various other

---

104 Mark S. Alexander, "A History of the *Argentine Baptist Mission* 1982-2003 in *The Argentine Baptist Mission—One Hundred Years of Ministry in Argentina*, pp. 228-229

activities when it began to rain. The missionary announced, "I'm sorry, but we have to leave right now or you might not be able to get out for a week." All the visitors got a goodbye kiss from everyone before dashing off to safety.

One of Ben's favorite experiences took place with a team of one pastor and three women for whom he interpreted, first in southeastern Patagonia and then further north and west in San Juan, in the foothills of the Andes. In Comodoro Rivadavia Ben was able to see how the work had grown in the quarter of a century since he and La Nell had pioneered there. Many years later, in 2016, Leo and Mirta Cisterna, a couple from Comodoro who joined the church in La Falda, gave Nelda a picture of her father with the Mississippi team, and told her that Leo, for whom his wife had long been praying, had made his profession of faith during that evangelistic effort.

But Caucete, a poor town in San Juan, was the jewel of the trip. The church, pastored by Héctor Sambrano, a dynamic young man whose family the Bedfords knew from Rosario, had taken the recommendations for preparation very seriously and had dozens of visits lined up in homes of nonbelievers, the municipality and the hospital. The pastor from Mississippi and Héctor were both musicians and sang several duets during the campaign. Besides the services at the church, they visited homes morning, afternoon and night. There were ninety-six professions of faith in that handful of days, and ninety of those persons later went on to be baptized.

At the first home they visited, they were received by the owner, a short man who looked a bit nervous. He hoped they would not mind that he had invited a few friends and relatives. They found thirty persons packed into the small living-room area. The women gave their testimonies and the pastor delivered a short message. When Ben gave the invitation, he quoted John 3:16 and told the listeners, "I love this verse and I like to say it with my name instead of 'the world': 'For God so loved *Benjamin Bedford* that he gave his one and only Son, that whoever believes in him shall not perish but have eternal life.'"[105]

---

[105] The Bible, New International Version

After a short silence, the host asked, "Would you mind quoting it again with my name instead?" So Ben did, and person after person requested the verse with their own name in it. Seven of them made professions of faith that day in that home.

The Lost Decade

The elderly woman rummaged around in her handbag for her wallet. Then she handed it to the girl at the grocery store counter. She had no idea what the price meant. In this case, the cashier was honest and sorted out the right amount. Others were not as fortunate.

Argentines are notoriously adaptable, but recent events were too much for many of them, especially among the elderly. The so-called Lost Decade describes the Latin American debt crisis that came to a head in 1982 with Mexico's default and the unwillingness of creditors to refinance loans, coupled with the requirement to make repayments from the assets of the debtor States. Argentina's foreign debt rose from around 7.8 billion dollars in 1975 to 45 billion by the end of 1983. In the Greater Buenos Aires Metropolitan Area alone, poverty rose from 5% in 1975 to 37% in 1982. The military bequeathed a true disaster to the new democratic government.

Efforts to control inflation met with only sporadic success. Between 1970 and 1985 the currency changed names three times, knocking off zeros at each stage—two in 1970, four in 1983, three in 1985.[106] People had to make complicated mental conversions and it was no wonder that they often lost track of what things cost and how much money they really had. Many were still middle class in their own minds but poor in reality.

A Human Needs Conference was held at the Baptist Camp in 1986 in the middle of this continent-wide crisis. It sought to give Christians tools and projects with which to help their neighbors.

---

[106] In 1992, the name went back to pesos from australes, removing four zeroes.

Missionary Sarah Wilson, who had devoted her entire career to social work, was one of the prime movers.

As Area Associate, Ben was in charge of much of the logistics, including the literature. A fat binder with the program schedule and articles written by professors, pastors and social workers from every country was to be put together. Some of the submissions were in Spanish and others in English. La Nell's time was already stretched to the limit, so Nelda was pressed into service. She retyped, translated and edited all the papers and spent hours at the office photocopying and collating, fortified by cups of strong black coffee from the ground-floor café. She was able to keep in touch on the office telephone because Ben had finally sorted out the mystery of the disappearing line. Almost every weekend, and often in between, the line would be dead. It turned out that the Provincial Legislature next door was "borrowing" it because its own lines were so congested. After several forceful encounters, the line was finally left alone.

Conference attendees returned home armed with ideas for programs to be implemented at the church, association and convention level. Budgets were planned keeping this important item in mind. The Argentine Convention already participated in the World Hunger offering and had long had a Children's Home and a Nursing Home, as well as many Good Will Centers. There had been special drives over the years. Ben remembered *Operación Amor*[107] in the 1960s, during which he drove through the South Zone with mattresses tied to the top of the Rambler station wagon. During Bahía Blanca's terrible flood in 1985 wholesale and retail grocery businessman Andrés Arrojo and his family supplied the Convention with all sorts of goods at cost for distribution to the victims. When Mendoza was hit by an earthquake that same year, the Foreign Mission Board contributed tents to shelter the homeless. Some churches, like the First Baptist Church of Quilmes in suburban Buenos Aires, offered medical services and others provided lawyers to help people with their legal problems.

As in most churches in the country, the Bedfords' congregation in Barrio San Martín had a community service area. Among other things,

---

[107] Operation Love

members brought clothes and groceries for distribution among those who needed them in the congregation and the neighborhood. But the times called for more than the usual efforts. Like many others, the Bedfords looked for additional ways to help on a personal basis. La Nell came up with a practical idea: buying two to three times the usual amount of groceries. Half of this went to their pastor and his family who, like most of their peers, were struggling to make ends meet with a very low salary. They shared the remainder with the people who now came daily to their door asking for help.

Trial Run

Although it still seemed quite distant, retirement was only five years away. They had considered two possibilities. One was to settle in the mountains of Córdoba, perhaps in La Cumbre. Their friend Dr. Daniel Tinao dreamed of building a house there with them, near the golf course. The other, somewhat more practical choice in view of things like medical coverage, was in the U.S., perhaps in the high, dry weather of Albuquerque.

During their short furlough at the end of 1978, Ben and La Nell had participated in an Associational World Missions Conference in Albuquerque, hosted by the Hoffmantown Baptist Church. They had renewed their acquaintance with that congregation when they spoke at a Missions event during the year Ben had taught at the Seminary in Fort Worth. At that time, they were invited to spend their next furlough there: "We'll put you up!" That was also when they met the Maxwells, to whom they and countless guests of the Bedfords were forever after indebted for a delicious chocolate turtle recipe.

But there was a major change to which they had to adjust before they travelled. The Foreign Mission Board had decided that it was time to redistribute Areas again. Now Brazil was coupled with the Caribbean and all Spanish South America was placed under a new Director, Dr. Bryan "Breezy" Brasington, with his wife Vickey. Ben would be his Associate for Southern Spanish South America, which meant adding Chile to the three countries already under his wing. They were able to squeeze in one Mission Meeting there before they left, going by rail from Santiago down south to Temuco. Missionary Grundy Jones took the same train and gave them a good briefing on the way.

Furlough began with a trip to FMB headquarters in Richmond, Virginia. They were scheduled to leave on Pan American but the flight was cancelled due to mechanical problems and they were switched over to Aerolíneas Argentinas. However, five minutes after they left they were forced to return and wait around another three or four hours. They spent a fitful couple of hours in the hotel before finally leaving so late that they had to spend the next night in Miami.

Upon hearing their destination, the gregarious taxi driver who picked them up at the airport in Richmond searched through his vast repertoire for a subject that might interest them.

"What do you think about that Tammy Faye Bakker, then?"

He was astonished to find that the Bedfords had no clue about the huge story that had recently broken concerning the mediatic evangelist couple, and gleefully filled them in on the sex scandal and accounting fraud that ultimately led to their divorce and Jim Bakker's imprisonment.

In between trips, Ben and La Nell got to know Albuquerque. At first, they stayed in an apartment on Wyoming Street and later moved into a large, comfortable older house on Avenida La Costa whose equity had been donated to the church. Besides David and Nancy, they made visits to and received visits from all their surviving siblings, and even spent a few delightful days vacationing with their best friends Bill and Opal Ferrell in Arkansas.

Body Life, Hoffmantown Baptist Church's bulletin, ran an article on the Bedfords' New Mexico connection them in its November 18, 1987 issue:

> *As we celebrate Missions Day this Sunday, we will be blessed by the presence of two of our foreign missionaries, Dr. and Mrs. Benjamin Bedford, who are presently in Albuquerque on a seven-month furlough from their assignment in Córdoba, Argentina.*

After a brief overview of their careers, it finished up:

> *The Bedfords will be leaving us in December and ask us to pray for them as they return to Argentina, as well as for their*

three grown children and four grandchildren. In December, their daughter, Nancy, will receive an M.Div. degree from Southwestern Seminary and will be returning to Argentina with them where she has been invited to teach Greek and Theology in a Bible Institute in Córdoba. La Nell and Ben also would like to express their gratitude to our church family for providing them with a home to live in and a car to drive while in Albuquerque. In turn, how thankful we are that in this small way we have had an opportunity to show our love and appreciation to these two unselfish, dedicated servants of the Lord, who have been willing and able to go into the world to do His work!

When it was time to go, the Bedfords left the borrowed car and all the keys in the garage, slipping out under the closing door. As they backed out of the driveway in a rented Mercury with a huge trunk, La Nell remarked, "That seems like *our* house."

Perpetual Motion

Although they say there is no such thing as perpetual motion, the Bedfords felt that they came pretty close to achieving it. Back in Córdoba, they resumed their local activities, with La Nell teaching at the church in San Martín and Ben preaching and promoting evangelism all over the Association, punctuated by a steady round of travels.

The schedule included two trips per year to El Paso for Board meetings at the Spanish Baptist Publishing House, monthly trips to Asunción on Hospital business, and two mission meetings per country per year, plus meetings in the various countries in relation to the Stewardship Campaign and the Mississippi Partnership. Sometimes Ben wondered whether all that time sitting in chairs and around tables was well spent. Nearly thirty years later, at Lloydene Balyeat's ninetieth birthday party, his old friend Dan Carroll, with whom he had shared countless hours in Mission, Seminary and Publishing House committee meetings, told him:

"One of the things I best remember about you is your sitting through those meetings, listening to all the discussions and opinions. After a couple of hours, you would say, 'I think what I'm hearing is….' All of a sudden, everything would become clear and we would reach a decision."

At times the Bedfords went together and at others they travelled on their own. La Nell was pressed into service to speak at several spiritual retreats for the missionary women. Vickey Brasington wrote her after one of these in which she had given a series of talks on menopause:

Dear La Nell:

It has been our prayer that you have found a few minutes to catch up with yourself. It was a wonderful two weeks, but no one can say that they were very restful—exciting and fulfilling—but not restful.

How can I begin to say "thank you" for all you contributed to the Retreats? You did make a most delightful and meaningful contribution. That was evidenced not only by the comments I personally heard, but in the expressions on the Evaluation Sheets. You significantly touched many lives. I also appreciate the time and energy you spent with our ladies during your free time.

You have made an excellent team member and I look forward to our third retreat here in Ecuador next May. We really should all be "great" by then.

They resumed their visits to the individual missionary families, at times for general pastoral purposes and at others to help with specific problems that cropped up along the way. They now had more than 300 missionaries and their families in their care.

Just so they would not get bored when they were at home, they embarked on a small building project to add stairs, a bedroom and a bathroom to the house in Cofico. Nancy was living with them, teaching at the Bible Institute and studying German at the Goethe Institute. Their grandchildren were growing up. The youngest was now in kindergarten and the oldest had made a profession of faith while they were on furlough. Ben had the privilege of baptizing her at the church in La Falda.

The Shoestring Republic

"You are the first to want to get to know the north before the south," commented one of the missionaries during the Bedfords' initial extended trip to Chile. Since the country had been added to their area of responsibility shortly before their furlough, they had not yet had time to do more than attend Mission Meeting and get a general idea of the work and the people who carried it out. Now they had set aside a month in which to visit the missionaries working in the north.

Baptist work in Chile had begun in the late nineteenth century with Scottish believers:

> Chile was undergoing changes. 1883 saw the end of their war with Peru and Bolivia. In 1881 Chile signed a peace treaty with the Mapuche Indians which opened up the land between Concepción and Valdivia. An army outpost was opened in what became the town of Temuco. The government offered land in this area to Europeans for homesteading.
>
> A group from Scotland moved to this area. In the group was a Baptist pastor, William McDonald. He was their pastor and school teacher. McDonald wanted to start work with the Chilean people. At first he worked with the Christian Missionary Alliance, but broke relations with them over doctrine. He then started 3 small churches around Temuco and in 1908 he organized them into the Chilean Baptist Union. He was interested in getting help from the SBC-FMB. He made contact with Dr. William Bagby, missionary in Brazil. They met in Argentina and out of this meeting came the first SBC missionaries, William and Mary Davidson, in 1917.

William McDonald wanted to start a Baptist school for children from Baptist families and provide educated leadership for the Baptist work. Plans were made and two single missionaries were sent, Agnes Graham and Cornelia Brower. Property was bought and the first building was constructed. The building included classrooms and rooms for boarding students. Classes began in March 1922.[108]

Now there were missionaries throughout the country so that, in addition to spending time with some wonderful people, the Bedfords got to see amazing sights in the neighboring country. Argentina and Chile are the two southernmost countries in the world, and they march side by side from Tierra del Fuego (whose tip is only 620 miles north of Antarctica) to Bolivia, separated by the majestic Andes. Bolivia is to the northeast, Peru to the north and the Pacific Ocean to the west. It is so narrow (211 miles at the widest point and 40 miles at the narrowest) that it has been called the Shoestring Republic. Nevertheless, it has a booming tourist industry; it is rich in minerals, notably copper; and it is a major exporter of fresh fruit and wine:

Spindly Chile stretches 4300 km[109]*–over half the continent– from the driest desert in the world to massive glacial fields. A mosaic of volcanoes, geysers, beaches, lakes, rivers, steppe and countless lands fill up the in between. Slenderness gives Chile the intimacy of a backyard (albeit one fenced between the Andes and the Pacific). What's on offer? Everything. With easy infrastructure, spectacular sights and the most hospitable hosts around, the hardest part is choosing an itinerary. Seek out its sweeping desert solitude, craggy Andean summits and the lush forests of the fjords for a sample. The mystical Easter Island or isolated Isla Robinson Crusoe offer extra-continental exploits. But don't forget that Chile is as much about character as it is setting. Its far-flung location*

---

[108] Letter to Benjamin Bedford from Grundy Janes, February 8, 2017
[109] 2700 miles

fires the imagination and has been known to make poets out of barmen, dreamers out of presidents and friends out of strangers.[110]

Ben and La Nell travelled relay-style, being met at each point by different missionary families that took them from one home to another and showed them around their field of work. Ken and Divina Park picked them up at the airport in Santiago and drove them 420 miles north to Copiapó. The two men were of similar height and balding patterns, so that they were sometimes mistaken for each other. They later served together on the Board of the Spanish Baptist Publishing House.

Their next hosts were the Andrews, 180 miles south in La Serena. Mark's father had been at the Seminary with Ben and had served as a missionary in Concepción for many years. Invited to preach at their church, Ben used the famous "Vinegar, Vinegar" anecdote from his childhood to illustrate the effects of guilt.

"I wish I had a story like that to use in my sermons!" exclaimed Mark.

The Andrews took the Bedfords back north, this times 435 miles to Antofagasta, handing them over to Martha and Vic Bowman. The work there had been started by the Harts after beginning their missionary career in Argentina, and their daughter had established a clinic in that Chilean city. The Bowmans drove them 350 miles further north, all the way to Arica, near the border with Peru. From there they returned to Santiago and flew back to Córdoba.

On another trip, Ben and La Nell took a bus for the breathtakingly beautiful stretch between Santiago and Viña del Mar on the coast. Mary Jo and Bill Geiger, head of the very fruitful Christian Education Board of Chile, met them there and took them to nearby Valparaíso, where a devastating earthquake had occurred in 1985 with a toll of 177 dead, 2,575 injured, 85,358 houses destroyed and about a million persons homeless.

---

110 Danny, Palmerlee. *South America on a Shoestring*, Lonely Planet 2007, p. 410

At times, they also travelled in their own car, like the time they crossed the Andes from Argentina in Mendoza and drove 600 miles south to Puerto Montt and Puerto Varas, "The City of Roses," in the Lake Region, where they made several visits. One of their hosts, Archie Jones, a field missionary, had begun his career in Ecuador and had gone to Chile when he remarried. His children had asked that his new wife at least be older than the first son and she was, albeit by a slender margin. Ben and La Nell returned home by riding a barge between the mountains from Lake Todos los Santos in Chile to Lake Nahuel Huapi in Argentina, disembarking in Bariloche.

Perhaps the most spectacular trip took place a couple of years later. The Bedfords met up with the Brasingtons and the Charles Alexanders in the Argentine Patagonia, in Comodoro Rivadavia to be exact, where they visited their old church once again, now in a new building, at whose inauguration Ben had spoken in 1987. They drove south to Río Gallegos for a brief visit and then even further south into Tierra del Fuego. They bought fruit and all the makings of a scrumptious picnic before crossing over to the Chilean side by ferry to visit Mike Dietz in Punta Arenas, after which they had planned a brief sightseeing excursion in the Torres del Paine National Park as they worked their way back up north. However, the border guards would not allow the Bedfords to take food across because they had Argentine documents and they were forced to throw it all away under their watchful eyes, but the food bought at the same store by those traveling on U.S. passports was allowed through and shared with the less fortunate. Back in Argentina, they visited the magnificent Perito Moreno Glacier in Santa Cruz Province. They parted ways in Bariloche, where the Alexanders and Brasingtons took a barge to Chile and the Bedfords drove on north to Córdoba, their minds and souls full of the incomparable beauty and majesty they had been privileged to behold: pristine glacial lakes, luxuriant evergreen forests, jagged snow-clad peaks and extinct volcanoes.

Musical Chairs

In the space of a few months all of the Bedfords' children changed continents and hemispheres. Nancy left home to pursue a doctorate in theology at the University of Tübingen in Germany. Hers was among the last doctoral theses supervised by renowned theologian Jürgen Moltmann before his retirement. She faced the challenge of taking all her classes, writing her dissertation and having her oral examinations in German, which she had only begun learning a couple of years before.

Alberto considered that his cycle as administrator in Villa Bautista had ended and persuaded Nelda to try their fortunes in the U.S. for a few years. They decided to settle in Albuquerque so that they could be near her parents when they retired. It was a wrench for the Bedfords to see them off at the airport in Córdoba. When they walked back to the parking lot, they saw Alberto's father leaning over the roof of his car, sobbing quietly as he pounded it with his fist, mirroring what they all felt.

For their part, David and Patricia were appointed as missionaries to Brazil. Patricia suffered her third miscarriage the day after they arrived in that country and it seemed that they would not to be able to have any more children. They heard that adoptions could be arranged at no cost through the Minors Court in Campinas, where they were interviewed and approved on a Monday in May of 1989. According to the authorities, it would probably take anywhere from three months to one year to match them up with a child, but on the Friday of that very week they received a call informing them that there was a baby they would like for them to consider, born on the day they had applied to be adoptive parents. They rushed to the maternity ward and it was love at first sight, but they had to get permission to wait until the next day to take him home so they could buy a crib, clothes, diapers and bottles. They named him Sérgio César Benjamin and took him to meet all the grandparents in Argentina when he was six months old.

The trusty Honda Civic was in the thick of it all. It had been Nancy's first car and had seen her through college and Seminary. Her parents bought it back from her when she left the U.S. and they asked her to leave it for David and his family to use in Illinois. When they were appointed as missionaries, they drove it to Richmond, Virginia for orientation. Ben saw them there and shot baskets with William at the gym while his parents were being briefed. After his own meetings, he drove the little car down to Miami and entrusted it to his old friend and former Seminary colleague Julio Díaz, now living and teaching there, until the Gaydous picked it up and drove it all the way to Albuquerque. A decade later, both William and Alejandro were to drive that amazing vehicle.

Of Wallets and Steak Knives

Two things happened that changed the pace a bit for the Bedfords toward the end of their time in Argentina. One was the arrival of Mark and Karen Alexander to work with the Córdoba Association. The other, a few months before their departure, was the appointment of Ted Stanton to succeed Ben as Associate to the Area Director upon his retirement. Until then the Bedfords would be showing the Stantons the ropes and ensuring a smooth transition. In practice, this worked out to moving at somewhat less of a breakneck speed as Ben had fewer speaking engagements and meetings in Córdoba and Ted began taking over some of the trips.

The First Baptist Church of Córdoba, located on Avenida Colón, one of the main arteries of the city, was without a pastor and the congregation approached Ben about helping out. Breezy authorized his acting as interim pastor as long as it did not interfere with his duties as Associate. The church understood that he would have to travel frequently, but he would preach whenever he was in town, and he and La Nell would help them unite, reorganize and plan for the future. As usual, strong and sweet bonds were soon forged with yet another congregation.

There was a lot of counseling involved in their work there. Soon after they began, Ben had a very frank talk with the young people about the potential consequences of sexual relations outside of marriage. A couple of university students lamented, "We wish that we had heard this six months earlier!" The young woman was pregnant and both sets of parents were very angry and upset with them. With much love and understanding, they were all eventually able to work through it. The young couple married and good family relations were restored.

Mrs. Olivera was a faithful and active member, married to a gruff, nonbeliever who was a retired police chief from Resistencia, Chaco. They lived on 9 de Julio, one street over and several bus stops down from the church building. One afternoon on her way home after a WMU meeting, Mrs. Olivera had her purse snatched by three boys. Because the long strap was around her body, she was knocked down and bruised in the process.

Ben and La Nell went to visit her at home. Her husband Eraldo was enraged.

"It's a good thing I wasn't there. I would have grabbed my gun and shot the vandals!"

The Bedfords commiserated and hoped that the scare would not keep her from attending church.

"Perhaps you could go with her to make sure she's safe," they suggested.

Ben talked soccer extensively and knowledgeably with his host, who ended up inviting them to share an *asado,* the sublime Argentine barbecue. Eraldo even gave Ben a handsome long *asado* knife that he treasured ever after.

For his part, Ben gave him some literature and Mr. Olivera began attending some of the services. He even agreed to participate in a spiritual retreat that the church arranged to have at Villa Bautista, the Baptist Camp. The congregation hired a bus but the Bedfords went on ahead in their car to get everything ready. When the Oliveras' grandson got off the bus, he explained why Eraldo would not be going after all. He had been hospitalized with a heart attack.

As soon as they got home, the Bedfords visited Mr. Olivera at the hospital, where he was scheduled for surgery.

"Pastor, I'm ready to make a decision now."

"Are you sure you're not just afraid of the operation?"

"No, I'm ready to give my life to Christ."

When he recovered from surgery, Eraldo wrote out his testimony and asked to have it read at church. He was afraid he would get too emotional if he tried to do it himself, so one of the young men did it for him. Ben was soon to baptize grandfather and grandson.

The change in the retired policeman was astounding. He even began tithing right away, and he and his wife took it upon themselves to care for another church member, a wonderful lady who had been abandoned by her husband, had a disabled child and had been diagnosed with cancer. The Oliveras made sure she had all the medicine and groceries she needed. Eraldo said, "When all this clears up, we will be able to give more than the tithe at church." And they did.

Ben used to joke that Eraldo's wallet had been converted along with his soul. Mr. Olivera continued to write them for years after the Bedfords left. Ben loved to tell his story to illustrate the transforming power of Christ, often taking the famous barbecue knife as the opening conversation piece.

An Abrupt Halt

Ben looked over Nelda's shoulder as she typed another page of the book she was translating.

"Don't you think that *casa* would be better than *morada*?"

"Maybe so, but I'm quoting the Bible and don't feel free to change it."

"Oh, sorry!"

He was spending a few days with his daughter and her family in Albuquerque on the way to El Paso, and while his suggestion about the translation might not have been his best idea ever, the next one was excellent.

He got in touch with Gerald Farley, Business Manager of Hoffmantown Baptist Church, to inquire about the possibility of buying the house that he and La Nell had lived in during their previous furlough. There were some technicalities that would keep them from being able to finalize the paper work for several months, but the church was glad to arrange the transaction and made the house available to them immediately. So Ben took his daughter to a notary public and got her a power of attorney authorizing her to sign the papers for them at closing. The Gaydous gave up the house they were renting and moved in. They made the regular mortgage payment and the Bedfords paid the second mortgage, a beneficial arrangement for all involved.

Everyone was looking forward to November of 1990. Alberto's parents were going to visit, while La Nell and Nelda would be touring Europe for a month. Everything was planned down to the last detail—itinerary, train passes and hotels. However, things started going off plan in October. The U.S. had entered a recession in July that lasted eight months, and its sluggish reaction the next year was commonly referred to as a jobless recovery. Much of Albuquerque's business depended on government contracts. When the economy began to suffer and the government cut back on expenses, businesses began failing, with a disastrous domino effect. The shop where Alberto worked was one of the casualties. Everyone was laid off and the company was sold. He had six months of unemployment compensation, and he applied for any and every job he heard of with no success, the usual reason being that he was overqualified and would quit as soon as something better became available.

After attending an Area conference in Richmond and meeting with Paraguay's Baptist Hospital partner in Jacksonville, Florida, Ben and La Nell flew to El Paso for a series of meetings at the Publishing House. La Nell left early for Albuquerque. On the Thursday before the Saturday that they were to travel to Europe, Nelda did some last-minute shopping with her mother and mother-in-law. La Nell courteously insisted that Lola sit in front but, as she climbed out of the two-door Honda's back seat in the parking lot, the seatbelt strap somehow tripped her up and she fell onto the asphalt.

Years of dealing with pain had made La Nell rather stoic so that the others did not realize how badly she was hurt. They bundled her up into the car and took her to the emergency room to get her checked out. It transpired that she had broken her hip and would require a prosthesis to replace that joint. Ben rushed back from El Paso to be at her side and they bought her a comfortable recliner for her post-surgery recovery.

The trip to Europe was cancelled and there was quite a crowd for the holidays. One of Nelda's co-workers was revealingly horrified: "Your parents *and* your in-laws in your house *at the same time*?!" But Nelda had hit the jackpot in the in-law department and the two sets of parents were good friends. It snowed and the elder Gaydous were thrilled for their only Christmas in the northern hemisphere to be a white one. The celebration was only slightly dampened by a burst pipe. Meanwhile, the children basked in the attention of all four grandparents.

While they were there, Daniel made built-in drawers and shelves for the den, a desk and bookshelves for the study, and some beautiful storage cabinets in the garage that became the envy of the entire neighborhood. The Bedfords improved their future home and the Gaydous recovered travel expenses. And Daniel was able to browse to his heart's content through the well-stocked aisles of The Home Depot.

Many Farewells

Someone had gone to a lot of trouble to cart an impressive display of elegant and fragile china to the Baptist Camp in Paraguay during the summer Mission Meeting. There was a magnificent spread and amazing decorations. It was the first of the Bedfords' official goodbyes over the six months before they left permanently for the U.S. The missionaries gave Ben and La Nell a gorgeous *ñandutí* lace tablecloth with matching napkins for guests to ooh and aah over for years to come. They had also set up times and assistants to walk La Nell around the Camp's excellent swimming pool, great rehabilitation after her hip replacement surgery. José Missena, the prominent Paraguayan leader with whom Ben had worked in the Seminary, on evangelism and on the Stewardship Campaign, told him, "You have done more for Paraguay than anywhere else these past years."

Because of the accident, they had missed the Argentine Summer Mission Meeting at which their farewell party had originally been planned (they were honored together with another soon-to-be-retired couple, Mark and Cecile Alexander, several months later in Buenos Aires). At her last visit to the doctor before returning to the field, he had asked, "Do you have stairs in your house?

"Yes," La Nell had answered rather apprehensively.

"Excellent! Go up and down them as much as possible. It's great exercise."

It must have been, because in a few months' time she was walking with no trace of a limp. She was even able to take up golf, tennis and ping-pong again.

The missionaries in Chile gave them another beautiful tablecloth, this time in soft pastel colors, and the Uruguayan Mission presented them with some elegant candlesticks and a little chest full of hearts with handwritten messages from the missionaries. These are representative:

> *Ben, from the first time I knew you personally in Costa Rica I have been impressed with your humility as demonstrated again and again in various situations. I consider this one of the greatest of Christian virtues. For this reason and many others it has been a genuine joy to work with you through these nearly 40 years.*
>
> *Dearest La Nell, one of the sweetest things that you have done is be attentive to our birthdays and anniversaries. Thank you for being faithful to remember and pray for us on these special days.*
>
> *Ben, I have always appreciated your warm, humorous way of communicating your wisdom and concern to us. I am certain that the Lord will continue to bless you in the future.*
>
> *La Nell, you are a beautiful person, both physically and spiritually. That's how I think of you. Thank you for being a genuine friend and supporter of our ministries through the years. Don't forget us.*
>
> *Ben, we have greatly appreciated your gentle spirit and your genuine concern that you have shown through the years. You have been a friend, as well as a "boss." Thank you for your support of our ministries. May God continue to use you both. We love you.*
>
> *La Nell, I congratulate you on the efficient, faithful support you have given Ben as his "traveling secretary." I have been impressed with your positive outlook and friendly personality. I hope we can get together after retirement to share and just enjoy your company.*

At the last Argentine Convention they attended, at the Seminary facilities, they were recognized together with John and Mary Evelyn Divers, their one-time neighbors who were about to retire. Both couples received beautiful plaques commemorating their years of service in the country. During their next conversation, the President of the Convention, Carlos Caramutti, asked La Nell where they had put it.

"Under the bed."

"Under the bed? Why?!"

"After forty years of service, I didn't even rate a name. It says, 'Dr. and Mrs. Benjamin Bedford.'"

Appalled by their unthinking *machismo*, the Convention decided to redo the Bedfords' and the Divers' plaques. From then on, there was equal recognition for men and women in Baptist work. Far from being upset with La Nell, they admired her authentically Argentine straight-speaking spunk.

The Women's Convention recognized La Nell's faithful service in the Women's Missionary Union activities with a charming commemorative folder with pages and signatures for Rosario, Comodoro, Buenos Aires South Zone and Capital in beautiful India-ink calligraphy.

The First Baptist Church of Córdoba pulled out all the stops. They moved the pews out of the way and set up tables for a goodbye party after the evening worship service, at which they shared the Lord's Supper and Ben got the best possible parting gift when three persons made professions of faith at the end of his last sermon. Amado Apestegui, Chairman of the Pulpit Committee, wrote an article about it for the Baptist Convention's magazine. After a brief summary of their careers, he said:

> As we can see, a whole lifetime and the best years of their youth in Argentina at the constant service of God and of the People of our Country. This past year we have had the privilege of having them with us as Pastors of this Church.
>
> May 26 was the last night; they are returning to their Homeland. At the end of his message, in response to his call, 3 souls surrendered their lives to Christ. After some words on behalf of the Church, when La Nell was invited to tell us something she answered, "I can't," and I thought I saw not only her feelings but tears running down her cheeks. It was the best response from a transparent message that joined us in fraternal love. Thanks be to God: once more we find that the love of Jesus Christ has no borders. We would have liked to have them with us for a longer

time but it was not God's will. May the Lord continue blessing them richly in the new place He has for them.

Like the Apostle Paul, they can say, "I have fought the good fight" in Argentina; "I have finished the race, I have kept the faith."[111]

There was no time to get sentimental about leaving their home of the past six years. The lease on the Alexanders' apartment was up and they needed to move in immediately, if not sooner. The moving van had scarcely removed the Bedfords' belongings when Mark and Karen began hauling in theirs. Ben and La Nell spent their last night in Córdoba at the Argentine Automotive Association's hotel.

Their destination kept them from dwelling on what they were leaving behind for they were driving to their beloved Rosario, where they had speaking engagements the next day. After Ben preached at Distrito Sud Baptist Church, home of their first pastorate in Argentina, their good friend Alberto Pizzicatti, chairman of the deacons back then and later Seminary colleague as business manager, treated them to lunch and then they treated him to ice cream, fondly reminiscing over forty years' worth of memories. They had afternoon tea with José and Delia Ragni, with whom Ben and La Nell had built so many church buildings and prepared so much Sunday School material and who had been the first ones to be baptized at the 1958 inauguration of the new building of the First Baptist Church, where Ben preached that night.

On Monday, they drove to Buenos Aires to oversee the removal of the furniture from their little pied-à-terre, turned in their car and signed the closing papers for the sale of the apartment in the same amount for which it had been bought.

Now it was really time to leave. In their farewell letter to the Argentine Mission, Ben and La Nell wrote:

Our relationship with the Argentine Mission these forty years has been one of joy and fulfillment. It has given us the opportunity to have fellowship and to work with some of God's choicest

---

[111] *El Expositor Bautista*, July 1991, p. 23 (Scripture quoted 2 Timothy 4:7)

people. The relations with the national brethren have always been good but the degree of cooperation and maturity which now exists should enable the work to develop at a more rapid pace. This will permit the Mission to use its expertise in varied facets of the work.

Words cannot express our appreciation and gratitude for the dinner, gifts and many expressions of love. You are our family. When one leaves a family there is always pain. Of course, part of the healing will be the contact we can have through your letters and visits. Please keep us on your mailing lists and share with us any information which is not confidential.

Your prayers for us in these months of adjustment are greatly needed. Know that we will continue praying for you as you witness for our Lord here in this beloved land.

With Love, prayers and deep appreciation

It was a very good thing that they had a joyful event to look forward to: on their way to the U.S. they were stopping in Campinas, Brazil for the birth of their sixth grandchild, David and Patricia's miracle baby. David had been in a minor accident that had wrenched an arm caught in the steering wheel, so Ben got to drive them home from the hospital with their beautiful little daughter Sabrina. Unfortunately, the girl who took the message at the other grandparents' house got it all wrong and passed on the news that the baby had died at childbirth. The distraught Robertos changed their tickets and rushed to console their daughter, only to find everyone in excellent condition and that celebration was in order.

Ben and La Nell moved into the Mission's guest apartment to make way for the in-laws and Sergio insisted on going with them. During the day, Ben and Julio entertained Sergio and William (when he got back from school) in the back yard and at the park, while the women pampered Patricia and helped look after the baby.

While they were there they received word through the Foreign Mission Board that Ben's brother L.D. had suddenly passed away. David went downtown with his father so that he could make a long-distance telephone call to his sister Jewel. On the way back, he took his mind off his sadness by wondering what it was like for his son to live in a country of whose language he was not a native speaker.

"What do the Brazilians think of your Portuguese?"

"Some days they can tell I'm not Brazilian," quipped David.

The Return of the Natives

After being lost for several days between Houston and Albuquerque, and making an inexplicable detour to Phoenix, the Bedfords' shipment arrived, safe and sound except for the china cabinet's marble top that the insurance eventually replaced. The Gaydous had moved out a few days after Ben and La Nell arrived—Alberto having finally found a job in Texas—so the plan of living in the same city was not to be. The Bedfords joined the Eastern Hills Baptist Church and began the process of settling in.

It was very strange to think that they were there permanently. They were feeling the effects of what sociologists had come to call the "marginal man theory" to describe individuals suspended between two cultural realities and struggling to establish their identity. New Mexico had given them their start. Its public education system had seen them through school and provided La Nell with a scholarship for college. Its churches had trained them, given them their first opportunities for service and helped Ben with his university tuition. They had sent them out into the world with their blessing in their early twenties and now they were welcoming them back in their mid-sixties.

The Bedfords suddenly realized that they did not know much about their state outside the greater Clovis and Portales area. Until their short furlough in 1987, Ben had been to Albuquerque once, when he was in college, representing Eastern New Mexico University at the BSU State Convention, and they had been to several camps at Inlow, near Tajique, and Glorieta, near Santa Fe.

Ted Stanton was replacing Ben as Associate and had already taken on the tasks in the field. Ben and La Nell were to spend this last year on speaking engagements and Missions enlistment activities.

This proved to be a wonderful transition, for their responsibilities took them far and wide to meet with every Baptist association in New Mexico. They spoke to leaders and laymen of the many and varied types of services that were needed, from career missionaries to short-term volunteers, to partnerships between churches and associations. When Ben travelled alone he drove the trusty little Honda, taking the odometer to unimaginable readings. When they went together, they drove their brand-new white Buick that floated along the highways like a dream.

In November, they sent out their traditional Christmas newsletter:

Dear Friends and Loved Ones:

A few months ago we wrote you saying that it was our last report from the field. Now we are writing our final letter as active missionaries of the Foreign Mission Board. On July 12 we arrived from the field to begin our final furlough which will end on August 31, 1992, following 41 years, 4 months as missionaries, including 20 years in evangelism and church planting, 10 years in theological education and 11 years as associates to the Area Director for the South Cone of Spanish South America. September 1, 1992 we will become emeritus missionaries. We are grateful for the opportunity to serve God, Southern Baptists and the people of Latin America for these many wonderful years.

The overwhelming needs of the world, the unequalled opportunities of service possible through the open doors should not be ignored by Southern Baptists. As we approach this Christmas Season we urge you to:

PRAY as never before for world missions.

GIVE sacrificially to the Lottie Moon Christmas Offering for foreign missions.

URGE your church to set a worthy goal for this offering.

DO all in your power to lead your church to increase the percentage of your budget which goes to the Cooperative Program.

OFFER YOURSELF in service to God to do whatever He calls you to do and to go wherever he leads you to go.

Please continue to pray for us as we enter a new phase of our ministry. Pray for our children: (1) David and family who are serving as missionaries in Brazil; (2) Nelda and family as they seek to serve the Lord in their local church in Austin, TX; and (3) Nancy as she finishes her ThD in Tübingen, Germany.

Let us continue to hear from you at the address listed at the end of this letter. We want to express our gratitude to the First Baptist Church of Clovis, NM for processing and mailing our letters through the years.

Bilingual Acrobatics

Speaking more than one language has many and varied advantages but can also give rise to strange situations. Ben remembered a sermon on spiritual gifts that he delivered as a guest speaker on one furlough. From his wife's and daughter's expressions, he could tell that something was not right. Afterwards, he discovered that he had used the Spanish word *dones* for "gifts" throughout the message. Fortunately, the congregation understood the term from the context and merely assumed that he was very erudite and preferred using the original Greek word.

Interpreting for another person may be difficult—in fact, studies show that it is more stressful than being an air traffic controller—but interpreting for yourself can be even worse. Friendship Baptist Church had asked Ben to preach a bilingual sermon the Sunday night they first invited him to speak and he was having to make a supreme effort to remember exactly what he had just said in English, say it again in Spanish, and then shift gears to the next point. La Nell got off easy with reading the Scripture in Spanish.

The interim pastor, with whom Ben was acquainted from associational activities, lived a couple of blocks away from the Bedfords and had told them that the church was looking for a bilingual pastor. He arranged meetings with various church leaders and the congregation called them in December of 1991. The church families reflected the broader cultural reality. In many cases, the grandparents preferred Spanish, the parents were fully bilingual and the grandchildren preferred English.

New Mexico has many fascinating aspects. It was inhabited by Native Americans for thousands of years before the Spanish colonists made it part of the Viceroyalty of New Spain beginning in 1598. Spanish explorers called this region New Mexico as early as 1563, incorrectly believing it had wealthy Mexica Indian cultures similar to those of the Aztec Empire. However, the name remained. Later it formed part of an independent Mexico, which did not adopt its own name until 1821. New Mexico became a U.S. territory and eventually a state after the Mexican-American War. It has the second highest percentage of Native Americans in proportion to the population after Alaska and the highest percentage of Hispanics, including descendants of the original Spanish colonists from more than 400 years ago. These cultural traits are expressed in the state flag, whose scarlet and gold colors come from the royal standards of Spain and the ancient sun symbol from the Zia, an ethnic group included in the broad appellation of "Pueblo."

At first there were no services in Spanish, but two Sunday School classes were offered in that language for adult men and women, taught by Mr. and Mrs. García, respectively. La Nell was immediately recruited to teach the young people and young married couples in English. They were her favorite age group and she invited them to get-togethers in their home from time to time. Eventually a Spanish service was added during the Sunday School hour and subsequently the evening service began to be conducted in Spanish to accommodate the changing demographics of the congregation.

Two factors opened up the work with Hispanics in the neighborhood. One was the Good Will Center a few blocks away on Edith Street, sponsored by the Convention, to which the Goodes, social workers and state missionaries, dedicated a considerable amount of time. Its work was dear to Friendship's heart, for it had gotten its own start as a Goodwill Center sponsored by nearby Riverside Baptist Church. The Garcías' daughter-in-law volunteered regularly, and La Nell began giving sewing lessons and teaching a Bible study in Spanish at the center every Friday. The church had a pantry and a clothes closet; on Thursdays, which was Ladies' Day, the women would organize care packages. On Thanksgiving and Christmas local businesses donated twenty to thirty turkeys that the church distributed to needy families.

The other rather unexpected factor was funerals. It all began with a death in one of the church families. The service was held in Spanish for the benefit of the many friends and relatives who did not speak English. After that, Ben was often asked to speak at funerals, even in Catholic churches, when the priest graciously agreed to hold joint services. An elderly member of the church who had nearly reached the century mark had a brother whose wife died. The sister-in-law had pastored a Pentecostal church that met in their home and the family asked Ben to hold a bilingual funeral service. Many years later, he received a call from a young lady who had tracked him down as the pastor who had preached at her grandmother's funeral. Now her mother had passed away and he was the only one she could think of: "Could you please preach the sermon?"

Besides the sanctuary, the church had three more buildings, for Sunday School classes and the young people's activities. Perryton Baptist Church, from the Texas town of the same name, helped put a new roof on one of them as a mission project and, in return, Ben preached a revival for them. Friendship had recently acquired three acres of land, where softball and soccer fields were set up, as well as a basketball court. Their soccer team had an intense but friendly rivalry with nearby Iglesia Bautista Sinaí, led by Pastor Belmonte. The softball team played against peers from various denominations, sometimes in their own facilities and sometimes at a park with an officially marked field.

Friendship Baptist Church belonged to both the Spanish and English Associations and Conventions, and participated actively in each. Ben was twice elected President of the Spanish Association and served many times in its Christian Education Department.

The Bedfords officially retired in 1992. They attended a moving ceremony in Richmond, Virginia where they marched in with some 400 fellow retirees who were being honored. They received a commemorative plaque and their pins for forty-one years of service as missionaries. La Nell was chosen as one of the speakers and she talked about taking advantage of opportunities along the way, sharing the stories of how the Ragnis came to know the Lord through construction projects and the Torres through their daughters' orthodontic treatment.

This was eight months after beginning the pastorate at FBC. They decided to accept a salary of no more than $1,000.00 per month, the limit before having to pay taxes when receiving Social Security benefits. The full pastoral salary remained in the budget to keep the congregation in practice for the future. In the meantime, the difference was given to Missions and building projects.

A young man by the name of Jay Sparks worked in the Association during his two-year mission stint with the Home Mission Board. During that time he had also married, and his wife felt so comfortable in Friendship Baptist Church that they eventually joined there. After a time, the congregation decided to call them to co-pastor.

Reconnecting with Family

Three separate areas had to be set up to accommodate everyone: the long table in the dining room, the round table in the breakfast room and a card table in the den. People drifted back and forth and regrouped periodically to catch up with one another. The Bedfords had originally invited Ben's siblings and their spouses, but all of L.D.'s family, cousin Howard and niece Carla wanted to go, so of course they were included. A big group slept over and the rest stayed at a motel a couple of blocks away. They also hosted the somewhat smaller Watson crowd which came on another occasion.

One of the reasons that Ben and La Nell had decided to retire at sixty-five rather than seventy was to support and spend time with their aging siblings, all of whom were older than they except for Tom. Besides having them in their home, they made trips as far away as California to see Ira, and to Missouri and later Minnesota to visit John. They frequently stopped by Clovis for Billie and Mary, Lubbock for Kenneth and Odessa for Jewel.

Besides their mothers, before retiring they had already lost La Wanna, Maurice and W.L. on the Watson side, and A.T. and L.D. on the Bedford side. Over the next twenty years, one by one the remaining siblings and their spouses passed on, until they were the only ones left of their generation. They offered love and consolation to the families and attended the funerals, at most of which Ben was asked to speak. They became increasingly close to their nieces and nephews, maintaining frequent contact through visits, cards on birthdays, anniversaries and Christmas, and telephone calls, especially once Ben discovered the joys of the cell phone.

Of course, they had three of their very own grandchildren in Texas. Besides visits with the whole family and the thrill of Ben baptizing Veronica and Alejandro at the First Baptist Church in Austin, there were individual stays for maximum personal attention. There were trips to Carlsbad Caverns and even to the Grand Canyon. Moreover, there were many interesting things to offer visitors right there in Albuquerque, such as the October Balloon Fiesta, the largest hot-air balloon event in the world, and a variety of parks and hikes in the beautiful Sandia mountains, bare-shouldered and austere toward the city and draped with pine forests on the other side.

Little by little they went along making improvements to the house to make it even more welcoming. They replaced the drab old kitchen cabinets with new wooden ones stained in a light shade and installed new appliances. They took up the depressing old linoleum and had beautiful clean tile laid down. Eventually they changed the worn carpets and modernized the bathrooms. They replaced the back yard's warped wooden fence with a wall and wrought iron gates. One year they added a delightful sunroom whose ping-pong table gave them both fun and exercise, and which could do double duty as an extra dining area when they hosted a crowd.

Superficial Changes

As usual, the Bedfords soon found themselves involved in an increasing number of overlapping activities. Their new connections in the local and state associations and Convention as part of their Missions enlistment responsibilities had not only led to taking on a pastorate with all that it entailed but, as soon as word got around that Ben had a doctorate in Theology, he was also approached about teaching at Southwestern Seminary's new satellite campus in Albuquerque. Some students would be taking classes in person and others by video. They urgently needed someone to teach the New Testament course for the Master of Divinity students. Classes met once a week, on Mondays, from 9:00 a.m. to noon, and from 1:00 to 5:00 or 6:00 p.m. Because Golden Gate Seminary was already working in New Mexico, the program was transferred to that institution the following year. Ben was Adjunct Professor for two years in all, teaching Missions and Cross-Cultural Communications in the second year.

At the same time, he entered what would become a twenty-year relationship with the Contextualized Leadership Development (CLD) program, at first teaching whatever courses were needed and later becoming Director. A report to the Central Baptist Association's Annual Meeting gives a brief overview of the CLD's history and mission:

> *What is Contextualized Leadership Development? Nearly twenty-five years ago Golden Gate Seminary recognized that if it was to fulfill its mandate with the Southern Baptist Convention to provide for effective leadership in the churches of the West, then graduate level programs in English would not be enough to*

address the needs of those churches. Training would need to be offered at the post-high school level, in languages most useful to the churches, at sites close to the churches and at a cost affordable to the students. Begun first in the early 1980's in partnership with the North American Missions Board of the SBC, Ethnic Leadership Development (as CLD was then called) offered basic training to Christian leaders for church planting, evangelism and ministry.

Golden Gate authorizes local churches and associations to open CLD centers wherever such training is needed and adequate resources for that training is available, to provide relevant meaningful ministry within every cultural and ethnic group.

Central Baptist Association has furnished classroom space, library space (presently being moved to Sinai Baptist Church in order to provide needed space for the Association) and office space for the CLD Director. The program has an Advisory Committee which consists of the DOM [Director of Missions] and other leaders. It acts as a local trustee body.

So retirement came and went as nothing more than a change of location and financial arrangements: the work was the same as it had always been. The Bedfords became in essence area missionaries, visiting churches from Santa Fe in the north to Gallup in the west, encouraging, counseling, promoting, preaching and teaching.

One of Ben's close colleagues during those years was Dr. Thomas Eason, who with his wife had been language missionaries with the Baptist Convention of New Mexico and the North American Mission Board. While Ben served as director and instructor of the Albuquerque Center, Dr. Eason did the same in the Las Cruces Center. Each January the Seminary provided a directors' conference, and the two men would fly from Albuquerque and El Paso, respectively, to meet up at the Oakland, California airport. Dr. Eason rented a car and provided transportation while they were at the Seminary, while Ben made housing arrangements and navigated the turns and highway changes with a map, only occasionally making unplanned detours. One year they met at their usual spot in the airport and went to the car rental booth. The attendant looked over the reservation information and asked for a current driver's license. It turned out that Dr. Eason's license had expired two days before. He and Ben simply switched driver and navigator roles on that trip, and all was well.

Ben loved his students and the opportunity to teach and train pastors and teachers, and they in turn loved him. One of them, Steve Long, attorney turned pastor, tells of their relationship. A notice in the church bulletin board informed him of the Seminary's new satellite campus in Albuquerque. As part of the admissions process to the Master of Divinity program, he was required to write a statement of his call. He explained that he felt called to teach but was not sure about being a pastor. They suggested the Master of Theology program but allowed him to stay in the M.Div. Over the years Ben introduced him to pastoring and he discovered that he loved it.

Ben is one of the best teachers I've ever had. He also pastors the students. When he prays you know he is talking to God. He also has a great sense of humor. I remember before a test he told us about one of his profs who always prayed before an exam that God would bless them according to the amount of study they did.

He is always passing on practical advice, too. At the first class I had with him he made it a requirement that we keep and turn in a notebook with all our class work and assignments. He assured us that from time to time in our ministry we would want to review something we had done in class. And he was right.

I remember how devastated he was when a church he was pastoring had a fire and all his class notes and sermons over the decades, as well as his books, burned.

We were the beneficiaries of the entire corpus of the wisdom of God and spiritual experience he acquired over a lifetime of serving Christ. I sat under his teaching long enough to discern that he was a brilliant theologian. But he applied that theology in a humble and unpretentious way so that to the simple he was simple; and to the brilliant he was profound.

The thing I dreaded most in pastoring was hospital visits. I didn't even like to visit family in the hospital. I accompanied him on a hospital visit and he admonished me about being sensitive to pray for other people in the room, including the hospital staff. I learned to do hospital visits by watching him and came to love that part of the pastoral ministry. Ben was not only my professor, he was the ministry supervisor in my M.Div program. I designed a supervised ministry experience that focused on pastoring and Ben walked with me through it.

As my daughter graduated from high school and went on to college, he told me how he used email to keep in regular contact with his daughters.

He organized and was the director of the Golden Gate CLD program and taught classes in Spanish as well as English. He never lost his love for Hispanic people. I've heard that the accent of Argentinians causes other Latin Americans to perceive them as arrogant. If that's true, and if Ben acquired that accent, his humility and genuine love for people must have overcome it because the Hispanic people here loved him.

I think it would be accurate to say that Ben never really retired—he just quit getting paid. You may certainly quote me. It would not be an overstatement to say that Ben continues to be one of the most influential people in my life because of the privilege I had of spending so much time with him.[112]

---

[112] Stephen C.M. Long, from an email message to Nelda B. Gaydou, dated February 2017

Fire and Demons

Nancy hooked up the computer monitor that her parents had carted with them all the way from Albuquerque to Tübingen, Germany. Straining to see the letters on her laptop's tiny screen had been giving her migraines. Unfortunately, when the computer was turned on nothing happened. But the monitor did work with Ben's laptop on which he was finally learning to master Word and PowerPoint. He realized that his daughter's need was greater than his own and left it with her.

The Bedfords had taken a month off to visit their very own theologian, who was reading and absorbing knowledge at an impressive rate. During their absence, La Nell's brother Tom and sister-in-law Iris were staying at their house and filling the pulpit at their church.

One night, not long after they returned, they were rudely awakened by the insistent ringing of the telephone at around 2:30 a.m.

"Come quick, Pastor! The church is on fire!"

Ben dashed over to find that the window of his study had been broken and the curtains set on fire, which then spread through the office, damaging many of the approximately one hundred books he kept there, to say nothing of countless sermon and class notes. A neighbor had heard the noise when the vandals broke a window in the sanctuary, and scared them off before they did any more damage. Two boys and a girl took off in a pickup truck while he called 911.

It turned out that the neighborhood's Pentecostal and Catholic churches had also been set on fire that night as part of a gang's initiation rites. Eventually the girl who had been in the vehicle but had not actively participated in the arson was tracked down by the telephone that had been snatched off Ben's desk through the broken window. She was sentenced to community service and the judge asked that it be carried out at the church, so she spent a good many hours cleaning the premises. Most of the damage to the office and auditorium was from smoke and water. Services were temporarily held in the Fellowship Hall and Ben was able to rescue a few of the books, now with wavy pages. The church's insurance did not cover them, and although the Bedfords' personal insurance did, enabling Ben to replace some of the commentaries, most of the books and notes were gone forever.

Friendship Baptist Church held a home Bible study and the hostess' niece, who attended from time to time, had recently bought a house on San Martín (coincidentally the same street on which the vandalized Catholic Church was located). She invited Ben to her home to give a Bible study and asked him to go early to pray. She explained that her family was going through a rough time. Her husband's uncle had recently died from complications of a horrendous work accident in which he lost an arm to a meat grinder. Now all sorts of strange things were happening in the house, and they feared that it was possessed by demons. Although he arrived early as requested, the house was already packed with people, including a couple of Pentecostal preachers. The entire crowd stared at Ben expectantly.

"I am no exorcist," he explained, "but the Bible teaches that Jesus and the disciples cast out demons on several occasions. What we know for certain is that Jesus is far more powerful than Satan. He can heal everything and allow us to live without fear. I know of no ritual. What I will do and what you must do is ask Him to protect you, remove all fear and give you peace."

They followed this advice and had no more trouble. The homeowner's father, a man who had always violently opposed anything having to do with church, was visiting from California. He made a profession of faith that night and returned home a changed man. Interestingly, there were a couple of similar incidents of this type in store for the Bedfords, one in a mobile home in Santa Fe and another in a house in Chicago. In both cases inexplicable things occurred, such as television sets turning on spontaneously and doors opening and shutting on their own, making the proprietors afraid to be there alone. Each time, Ben told them to depend on the Lord, who promised to protect his own, and that it was a matter for prayer and faith. Each time, the trouble stopped.

Reluctant Flower Girl

The little flower girl pouted and refused to pose for the wedding pictures unless the bride held her. Three-year-old Sabrina had entered the halls of the First Baptist Church of Austin triumphantly, feeling like a princess in her fancy long dress with the exciting bell skirt. But when she saw her aunt in her beautiful bridal gown, she realized that she was not going to be the star of this show after all. For Nancy, now officially Dr. Bedford, had returned from Germany with a husband, Daniel Stutz. They met and fell in love while they were studying German at the Goethe Institute in Córdoba, and wrote each other after she went to Tübingen. The next year he followed to nearby Stuttgart, from where he could visit her frequently. He was there on an academic scholarship for a Master's degree in International Law that he had received by earning the highest grades of his class in the prestigious Law School of the University of Córdoba. He was able to work for room and board by claiming Italian citizenship through his maternal grandparents, which enabled him to work legally throughout the European Union. Now that they had both finished their European degrees, they were ready to start their lives together, beginning with half a year in the U.S. To travel there, Daniel would need a green card and to get it they would have to be married. So they had a charming civil ceremony and celebration in Germany with their friends and spent what Nancy called a "consular honeymoon" doing immigration paperwork.

Now the religious ceremony was about to take place in the beautiful little chapel of the church that had supported Nancy spiritually and financially throughout all these years, full of friends and loved ones. David and his family, back after a term in Brazil, were living in Fort Worth, where he was working on a Master of Theology.

Everyone participated: La Nell made the wedding dress; Ben performed the ceremony; Patricia sang; Nelda delivered a short message on marriage; and David filmed the whole thing, which took place in both English and Spanish for the benefit of Daniel and his family back in Argentina, none of whom spoke English. One of the most charming aspects of the ceremony was that the bridesmaids and groomsmen were all Nancy's nieces and nephews. The two youngest led the way, Sabrina the flower girl and Sergio the ring bearer. They were followed by Veronica on Alejandro's arm and Andrea on William's. But nothing overshadowed the bride's glow.

It was September and Nancy had teaching jobs lined up in Buenos Aires beginning the following February, at the Baptist Seminary and at ISEDET.[113] Until then, Daniel would work and they would house-sit for her parents while they were in Argentina for several months on two exciting projects.

---

[113] Instituto Superior Evangélico de Estudios Teológicos, a theological institution supported by the Anglican, Lutheran, Methodist, Presbyterian, Waldensian, and Reformed churches

Surprising End of a Mission Trip

Albuquerque-Phoenix-Chicago-Miami-Buenos Aires was a rather roundabout route, but the Bedfords were not complaining, as the tab was being picked up by the Foreign Mission Board and this was the most economical ticket. They were off to spend four months in their beloved Argentina promoting a fund for the future financing of the Seminary. They arrived in October and set up headquarters in a Seminary apartment, but before getting into their fundraising activities, they would be leading a Missions project.

The Córdoba Association had long been interested in another partnership program along the lines of the highly successful experience with the Mississippi associations. Mark Alexander talked to the Foreign Mission Board and to the Bedfords, who worked with the Central Baptist Association of New Mexico, and together they formed a team of around forty volunteers. The two largest groups were from Albuquerque—nine from Friendship and ten from Del Norte Baptist Church. Among the others were Lynn Ferrell and her husband Bob Naughton (and their children Michael and Monica), then living in Los Alamos, and a couple from the church in Perryton, Texas that had helped with the roofing project at Friendship.

The various members of the team were to meet up at the Dallas-Fort Worth airport and leave together, but a huge snow and ice storm rolled in. Part of the group made it out before it hit and the other was delayed, so they ended up getting to Buenos Aires at different times. International flights arrive and depart from the Ezeiza airport, located just west of the Capital's city limits, but domestic flights normally use Aeroparque, a little over a mile northeast of the downtown area. There are thirty miles of heavy traffic between them so the Bedfords split up,

La Nell herding the first group to Aeroparque and Ben waiting for the stragglers. When it was obvious that no one else was coming out of the customs gate after their plane landed, Ben began making inquiries.

"Oh, yes, the North Americans! We forgot to tell you that they managed to catch a flight going directly to Córdoba from here and are already on the way."

Ben grabbed a taxi and raced across town to join the others. In Córdoba, the volunteers stayed with local church families. The Spanish speakers were spread out among the teams to interpret for those who spoke English only. The interpreters' ranks were beefed up by Mark and Karen Alexander, Ken Evanston from Uruguay and several English-speaking Argentines. The volunteers laid foundations and built walls for a church building, visited countless homes, shared their testimonies, sang and preached. Approximately 200 persons made professions of faith. For many of the volunteers, like Zella Boyer and Michael and Mary Splichal, it was a pivotal experience that changed their vision of Christian service forever.

Benjamin "Benny" Montoya was among the most enthusiastic:

The year 1994 was a highlight of our Christian life. Our pastor had been a missionary in Argentina for 40 years before moving to Albuquerque, New Mexico. Brother Bedford formed a committee in New Mexico for a Mission Trip to Argentina. Christian members and pastors from different Baptist churches volunteered. My mother Lidia, daughter Marie and I were blessed to be part of the crew. There was a total of 40 persons on this Mission Trip. Some of the members and pastors who didn't have the resources were helped with the leadership of Pastor Bedford.

We were all assigned to stay with different families in Córdoba, Argentina. A youth pastor and I stayed with a young Argentine family and their two young girls. I was very humbled to stay with them because of their faithfulness. Also, they were very poor, comparable to a low-income family in the U.S.A. The husband was a taxi driver and was always busy. He worked all hours but still had the responsibility to set up his garage for church, by setting out benches and cleaning up the place.

Every day we got up early for breakfast, which was usually bread and hot yerba mate. The family was aware of my health problems as a diabetic and with their few resources would go out and buy eggs for breakfast. Our work was different from the other crew. We pulled nails out of pallets and salvaged the boards to be used on the church being built.

After work, we cleaned up and would eat supper while visiting a different family every night. We would give our testimony and just visit until 9:00 or 10:00 p.m. I had the privilege of interpreting for my friend the youth pastor and the people we were visiting. This reminded me of how difficult Pastor Bedford's task was preaching bilingually at our church.[114]

When it was time to leave, some of the volunteers opted to stay behind and do some sightseeing at the spectacular Iguazú Falls in the tri-border area, finishing up with a visit to Ben and La Nell in Buenos Aires. The Bedfords were loaned an office, where La Nell typed hundreds of letters and made hard copies on a portable printer, no larger than a three-hole paper punch (borrowed from Nelda and Alberto), as well as an Estanciera to drive around.

After speaking at numerous churches and associations in the Capital, they made a trip south as far as Río Negro, Neuquén and Esquel before heading to Córdoba for summer Mission Meeting right after Christmas. They had a marvelous time catching up with everyone. During the New Year's Eve Party, Mark Alexander spoofed their fundraising with the sham auction of a chair in which pioneer missionary Sydney Sowell had supposedly once sat. Ben even took the teenagers on a hike to a favorite spot on the Cuadrado, one of the mountains behind La Falda.

They had been assigned a room in one of the camp dormitories, but when they realized that the Hudsons were rather cramped for space with their son's visit, the Bedfords offered to let Timothy have their room while they stayed at Nelda and Alberto's unoccupied house a few

---

114 Benjamin Montoya, from an email message to Nelda B. Gaydou, February 2017

blocks away. Ben was not feeling very well. He called the doctor over the weekend, and was promised a house call that never materialized.

On Monday, they were to have the senior Gaydous over for tea so they dashed to La Falda for supplies. Ben made a nostalgic purchase of coffee at the Bonafide store he had frequented so often, but by the time they got to the bakery he was feeling very miserable indeed and asked La Nell to run the errand.

When she got back into the car, he said, "I think we better go by the hospital."

The receptionist put Ben in the waiting room. When the doctor opened the door, a nimble woman dashed in before him and he was forced to stay a bit longer. Now the doctor spotted him and walked over.

"Are you O.K.? I'm sorry I couldn't find the house yesterday."

"I just wanted to pay you for your time."

"No worries, but you better come in. I want to look you over. You look very pale to me."

After a brief examination, the doctor told him he needed to check in for testing.

"But I don't have anything with me! My wife is waiting outside in the car and she's not really up to driving it."

The doctor insisted and went out to the car to talk to La Nell in person. She steeled herself and drove the car to pick up supplies. By the time she returned, Ben was in intensive care. He was hemorrhaging at an alarming rate and it was not clear from where. A frantic round of testing was set in motion. Eventually a tear was located in the small intestine and by then the threat of general organ failure was looming large. The hospital staff asked if they had a problem with blood transfusions.

"As long as they don't give me AIDS, no problem," joked Ben wanly.

With their own children far away, the senior Gaydous, the Mission family and the people from the La Falda and Villa Giardino churches rallied round. The Bongiovannis were particularly helpful. Besides their kindness in keeping La Nell company and generally acting as surrogate children, they both had the same blood type as Ben and donated for the transfusions. On the first attempt the blood went right through him like water. The medical staff suspected that the bone marrow was not working and started alternating courses of fresh blood and plasma. Daniel, a kinesiologist, was allowed behind the scenes, so he went in at all hours of the day and night to get the latest updates and most accurate prognoses. One night, the doctor told him that he was afraid Ben would not make it to the morning.

La Nell had been nearly frantic with worry, terrified of losing her husband. Now, seeing him full of needles and tubes, and in great pain, something gave way and she changed her prayer: "Lord, he is yours. If you must, take him—don't let him suffer any more." That night was the turning point; the balance came down on the side of life.

When Ben was strong enough to be moved, Rubén and Sarita Simari drove the Bedfords to the Córdoba airport and even got permission to take their car directly out to the aircraft on the runway. Their old neighbors the Divers picked them up in Buenos Aires. After a few days, they flew back to Albuquerque. Ben was extremely weak, and his arms were black and blue with bruises and hard as rocks. Their doctor took a good twenty to thirty minutes to read everything in the medical file from the small La Falda medical facility. Finally, he looked up.

"They did everything we would have done. You were in good hands."

Another Twist of the Kaleidoscope

As Ben recovered, the Bedfords settled back into the pattern of church, associational and teaching activities. Meanwhile the kaleidoscope of life shifted and resettled several pieces of their personal lives.

By May Ben felt strong enough to accept an invitation to participate in the ceremony to turn over the Baptist Hospital in Asunción from the Mission to the Paraguayan Convention. He was teamed with Betty Missena to present an overview of the Hospital's history. It was an emotional and gratifying experience.

Shortly following his return, Bill and Opal Ferrell stopped by for a lovely visit after being with Lynn and her family in Los Alamos. They talked and laughed and played 42,[115] slipping effortlessly back into lifelong patterns of companionship. Their next stop was Cedar Hill, Texas, where Opal's sister Edna Grogan lived. The novelty was that now Opal shared driving duties. When Bill had been diagnosed with cancer several years before, Ben had urged her to take classes and get her driver's license: "One day you will need to be able to take him to the doctor." So she had done it. While they were still in Texas, the Bedfords received the news that their friend and missionary colleague Charles Campbell had passed away. They relayed the message through the Grogans to the Ferrells, who were able to attend the funeral in nearby Tyler and lend their sweet support.

Ben and La Nell travelled to Mississippi during the summer and went to the hospital with Opal for Bill's last blood transfusion. He began to fail rapidly after that and was gone by September. Ben and La Nell flew, and Alberto and Nelda drove to Jackson where legions of friends and loved ones were gathering to honor him. Ferrells and

---

[115] A four-handed partnership game of dominoes

Bedfords clung together—it was one of their hardest losses. There would never be another friend like him.

Nineteen ninety-six was marked by all sorts of events. Ben and La Nell celebrated their fiftieth wedding anniversary in April with a delightful service and reception at Friendship Baptist Church. Nancy flew in from Buenos Aires, radiant with expecting her first child; the González and Zorzolis, old friends from Argentina, made the trip from El Paso; Ben's sister Billie and husband Marion were there from Clovis; their niece Frankie made a special appearance from California; even La Nell's college friend Earlene and Ben's best friend from junior high school, Walter Hyde, were present. David emceed, Patricia and William sang, and Nelda gave a reflection on their marriage. A huge binder held cards, letters, messages and pictures sent by friends from around the world. The church in La Falda even sent videotaped greetings.

In May, the Bedfords went to Austin to celebrate their first grandchild's graduation from high school—their precious Andrea was all grown up and headed for the University of Texas, but the rest of her family was returning to live in Argentina. In fact, Veronica had gone on ahead to start the school year there and was staying with her other grandparents. Alberto and Alejandro joined her, while Nelda stayed behind a little longer to see her firstborn safely settled into college before establishing a pattern of yearly visits to her daughter and parents. On the other hand, David and his family made Fort Worth their permanent home when he accepted a position teaching Spanish at Texas Christian University.

In August, La Nell flew to Buenos Aires to be with Nancy for the birth of Valeria, a rare and beautiful creature of extraordinary vitality. Ben joined them and they all got together at the Gaydous' house in Villa Giardino. The family was growing.

A Breather of Sorts

After all the comings and goings of the previous year, as they entered their seventies the Bedfords paused to catch their breath and enjoy a bit of "routine" work. To be sure, Ben had a little project going on the side, writing a commentary on 1 John, with sermon outlines and illustrations for 2 Timothy for the Spanish Baptist Publishing House. They were near enough to see David's family several times a year. William graduated from high school and started working on a degree in History and Archeology at TCU, and the "middle" grandkids were now in grade school. In time Ben was to baptize both Sergio and Sabrina. The advent of email allowed Ben and La Nell to be in constant communication with their daughters, to a large degree eliminating the psychological if not the physical distance.

One of the Bedfords' big material blessings was their health plan, which essentially covered everything not taken care of under Medicare. November's routine medical exam brought an unwelcome surprise: Ben's PSA levels were alarmingly high. Further testing confirmed prostate cancer and the urologist offered two choices—chemotherapy or surgery, with compelling arguments for and against each approach. The Bedfords decided on surgery, but there were no openings until January. The surgeon penciled Ben in and, meanwhile, they put the whole situation under prayer. In the face of the uncertain prognosis, they decided that the time had come to resign from the pastorate at Friendship.

A few days later the surgeon called: "I've had a cancellation by a patient who does not want to spend Thanksgiving in the hospital. Would you like to take his place?"

Ben did not hesitate and was soon under the knife. The

surgery successfully removed the tumor, which was still completely encapsulated, but the surgeon said that its condition was such that it could have burst at any moment and spread with deadly and irreparable effect.

Back in the Saddle

The Seminary in Buenos Aires had asked the Bedfords to help out during the 1999 school year (March through November) but that was still a year away. While Ben convalesced, La Nell continued to teach Sunday School at Friendship through the end of March, after which they joined the Del Norte Baptist Church, whose facilities were located not far from their home. La Nell was put to work immediately as the Adult III Women's Sunday School teacher. Kevin Warner, Minister of Worship and Education, reveals himself as a staunch admirer:

My story shows an interesting side to the PARTNERSHIP your parents have lived before my eyes.

As close as La Nell and Ben were to each other all the years we were together at Del Norte Baptist Church, there was an independent side to La Nell. And I mean that in a very positive way. She is not a withdrawn, shy introvert. La Nell is forthright and a straight shooter. When she had something to say, she said it. La Nell Bedford is a force to be reckoned with.

Now in our church every year we order offering envelopes for anyone who had given to our offering the year before. And it is most common that one box of envelopes is given to each married couple. My wife and I each put a check in to reflect our personal tithe from each of our own paychecks. But both of those checks go into the same envelope that has our names as Mr. and Mrs. Kevin Warner.

Not long after Ben and La Nell returned to Albuquerque they joined our church. And it also wasn't long before La Nell came to the Church Financial Officer and told her, "I want my own envelopes with my name on them so I can give my own tithe." And *I say, "Good for her!"*[116]

In May, the doctor cleared Ben to resume regular activities, so he promptly agreed to act as interim pastor of Spanish-speaking Emanuel Baptist Church until the end of the year and prepared to teach the fall semester in the CLD. He was back!

---

116 Kevin Warner, from an email message to Nelda B. Gaydou, February 2017

From Daycare to Graduate School

"¡Hola, Valeria!"

"¡Chau, preciosa!"

The neighborhood shop attendants all took time to greet the golden-haired little girl as she walked by hand-in-hand with her grandfather. A ten or fifteen-minute bus ride down busy Avenida Directorio got Ben from Floresta to Flores in time to pick her up from daycare at noon. According to her mother's schedule, he either walked her to the Stutzs' home or took her back for lunch and a nap at the apartment he and La Nell were using on the same block as the Seminary in Buenos Aires. Often they stopped by the Pumper Nic (the Argentine version of Burger King) to use its clean facilities and share a little treat.

La Nell was busy during the day at the President's office. Although she had originally been asked to teach Christian Education and help with the library, President Daniel Villanueva (who back in his student days had been Ben's capable teaching assistant) decided he could really use her organizational and linguistic skills for himself. She acted in essence as his administrative secretary and he kept her supplied with a variety of translation projects. Ben, on the other hand, was busy at night, since classes were scheduled late to accommodate the students' full work schedules.

The plan had been for Ben to teach New Testament but, in the event, Charles Allen came as visiting professor at the same time and covered those classes for one semester. This proved to be fortunate, because there were over sixty students needing to take Pastoral Ministry and Administration, which Ben was qualified to teach. He also gave classes in Johannine literature (works by the Apostle

John) and Ephesians at the graduate level, and two persons travelled from Asunción, Paraguay every week for one semester to meet this requirement for their doctoral degrees.

The Bedfords attended the Betel church[117] with Nancy, received visits from Nelda and made trips to their beloved Sierras in Córdoba, soaking up the atmosphere and reconnecting with a myriad of friends. Ben was even able to spend a week in Asunción at the invitation of his old friend Cacho Simari, now pastor of the Villa Mora church next to the Baptist Hospital. It was the annual Missions Emphasis Week which gathered pastors and leaders from the church's ten mission points in the interior of Paraguay, and Ben delivered the message at a special Sunday night service.

While they were still in Argentina, Dr. Gustavo Suárez wrote from the U.S. asking Ben to accept the position of Director of the CLD beginning January 1, 2000, so the Bedfords' main task for the next decade was all lined up.

---

[117] This church had combined the old Floresta church with the congregation that met in the Seminary chapel.

A New Crop of Leaders

The two men stood hip deep in the waters of the Pecos River, baptizing seventeen persons that bright summer day into the fellowship of El Buen Pastor Baptist Church of Santa Fe. Over half of them were from the Pecos area where the church was considering starting a new Hispanic work. The congregation had recently called Daniel Trejo as pastor and he had asked his teacher and mentor to share the moment. It had been a long process:

> *It was in the summer of 2004 that our paths first crossed. I was studying at the Seminary in Santa Fe and the next classes were to be given at the Association's facilities in Albuquerque. That is where I met Brother Benjamin and, when we were introduced, it was the first time I came across a humble Argentine. Just kidding! Here was a gringo speaking perfect Spanish with an Argentine accent, with a humility and love of God that I learned from him and that defined him as a man of love and passion for GOD.*
>
> *Several years passed and he was called as interim pastor at El Buen Pastor Church in Santa Fe, New Mexico. It was around 2006 and I belonged to another church—the First Baptist Hispanic Church of Santa Fe, pastored by César Gutiérrez. I was still studying and Brother Bedford and I were getting to know each other better.*
>
> *One day when we were eating together, he spoke words that marked my life. He said, "Daniel, have you not felt God calling you to be a pastor?" My wife and I looked at each other. I swallowed the piece of meat I had been savoring and didn't say anything, but I thought to myself, "I think that Brother Bedford has eaten garlic*

and onions today and they disagreed with him!" After praying for a moment, I took a sip of my Coke, waiting for inspiration, and answered, "No, I've never felt anything, Brother." And we kept on eating.

Almost a year later Brother Rafael Murillo and Brother Bedford invited my wife and me to a restaurant, and asked us if we wanted to accept the call as pastors of El Buen Pastor Church in Santa Fe. After some serious praying, my wife Marisela and I decided to take on this new challenge, to say yes to the call that God was making. When everything had been arranged, my wife and I were installed as pastors. Our ordination took place in January 2008. Brother Bedford was very happy—I'm not sure whether for me or for himself, because he was going to get a rest from the church. Just kidding—he will never rest because he is completely devoted to our Lord Jesus Christ.

He did not abandon me after the ordination. Now he would be my counseling pastor and my spiritual father. For one year he helped me, no longer as pastor but as a mentor. And after a year, the day of harvest arrived. We were to have the first baptisms and we made preparations for this great event in the Pecos River.[118]

Raúl Velásquez is another former student who remembers being put on the spot:

When I was invited to begin the Seminary, I said that I did not want to study to be a pastor, but to learn more about the Bible and be a blessing to those who do not know the Lord. I met Brother Benjamin and received Seminary classes through him, studying from the year 2001 to 2007.

One day I was talking to Brother Benjamin about my work with a group of brothers and that I was hoping to find someone to serve our group as pastor. I kept on talking and, after listening for a while, Brother Benjamin interrupted me and said very seriously, "Raúl, the Lord is calling you to preach." Those words kept

---

118 Daniel Trejo, from an email message to Nelda B. Gaydou, February 2017

resounding in my ears and in my heart, and through them I was able to understand that the Lord was calling me to the ministry.

Today I am the pastor of the Rosa de Sarón Church in Santa Fe, New Mexico, and the Lord continues to bless. I keep seeing people give their lives to Christ as Lord as a result of those words that Brother Benjamin, guided by the Holy Spirit, put into my ears and my heart. I always remember his counsel, ready help and service.[119]

Their stories illustrate the first and fourth of the five expectations listed in Ben's job description as Director of the Contextual Leadership Development (CLD) program, also known locally as the Albuquerque School of Theology:

1. Discover, train and mobilize personnel from churches in Central Baptist Association and Santa Fe;
2. Plan and coordinate all classes in accordance to policies of Golden Gate Baptist Theological Seminary;
3. Recruit, train and assign qualified instructors for each school team;
4. Develop a working relationship with the Baptist Convention of New Mexico, Central Baptist Association and Santa Fe churches;
5. Develop, implement and evaluate an educational strategy that will enable training for church members producing pastors, church planters and lay leadership.

The logistics involved were challenging, to say the least: deciding which classes to offer each semester in which language (English or Spanish) according to the students attending and their program requirements; finding qualified teachers for all the courses; choosing venues to help cut down on student travel and so on. The CLD offered two diplomas—one in Christian Education and one in Theology. Golden Gate required that teachers have at least a Master of

---

[119] Raúl Velászquez, from an email message to Nelda B. Gaydou, February 2017

Divinity and it was always a scramble to fill the slots. Eventually the Seminary agreed that seasoned pastors who had earned both diplomas could teach some of the classes. Ben was once again the faculty wild card, often teaching two or three classes per semester: Old Testament, New Testament, Baptist History, Evangelism, Revelation, Preaching, Pastoral Care, or whatever else was needed. Additionally, detailed records had to be kept of course work, professors, students, grades, finances, and so on.

At first Ben was given a little cubbyhole at the Baptist Office in downtown Albuquerque but the Convention soon sold that property and bought a new place on Wyoming Street where there was no room for him. However, the Association rented space in the Baptist Foundation's building and set him up there. The facilities allowed holding up to three classes at the same time, and classes also met in various church buildings, especially in Santa Fe. One semester Ben had two students from Albuquerque and two from Gallup in the same class so they took turns meeting in the two cities.

Ben's largely nominal salary was in fact paid by the New Mexico Baptist Convention. Moreover, the CLD only represented part of his duties. There was no catalytic or ethnic missionary for the district at that time, so he was asked to assume many of these duties. He counseled pastors and churches, and participated in educational programs in local churches and associations from Española to Gallup.

In one of his reports, Ben wrote:

> *Some of the churches have used the CLD programs to help train local leadership. However, the real purpose of the CLD is to train workers for vocational ministry—full time or bi-vocational. Actually, this is the fourth level of training. The first three levels are: new members, training of the church body, and training for leadership within the church. I have sought to promote such training in associations, local churches, camps, etc. Though this has helped, we have only touched the tip of the iceberg. In the CBA [Central Baptist Association], I have worked with the Director of Missions, Ken Goode, in projecting a type of institute that will train local leadership through classes similar to the CLD program*

but less expensive, more inclusive, and more pertinent to current needs. This will leave the emphasis of the CLD program, along with the Baptist universities and seminaries, for the training of pastors. I feel that the growth of the churches, especially the ethnic groups, will largely depend on the success of these programs.

Ben clocked up an impressive number of hours and miles on the road. Besides teaching, he was often invited to preach at Sunday services, revivals and camps. He filled in at congregations that were temporarily without a pastor: Friendship Baptist Church, Iglesia Bautista Emanuel, First Spanish Church and Fruit Avenue Church in Albuquerque, and Iglesia Bautista El Buen Pastor in Santa Fe.

A pilot program was launched to establish Spanish Departments in English-speaking congregations. The first two were in Monterrey and Belen. The concept soon spread, with some groups remaining as church departments and others becoming autonomous congregations. The group in Monterrey was going strong under the leadership of a Peruvian pastor called Sherlock Vargas. When he was laid off from his secular job he moved to Albuquerque and was eventually asked to head a Spanish Department at the Bedfords' own Del Norte Baptist Church.

While Ben flitted from church to church, La Nell opted to stay at Del Norte (although of course she often went with him, especially in the evenings) to serve in what had always been one of her main ministries: Christian Education. When they returned from Argentina, she was assigned the Adult IV Sunday School class with the most elderly women of the congregation. The former teacher turned it over gratefully, with some rather fatalistic parting words:

"Do the best you can. Mostly they just sit there."

La Nell paid no attention and set about preparing. Soon she had a lively group of octogenarians and nonagenarians eager to learn, discuss and share a wealth of experience. Many of them were living in nursing homes and she visited them regularly. She also invited them to her house, laying out the best linen, china, crystal and silver to honor them.

When the Spanish Department was organized at Del Norte, La Nell was asked to lead the Adult Sunday School class, so she said farewell to her ladies and embarked on a new adventure, using the material from the Spanish Baptist Publishing House that covered the entire Bible in nine years. Besides native Spanish-speaking New Mexicans, there were people from Mexico, Peru, Guatemala and Cuba.

The Bright Thread of Family

Family was a bright thread running through the rich tapestry of the Bedfords' lives. La Nell spent two months in Buenos Aires in 2000 with her youngest daughter. Ever original, Nancy was expecting twins and had been ordered to rest and fatten up. Her husband Daniel, suffering under a workaholic employer wholly devoid of empathy, was lucky to get off with a severe reprimand rather than being fired when he insisted on taking the day off to be with his wife during delivery:

"I didn't even take time off for my mother-in-law's funeral. After all, it didn't make any difference to her. Your wife's family can take care of her!"

La Nell ran errands and whipped up tempting meal after meal, getting the babies up to a respectable birth weight. Sofía and Carolina arrived ten minutes apart by natural childbirth, and their grandfather made a quick trip to meet the last but not least of the nine grandchildren.

At the end of that year Alejandro arrived in Albuquerque to spend several months with Ben and La Nell before joining his sisters in Austin, where Joshua, the Bedfords' first great-grandchild, was born. Veronica had been the first grandchild to marry.

After seven years in Buenos Aires, Nancy and her family moved to Evanston, Illinois in time for her to start teaching in the spring semester of 2003 as the Georgia Harkness Professor of Applied Theology at Garrett-Evangelical Theological Seminary, where she remains to this day. In July, all five Bedfords attended Billie's ninetieth birthday party in Clovis. From there, Ben, La Nell and Nelda went on to Austin to be present at the birth of Veronica's second child, Thomas, who received the last of La Nell's legendary hand-sewn quilts.

In 2006 Ben, La Nell and Nelda finally took their long-postponed trip to Europe, touring England, Scotland, France, Spain and Italy for a month on public transportation. One of the highlights was attending the baptism of William's firstborn, Sofia, at a beautiful little church parts of which dated back to Norman times. He had married Ellie, a fellow archeologist from England, and they had settled down in Oxfordshire.

Next to tie the knot was Alejandro, in 2007, to Cintia, and his grandparents travelled to Argentina for the occasion. In an unlikely twist of fate, the ceremony and reception took place at the same venues as those of his parents, with both of his grandfathers officiating in the ceremony.

Two more great-grandchildren were born in 2008—Dorrie in England and Evangelina Dolores (better known as "Lola") in Argentina. Ben and La Nell met her on their last trip there, in 2009, after a visit to Chile sponsored by the Cooperative Baptist Fellowship, during which Ben taught a workshop on Christian Ministry and an intensive course on First John for Seminary credit, and preached at Easter services. The last great-grandchild (so far) was Lola's brother Nicolás, born in 2010. By then, the "middle" grandkids were in college, Sergio at TCU and Sabrina at Stanford.

It was fascinating to keep up with the growing family and there was nothing Ben and La Nell enjoyed more than news and visits from any and all of them.

The Nicaraguan Connection

"Vení. Contame cómo te llamás."[120]

La Nell was enchanted to discover that Nicaraguans used *vos* rather than *tú*, just like Argentines. It made her feel right at home.

Brenda Gray of Del Norte Baptist Church explained how they ended up there. Sometime in late 2004 or early 2005, a new choir member sat down beside her. Upon discovering that she was originally from Nicaragua, Brenda said, "We should make a mission trip there." Sofía knew the Bedfords through the Spanish ministry, so the Grays invited all three to their house for Sunday dinner. Sofía showed them pictures of the family ranch and said she was going for a visit in the spring. The Grays and Ben decided to go and look over the possibilities.

Sofía's brother José picked them up at the Managua airport in his jeep and drove them to his ranch, nearly three hours away. Ben spent the night in town and the Grays stayed at the ranch, in a room over the barn. José's wife, a doctor, showed them around the hospital and discussed how to go about a medical/evangelistic mission in that area. Nothing was really decided, but Sofía had planned a big gathering at her ranch according to family tradition. She had one of the cows killed and invited all the surrounding churches:

.... There was music, singing, lots of food, Ben preached, and Sofía's sister-in-law was saved! What a night!

The next day, José took us to Managua where we treated him to a meal at the mall, and then to the Baptist guest house for the night. It was the 4th of July. One of the missionaries just happened to be there and she invited us to a party that night at one of the mission houses. At the party, we explained why we had

---

120 "Come. Tell me your name."

*come, and very quickly they agreed to have us come do a medical/
GO team out in Nueva Guinea. Turns out they had never had
this combination but were willing to try it. GO stands for gospel
outreach. The GO team would go the day before the medical
clinic, passing out tracts, inviting folks to the clinic, and inviting
them to a Jesus film that evening.*

*That spring, about 12 people from our church went on the
first medical/GO mission to Nicaragua. We had a doctor, nurse,
pharmacist, 2 translators (La Nell translated for Dr. Gray), Ben
counseling, and the GO team. It was a huge success, and we were
invited to come back the next year.*

*Our trips continued for 5-6 years. We went to different parts
of the country each time, working out of churches or schools. We
hooked up with a couple who were national missionaries on a
couple of trips. After the first one, we had 2 doctors.*

*Everyone loved Ben. They greatly respected his age and
wisdom! He was a trouper! On one of the trips we slept on cots in
a half-finished school house in the middle of nowhere! We dug a
latrine and put plastic around some trees for a shower.*

*On one trip we celebrated Ben's 80th birthday and on another
Ben and La Nell were celebrating their 60th anniversary!!!*[121]

Richard and Mary Gómez were recruited by Ben from the First
Spanish Fruit Avenue Baptist Church. As a pharmacist, Richard was a
key member of the medical team and kept exemplarily accurate records.
He described the first trip to Nueva Guinea, a six-hour drive southeast
from Managua. Fifteen persons went from Del Norte, First Spanish
Fruit Avenue, Samaritan Purse, Iglesia Sinaí and even one volunteer
from San Antonio, Texas. Generous members of the Albuquerque
congregations helped pay for several of the airline tickets.

The GO (Gospel Outreach) team visited the surrounding
communities before each medical clinic, going from house to house
and covering each home with prayer. They distributed over 1800
copies of the Gospel according to Luke, in the form of booklets and

---

121 Brenda Gray, from an email message dated February 2017

audiocassettes, inviting everyone to an open-air projection of the film *Jesus*. Pastor Héctor Belmonte was particularly effective at witnessing.

The medical team set up its equipment in a new place each day, usually a school or church, registering and scheduling patients to see the doctors for medical attention and provide medication. There was both medical and spiritual counseling. After each patient was seen and the prescriptions filled, they were referred to the pastoral team. Ben started out on the GO team but ended up spending most of his time counseling with the medical team. On this first mission trip, 632 patients were seen and 1800 prescriptions filled. There were 106 professions of faith and another 100 persons expressed strong interest.

The second trip was to Río Blanco, some six or seven hours northeast of Managua. The team of eighteen was joined by two local doctors. The clinics saw 1340 patients and filled over 5850 prescriptions. During the week 140 persons accepted Christ and 70 more asked for additional information.[122]

With each trip logistics and efficiency increased, as did cooperation with local health care professionals and Baptist workers. Furthermore, the groundwork was laid for establishing new Bible studies, mission points and two autonomous churches, a wonderful and rewarding experience for everyone involved.

---

[122] Richard Gómez, February 2017

Lowering the Speed Limit

Just as the Department of Transportation adjusts the maximum speed limit according to type of road and projected traffic, as Ben approached his eighty-second birthday he decided that it might be wise to moderate his pace a bit. Accordingly, he sent a letter to David Red, Leadership Development, Baptist Convention of New Mexico:

> *Dear David,*
>
> *The purpose of this letter is to present my resignation effective December 31, 2008. This includes not only my position as Director of CLD for Central New Mexico but also the other duties described in my contract with the Baptist Convention of New Mexico.*
>
> *It has been a pleasure and a blessing to serve in this position for nine years. I want to express my thanks and appreciation to all those with whom I have worked in the Convention, in the associations, in the churches, with the instructors and with the students, all of whom (both individually and collectively) have been a blessing and an inspiration in my life. I thank God for the privilege of serving Him during these years. Pray for me as I finish the year. I will do my best to leave everything in order. I will be happy to work with you in the period of transition. Be assured of my prayers and co-operation as you seek the best way to prepare workers for leadership in New Mexico.*
>
> *Yours in His Service*

Now relieved of administrative duties and a great deal of travel, he continued to teach at least one class per semester for four more years in the CLD.

Ken Goode, a missionary with the Central Baptist Association with whom Ben had worked closely over the past few years, put him in contact with the Director of Wayland Baptist University's extension program in Albuquerque, who was thrilled to have someone with a doctorate available. Although they usually had no trouble filling the faculty positions for the undergraduate programs, it was often difficult to find qualified teachers for the graduate courses.

Once again Ben was in the position of preparing and teaching whatever was needed: Theology, Old Testament, New Testament, Hermeneutics, Pauline Literature, Minor Prophets, Major Prophets, and so forth. As a bonus, he became acquainted with a whole new batch of promising leaders, pastors and teachers. Wayland offered classes in a variety of venues, including downtown and the Sandia base in Albuquerque, and in Clovis. There were students from every ethnic and age group, ranging from twenty-three to sixty-five years of age, many of them embarking on a second career. They came from every walk of life, even police officers.

One of the students in whom Ben saw great potential both as pastor and teacher was retired colonel Tom Lambert. Several years later, now pastor of the Forest Hills Baptist Church, he wrote Ben: "We miss you here in New Mexico, and at Wayland God used you to keep me in that program long ago. You were my first (and best) professor."

Crossroads

Ben had nearly reached his car when a large SUV suddenly aimed its beams right at him. His instinctive leap did not prevent the car from knocking him down and pinning his left heel under the front tire. The driver froze in shock. Fortunately, several of the supermarket's employees were on break in the parking lot and rushed over to help. One got the driver to move the vehicle off Ben's foot, one called 911, another fished his shoe out from under the wheel and several more helped him to his own car.

He assured everyone that he was all right and just wanted to go home, but the ambulance had arrived by then and both the paramedics and the police insisted that he go to the hospital. They had discovered that his left sock was full of blood and his right pants leg was torn at the knee, which was bruised and bleeding.

He used the ride to marshal his forces: he called La Nell to let her know he would be late; he called his neighbors the Fosters to ask them to get the extra car key from his wife, take the car home and stay with her until he returned; he called the people at the Missions Committee at Del Norte Church to let them know he would not make that night's meeting; he called Dr. Ira Pinkston, Worship Minister at Del Norte and a good friend, to request a ride home when he was discharged from the hospital; and he called his daughter Nancy to let her know what was going on and have her inform the rest of the family.

When the staff at the emergency room found that he wasn't dying, they put him in a little room and left him there for a couple of hours with an open wound, for the tire had ripped apart the flesh between heel and ankle. Eventually someone wheeled him to radiology, where they took about thirty X-rays of his right leg. Finally, they got around to cleaning the wound and stapling it shut. By then they were eager to get rid of him and he was even more eager to leave. Ira took him home well after midnight.

Nelda, who had just been in town visiting her parents and was now spending a few days with her daughters in Austin before going home, changed flights and returned to Albuquerque for several weeks to lend a hand and chauffeur her parents.

Ben's doctor referred him to an excellent foot specialist with an office in the same building who agreed to see him at once. He was not at all pleased with the look of things, and immediately removed the offending staples and took blood and tissue samples for a culture. The next appointment was at his other office across town and the news was not good: the tests confirmed MRSA (Methicillin-Resistant *Staphylococcus aureus*), a hard-to-treat bacterial infection probably contracted at the hospital and potentially leading to the loss of the foot or even death.

Immediate surgery was required to trim the tissue and scrape the bone in an attempt to prevent the infection from spreading further into the bone and on into the bloodstream. It was performed successfully that very night. Ben's wife and daughter were with him when he awoke in the recovery room. True to form, he was soon witnessing to the nurse. Every day La Nell dressed carefully to look her best for her husband, for nothing perked him up like his beautiful wife's devoted attention.

The doctor was able to set Ben up with a marvelous portable device that continuously applied suction to the wound and sped up the healing time markedly, allowing him to be discharged within a few days. A nurse would make daily house calls to clean the device and change the dressing. When they got home, the initial sighs of relief turned into gasps of dismay upon discovering that the kitchen floor was flooded and water was spreading into the adjoining rooms. While Nelda mopped, Ben called Lupe Ontiveros from the Spanish Department at their church, who immediately came to the rescue and repaired the leaky pipe.

When it was time for her sister to return to Argentina, Nancy took her place for another week. Meanwhile, Ben's Wayland classes resumed, meeting at their home several times. Then one of his students, Patrick McKinney, drove him to class until he was ready to get back behind the wheel. The people from church were wonderful, rallying round with visits, food and every possible offer of help, including replenishing their supply of firewood and stacking it in the garage.

Providential Circumstances

The accident actually simplified matters. For some time, the Bedfords' children had been urging them to make a move, preferably near one of them. They were concerned that their heretofore comfortable house was becoming too much for them: three bedrooms, office, kitchen, den, living room, dining room, breakfast room, sun room, two bathrooms, double garage, front yard and back yard translated into a lot of work for people in their mid-eighties.

So far, they had resisted changing their busy and happy lifestyle. They had already turned down two invitations to interim pastorates. The one in Colorado they had never seriously considered, but only a few months earlier they had received a tempting offer from Bernalillo, just north of Albuquerque on the way to Santa Fe. At first glance it had seemed an ideal way to round off their pastoral ministry. Ben would have finally been able to fully put into practice his intentional interim pastorate training. But remaining in their house would have meant a lot of driving throughout the week. The other option was to move out there. After much prayer, they decided it would be too much for their health and regretfully requested having their name removed from the list of candidates.

Now the accident had clearly revealed how difficult it was to keep everything going when one of them was out of commission. They all agreed that the most logical thing would be for them to relocate near Nancy, so the search for a suitable place began. She soon discovered that an apartment was available in the very building where she lived. It was undergoing foreclosure proceedings and, with the price going down a little every month, it was sure to be snapped up at any moment. After analyzing all their resources, the Bedfords made an offer in

May of 2012, six months after the accident. Between their savings, cashing in an insurance policy and most of the settlement from the accident, they managed to scrape up the amount needed for closing before selling their own house. In addition, the apartment had been vacant for two years and required repairs and refurbishing, so they borrowed $30,000 from Billie. Ben and La Nell made a quick trip to Evanston for the closing in May, returning to Albuquerque just in time for Wayland's graduation ceremony, where one of the graduates from the Master's program had requested being hooded by Ben.

The University wanted Ben to teach as long as possible, and he promised to do so until their house sold. Meanwhile, the income from teaching would cover the apartment's monthly expenses. The house was put up for sale in July; a firm offer was made in early October; Ben finished out the school quarter on October 31st, while La Nell rounded out seventy years of teaching Bible classes; the closing took place in November; and by Thanksgiving they were residents of Evanston, Illinois.

One year after the accident, Ben and La Nell were living in a wonderful apartment one floor down from their youngest daughter. Their indoor parking space was a couple of steps away from the hall entrance, the elevator was next to their apartment and the laundry room was two doors down.[123] They had a large master bedroom, a guest room/office, two bathrooms, a kitchen/breakfast room, and a spacious living room and dining room. Their furniture, including La Nell's piano, could have been made to order for the available space.

The only difficulty was getting the china cabinet up to the third floor. It simply would not fit in the elevator or negotiate the turns in the stairwells. Nancy's husband Daniel, who at that time had an office in the facilities of Reba Place, the Mennonite congregation to which the Stutz family belonged, secured temporary storage there until a solution was found. After a certain amount of head scratching, two carpenters from Reba sawed off the legs and put them back on after the cabinet

---

123 Municipal ordinances in the area do not allow individual washers and dryers in apartment buildings.

had been lifted on a platform with a winch and passed through the dining-room window from the green space between buildings.

Not only were the Bedfords in an ideal living situation, they were better off financially than at any other time of their lives: even after repaying Ben's sister, they had a respectable nest egg left over. It was a miracle.

Lake Michigan

Not since the early 1960s had the Bedfords lived so near a large body of water. Then they had been able to see the Atlantic Ocean in the Argentine Patagonia from the landing of their two-story house. Now they were about ten blocks away from Lake Michigan, which to the naked eye seems equally boundless.

It is the fifth largest lake in the world, and the second largest of the Great Lakes by volume or third largest by surface area. Unlike the other four whose shores are shared with Canada, it is entirely within the United States. Its extensive beaches have caused it to be known as the "third coast" of the country, and they are covered with soft, off-white "singing sands" whose music is a byproduct of their high quartz content. They also form the largest freshwater dune system in the world.

Some 12,000,000 persons live along the shores of Lake Michigan, mainly in the greater Chicago area. This includes Evanston, bordering to the south with Chicago, to the west with Skokie, to the north with Wilmette and to the east with the Lake. Before the 1830s the area was mainly uninhabited, although the Potawatomi Indians had trails running through it in a roughly north-south direction, with some semi-permanent settlements along them. The French explorers called it "Grosse Pointe" after a spit of land that juts into Lake Michigan about thirteen miles north of the mouth of the Chicago River.

The first non-Native Americans settled there in the mid-1830s. The township of Ridgeville was organized in 1850 but had no municipality. A group of Methodist businessmen, one of whom was John Evans, founded Garrett Biblical Institute and Northwestern University, which opened its doors for the first time in 1855 to ten students. They soon submitted to the county a plan for a city, requesting that it be named Evanston. The population quadrupled between 1860 and 1870, and increased by 70% between 1920 and 1930. Now its beautiful tree-lined streets are home to a population of rich ethnic diversity that numbers around 75,000, approximately 7% of which is Hispanic. Between Evanston and Skokie there are some 10-15,000 Spanish speakers. It was to them that Ben and La Nell felt called to serve.

Shortly before leaving New Mexico, Ben had been invited to speak to the Brotherhood group at the Spanish Convention, when he told them: "I took my first breath in New Mexico and I had hoped to take my last one here, but it seems that God has other plans, so please pray for me." When the Bedfords took their leave of the congregation at Del Norte, Ben said that if God had called Moses to lead the Israelites out of Egypt when he was eighty years old, he could surely call them to start a new work at eighty-five.

The Bedfords' arrival in Evanston practically coincided with that of Scott Kelly, a dedicated pastor with a special gift for working with students. He and Ben were to be weekly prayer partners for the next two years. Scott recalls those days:

> *I first met Ben and La Nell Bedford through Jonathan Turner, a former member of Evanston Baptist Church, shortly after I arrived in August 2012 to serve as pastor. Within a few months of my arrival, Ben and La Nell moved into their condo and began attending our church on Sundays. Within a short time, your dad began to talk with me about his desire to start a new church for Spanish-speaking people in Evanston. With the help of a small group of us from Evanston Baptist Church, Ben organized an initial informational meeting at the Robert Crown Center in Southwest Evanston.*[124]

The attendees included Jaime Shedd, an energetic and successful pastor and professor at the Moody Hispanic Bible Seminary who

---

[124] Scott Kelly, from an email message to Nelda B. Gaydou dated February 2017

told one of his promising students, Christian Castro, about the newly arrived retired pastor and his plans. Christian, who lived in the area, was enthusiastic about the possibilities and the decision was made to begin holding Bible studies on Sunday morning. At first there were just two families—the Castros and the Bedfords—and the idea was to alternate between their homes. The two men put together information and invitation packets to distribute as they went door to door in their neighborhoods.

The Bedfords' china cabinet dilemma had led to an interesting discovery: Reba Place rented the facilities in its activity center to various Christian groups. The location and the meeting place were perfect so they struck a deal. Ben and La Nell felt that the circumstances surrounding their move had been a miracle that went beyond their personal situation to allow new opportunities for sharing. Besides their usual tithes and offerings, they felt led to set aside for the new work an amount equal to the closing costs on their house. This was enough to cover the rent for the first two years and to purchase a piano, video equipment and some basic literature.

In spite of the increasing health issues that come hand in hand with advancing age, their personal life has entered another golden family time. Most days Nancy slips downstairs to join them for a cup of coffee after seeing the girls off to school and before plunging into her own busy schedule. They have seen their youngest grandchildren grow up, as Valeria has graduated from high school and begun an impressive course of study at the University of Chicago, and Sofi and Caro have gone through middle school and well into high school. The Bedfords have been back-up chauffeurs to school or extra-curricular activities, and have attended countless dance and choir recitals. David and Nelda visit them every year, and adult grandchildren, nieces and nephews stop by on a regular basis. In 2016 Ben and La Nell celebrated their seventieth wedding anniversary surrounded by loved ones.

Filadelfia

When Ben and La Nell did not appear by sermon time, the leaders were forced to improvise. Christian Castro tells the story:

> *While we were working in Evanston, I was also attending my church, Iglesia Bautista Filadelfia, with which the pastor was not yet acquainted. However, right about that time our church was left without a pastor. I took advantage of the opportunity to invite him to preach (at that time Filadelfia met in the afternoon, which gave us time for the new work in Evanston in the morning).*
>
> *Pastor Bedford accepted but when he didn't show we had to make some last-minute changes to the program. Practically at the end of the service, the embarrassed pastor and his wife arrived just in time for the final amen. We understood the situation perfectly: the pastor was new to the Chicago area and had spent an hour driving around looking for the address. Little did we know that for the next few years he would be our interim and then part-time pastor.*
>
> *The Pastor was also my teacher and tutor. During the breaks from my seminary classes, I would go to his house to look over subjects I had not taken yet. With great patience and dedication, he would explain them to me. We read, prayed and shared stories. During the first weeks of our friendship he also gave me several books that I still keep and use often in preparing my sermons.*
>
> *During the past years he has been the motor that has driven our church forward. He motivates us Sunday after Sunday in worship and Thursday after Thursday in Bible study together with his wife: a model marriage, a model Christian and a tireless pastor.*[125]

---

[125] Christian Castro, from an email message to Nelda B. Gaydou dated April 2017

After that initial fiasco, Filadelfia invited Ben to return the next Sunday and soon he was supplying the pulpit on a regular basis. In a short time, he was asked to serve as interim and finally as the permanent pastor.

The congregation was renting its meeting space. Since the host church used the facilities in the morning, after an early lunch the members of Filadelfia had Sunday School at 1:00 and the worship service at 2:00 p.m., with prayer meeting and Bible study on Friday. An Ethiopian congregation was also renting space in the same building and when it outgrew its allotted room, Filadelfia was asked to switch places.

The new situation had its drawbacks and they considered their choices. The first, of course, was to remain where they were. But their new quarters were somewhat cramped and far from insulated from the sounds of the ebullient Ethiopians. The second choice was to return to the space they had rented before. This would have been the option preferred by most of the members, but it proved to be impossible for the host church had been undergoing a division and resolution was still nowhere in sight. The third choice was to merge with the new work in Evanston and meet there, and this was finally decided upon after much prayer, although it involved changing not only the venue but meeting times and days as well. Since a Pentecostal church was renting the same space on Sunday afternoon, Sunday School and the worship service would be held in the morning. The only slot available for prayer meeting and Bible study during the week was Thursday. A bonus was having the space available for children's and youth activities on Saturday. In May 2014 Evanston Baptist Church moved out of rented quarters and generously donated eighty chairs, a sound system and a portable baptistry to the Filadelfia church.

The congregation, which had dwindled almost down to a handful under a conflictive former pastor, slowly but steadily regrouped and began to grow. There were experienced leaders, musicians and teachers among them. Christian and his wife Yessenia worked with the children and youth. The extended Castro family was from Guatemala, but there were also people from Mexico, Perú, Colombia, Venezuela and Puerto Rico.

301

One of Ben's joys was mentoring Christian in the pastorate. That energetic young man felt called to work as a bi-vocational pastor. His technological lay skills were extremely useful both at the personal and church level, as he often helped his pastor out when he ran into problems with his laptop or smartphone, and he managed the video and sound systems for the services besides laying out and printing the weekly bulletin for the church.

At first Ben had Christian preach about once a month. The time came when the congregation was led to call him as associate pastor. When Ben turned eighty-nine, he told the church he felt that the time had come for him to step down and tendered his resignation effective July 31, 2016, with the conviction that Christian was ready for full responsibility. An ordination council, which included Scott Kelly, was held and Christian was installed as the new pastor.

Ben and La Nell continue to attend Iglesia Bautista Filadelfia and enjoy the warm fellowship there, where the emeritus pastor is often called upon to fill in at the pulpit, the adult Sunday School class or the Thursday night Bible study. The church's newest project is to split the weekly study group in two, one meeting in Evanston and the other in Chicago, while Ben's latest personal project is a book on God's call.

Full Throttle Down Memory Lane

Three thousand two hundred fifty-eight miles in eight days—just another typical Bedford trip. Ben pored over maps for months planning the best way to see the most in the least amount of time. The idea was to visit as many significant sites in their early family history as possible. The time frame was dictated by Nancy's and the twins' 2017 spring break, and Nelda scheduled her yearly visit accordingly. The four of them, plus Ben and La Nell, piled into the Stutzs' new SUV and backed out of the parking garage in Evanston at precisely 6:00 a.m.

SATURDAY: Drove through rain and fog to Joplin, Missouri. Spectacular weather for the rest of the trip.

SUNDAY: Reached Dickens County in West Texas. Stopped at the gravesites of Benjamin Franklin Bedford and L.D.'s baby daughter Lanora in the Spur cemetery. The Patton Springs Elementary School that Ben attended is still standing in Afton. Discovered that Croton no longer exists—only a cracked concrete slab remains that may have belonged to the church or the gas station. The farms are all gone, the land reverting to its natural state and now being used for ranching. Ben amazed his family by remembering landmarks like Dickens' Peak and the exact spot where his family's Model I truck broke down in 1932. Beautiful hills, shrubby vegetation and colorful rock formations. `

Thirty miles away, Cone has also disappeared, but the cemetery still bears witness to La Nell's grandfather, Christopher Columbus Land, and her parents, John and Nora Watson. The rich flat land has not changed since they farmed there in the mid-1930s. The same is true for the countryside around her birthplace, Lorenzo.

MONDAY: Lubbock to Curry County in Eastern New Mexico. Open country: Pleasant Hill Baptist Church, Ben's first pastorate; Ranchvale Baptist Church, the first congregation to which Ben and La Nell were called together. Clovis: The buildings of Ben's beautiful old Clovis Junior High School and the First Baptist Church, his home congregation, are still standing. Visited Nancy "Tennie" Bedford's grave. Saw a chipmunk.

Roosevelt County: Portales: the old Ben Franklin store where Ben and La Nell met, the Baptist Student Union building that was at the heart of their early social life and the Administration building where La Nell worked on the Eastern New Mexico University campus; the First Baptist Church where they were married seventy-one years ago. Open country: the building of La Nell's home church of Bethel remains but now belongs to a Spanish-speaking congregation; Floyd High School is in a new building (the original one burned down in the 1970s). Royal treatment and grand tour when La Nell was discovered to be a distinguished alumna.

Brief overnight visit with niece Linda in Odessa.

TUESDAY: From the arid oil fields of West Texas to the lush Hill Country. Brunch with nieces Ladee and Lou in San Angelo. Amazing Texan hospitality. Great company and surprise view of the San Angelo River, running along the bottom of Dee's back yard. Peaceful old cemetery in Llano. Found 1844 tombstone of Ben's grandmother Mary Farris Bedford nestled among fields of bluebonnets. Met family connections Larry, Gail and Dean, who shared stories and documents.

WEDNESDAY: Crashed in Austin, Nelda with daughter Andrea, Ben and La Nell at the hotel. Only Nancy and the girls had enough energy to spend the day sightseeing downtown and at the University of Texas campus.

THURSDAY: Amazing view of Lake Austin and live oak-clad hills from beautiful Mount Bonnell. Delicious lunch at historic Kerbey Lane Café. Reached Fort Worth in the late afternoon and divided up, half with David and half with the Naughton-Ferrells.

FRIDAY: Relived decades of sweet memories and made new ones. Got copies of Opal's poem collection that her children published on the occasion of her ninetieth birthday.[126] Big get-together at David's house to celebrate family and friendship.

SATURDAY: Beeline back to Evanston. Arrived SUNDAY afternoon.

---

[126] Opal Y. Ferrell, *The Song in My Heart (Thank You, Lord)*, 2017

Crossing the Jordan River

And then one day, I'll cross the river
I'll fight life's final war with pain
And then, as death gives way to victory
I'll see the lights of glory and I'll know He lives.
          Because He Lives, William and Gloria Gaither

Ben and La Nell's postings have taken them to the ends of the earth and from sea to sea. Now they are in their nineties, and one of these days they will be called home by the King whose ambassadors they have been since childhood. I can picture their welcome: "Well done, good and faithful servants! Come and share your master's happiness!"[127]

Twenty-one years after it celebrated their fiftieth wedding anniversary, the following metaphor of their joint endeavor is more fitting than ever:

> The Creation story in Genesis describes the nature of marriage. Paul quotes it in Ephesians and, even more significantly, both Matthew and Mark record Jesus citing it: *"For this reason a man shall leave his father and mother, and be made one with his wife; and the two shall become one flesh. It follows that they are no longer two individuals: they are one flesh."* Can this really happen? It happens in the physical world and it happens in the spiritual world.
>
> Hydrogen and oxygen are two distinct elements. Hydrogen is a flammable, colorless, odorless gas, the lightest of all known

---

[127] Matthew 25:21 (NIV)

substances and the most abundant element in the universe. It has numerous industrial uses for things such as the production of ammonia, ethanol and aniline; the hydrocracking, hydroforming and hydrofining of oil; the hydrogenation of vegetable oil; the hydrogenolysis of coal; and it acts as a reducing agent for organic synthesis and metal minerals, to name only a few of its applications.

Oxygen is a colorless, odorless, tasteless gas essential to life processes and to combustion. It is so useful in industry that it holds the fifth place in chemical production volume in the U.S. It is used, among many things, to increase efficiency in the manufacture of synthesis gas for producing ammonia, methyl alcohol, acetylene and others; as an oxidizer for jet propulsion liquid; for resuscitation; as a heat stimulant; for decompression chambers and spaceships; as a chemical intermediate; and to counteract the effect of eutrophication in lakes and reservoirs.

But wonderful and useful as these two elements are, when they are combined in the right proportion, as H2O, they form an even more precious matter—water. Water is a fascinating substance, of tremendous power both for creating and destroying. Properly controlled, it gives life, health, comfort and beauty.

My parents and their marriage are like that. They are two wonderful individuals, each one a strong and gifted person with much to offer. My father is a deep thinker, a visionary, a leader with tremendous willpower and drive. My mother, with a mind as quick as lightning and formidable powers of organization, is a superb teacher and a gifted linguist.

Joined together in the right proportion, not merely as friends or co-workers, but in marriage, they have become something new. Because they are both so strong, there is the potential, as with water, for destruction and chaos. But because they have allowed God to do the combining and the using, they have fulfilled His purpose and become a powerful positive force. Their marriage has flowed through life like a mighty river, blessing the lands in which they've lived and enriching itself with the streams and fountains God has sent along the way to feed it.

They are not halves of a whole; they are complements of a unit. They have truly been joined together into one flesh and one spirit. Their passion for each other is obvious to anyone who knows them, but their passion for the Lord is even greater.

What joy and pride and gratitude I feel as their daughter, to be able to look at the united life they have led and are leading, and know that this is a life that is significant, that has made a real difference for good in the world.

As I consider them in their "retirement," still preaching, and teaching and writing, I know that they have made Paul's words their own: *"I only want to finish the race, and complete the task which the Lord Jesus assigned to me, of bearing my testimony to the gospel of God's grace."*

For me, my parents loom large in God's cloud of witnesses. Their joint life challenges us, in the words of the writer of Hebrews:

And what of ourselves? With these witnesses to faith, we must throw off every encumbrance, every sin to which we cling, and run with resolution the race for which we are entered, our eyes fixed on Jesus, on whom faith depends from start to finish: Jesus who, for the sake of the joy that lay ahead of him, endured the cross, making light of its disgrace, and has taken his seat at the right hand of the throne of God.[128]

---

[128] Nelda Bedford Gaydou, April 18, 1996

AFTERWORD
by Dr. Allen Benjamin Bedford

Our world is going through a difficult and discouraging time, in which we seem to be surrounded by self-absorption, greed and violence. The future looks dark both for humankind and the planet on which we live. Many wonder where we are headed and whether our efforts make any difference, but there are still hope and peace and joy to be had. That has been our experience, and we have found meaning as part of something that is much bigger than our individual lives.

Before actually sharing with you some of the ways in which God permitted La Nell, me and our family to participate in carrying out his plan during the last fifty-three years (the time covered in this book, 1964-2017), let me express our thanks and acknowledge our debt to many along the way. The first is to our parents. Since we spent our childhood during the Great Depression, many material things were lacking, but there was always an abundance of love. We received from them a great inheritance: how to become Christians and how to serve God and others. Our dads died when we were children and our older siblings made sacrifices to help us until we could fend for ourselves. We also wish to thank our teachers, professors, fellow students, church members, students and co-workers. From them we learned many things, including love, humility, sacrifice, knowledge, wisdom, and how to face victories and defeats. They were examples of faithful witness in service to our Lord.

Since I will be writing this from my point of view, I need to tell you about La Nell, my love, my wife for seventy-one years as of April 18, 2017. When we were married, we promised to be one in every aspect of our lives and that has been our goal all through the years. Our family has helped me to better understand the doctrine of the Trinity—how Father, Son and Holy Spirit work together as one to carry out God's Eternal Plan, while maintaining the personality of each. La Nell and I have worked as one in our home life and in our service in the Kingdom of God. However, while being one, we have at the same time expressed ourselves as individuals. As God added to our family unit David, Nelda and Nancy, they became a part of the whole but maintained their personalities and their contribution to the work. It would be impossible for me to describe for you all that La Nell has been to me, to our family and to the Kingdom of God. She has been a wonderful wife, companion, friend, mother of our children and co-servant in God's work. She taught our children to read and write in English before they started to school in Spanish and continued to help them in their education in both languages. She did a wonderful job as they learned to love literature and all three became authors—in English and Spanish. Most of all, they are dedicated Christians and are serving our Lord. She exerted a deep influence in their lives. She not only kept the home fires burning but was very active in the work in the local church, associations and conventions, serving in varied roles. She made a great contribution in Christian Education both on a local and national level as well as in the Women's Missionary Union. The book gives a glimpse of her efforts in so many areas.

When I finally answered God's call to preach, it was to be whenever, wherever and as long as He indicated. In the beginning, I thought of serving one church for forty or fifty years, but God's plan for me was different. I liked to preach, do evangelistic work, teach, be a pastor and so on, but I soon realized that the calling was not about me, but rather the privilege of participating in God's eternal plan. He gave me the opportunity to realize all my desires, but in his way, in his time, and according to his plan and purpose. As he does with everyone, God gave us the opportunity to participate in his plan. Now, as I look back over the past, I can see how God worked through his Holy Spirit in a way that was impossible to comprehend at that time, while we were immersed in what was happening.

When we got off the ship in 1964, we began a new era in our service. Our first two terms included Rosario and Comodoro Rivadavia—associational work in an established area and beginning a new work in a pioneer area. For the next eight years, we would live and serve in the greater Buenos Aires area, first as missionaries in the South Association and later on the faculty of the International Baptist Theological Seminary. This was a critical and challenging time for the growth and development of Baptist work in Argentina. There was a new vision that took shape in what was called the "Decade of Advance". Individuals, churches, associations, institutions, organizations and the convention came together in prayer, dedication and service. There was a rush of activities, such as planning, committee meetings, organization, finding and training personnel, budget, church buildings, equipment, and work toward realizing goals. All the above was and is necessary, but only as tools used by God. La Nell and I were in the thick of it all, trying to keep up with the opportunities and demands.

We were blessed to be teamed with a special group of pastors, leaders and lay persons. People were won to the Lord and churches were established. At times, it is difficult not to get too involved in doing rather than seeking to be useful in carrying out our Lord's will. I realize now that I should have listened more carefully to the voice of God saying" Be still and know that I am God; I will be exalted among the nations" (Psalm 46:10) and Jesus saying "I am the vine; you are the branches. Those who abide in me and I in them bear much fruit; apart from me you can do nothing" (John 15:5).

While continuing to work in Solano and the South Zone, we were requested by the Seminary to direct the in-service training to help prepare and place new workers in the new areas of service. Again, we found a group of men and women who were extremely qualified and dedicated in their tasks. I feel fortunate to have served alongside them.

After eight demanding years, both La Nell and I felt physically drained. In the humid climate, La Nell's arthritis had returned and she was having back problems. One night I went to the hospital thinking that I was having a heart attack, but it turned out be just exhaustion. They had been eight wonderful years, doing exactly what we liked. We thought it was what we had been prepared to do and we had been

311

blessed. However, we began to feel that God might be leading us elsewhere and our desire was always to do his will.

Soon, we felt called to answer an SOS call from the small church of Villa Giardino, in the interior, in the province de Córdoba, which had taken seriously the goals of the "Decade of Advance". They needed help in strengthening the church and reaching out to establish new congregations in the Punilla Valley. The invitation was to pastor the church in Villa Giardino, prepare its members to participate in outreach, undergird the ministries of existing nearby congregations that were without pastors, start a new work in La Falda, and look forward to new work in other areas as soon as possible. Besides the spiritual needs, the churches needed a place to worship, as well as equipment and literature. The task looked impossible (and, humanly, it was) but all things are possible with God. He only asks us to be instruments. Again, we were amazed at how God saved, prepared, and used people and circumstances.

The years we lived in La Falda were great but passed by in a flash. Our work there and in the Valley was not finished, but a great need had reappeared at the Seminary. The staff had dwindled because several of its members had departed for other places of service. Both the Seminary and the Mission requested that La Nell and I return to lend a hand in this emergency. We were willing, but La Falda and the area still needed help. I spent one semester of each of the next two years travelling back and forth between Buenos Aires and La Falda by bus to teach a double load of classes Tuesday through Friday, while La Nell stayed home and took care of the church work. Then we became full-time teachers, La Nell in Christian Education and I in Church Administration and New Testament, living in an apartment at the Seminary during the week and returning to La Falda on weekends until David and Janene Ford took on the church's pastoral duties.

In 1980, both of us taught a full load of classes, becoming involved in related needs and activities. We were happy and felt that we would dedicate our lives to this area of service until our retirement in 1992. However, in 1981 we received a call from Dr. Thurmon Bryant, Area Director for Eastern South America of the Foreign Mission Board, asking us to become his Associates. It was urgent, as the FMB was in the process of speeding up strategic plans for this area. We answered that we would need to pray about it and were granted one week. It was a very difficult decision, perhaps the hardest of our career. Convinced that it was God's will, we accepted and served as Associates until our retirement.

Those eleven years were filled with many challenges and blessings as we acted as liaisons between the FMB, Missions and missionaries. The most rewarding part was the privilege of knowing the missionaries and how God used them in his plan, through their individual ministries, special projects (Mississippi Partnership, Master-Life Conferences, Continental Campaign of Total Stewardship, Human Needs Conferences, Medical Partnership between the Baptist Medical Center in Jacksonville, Florida and the Baptist Medical Center in Asunción, Paraguay, Mass Media Conferences, and other specialized conferences) and institutions (Hospital, Publishing House, Seminaries and Good Will Centers).

In July 1991, we moved from Argentina to Albuquerque, New Mexico to begin the last chapter of our life. It was not a change of vocation, but only of location. During our first year in the U.S., I continued to serve the FMB in the area of enlistment, as a trustee on the Board of the Spanish Publishing House in El Paso, Texas and as Treasurer for Stewardship Campaign of the Americas. On August 31, 1992, after forty-one years and four months, La Nell and I became Emeritus Missionaries of the FMB.

From then until November of 2012, La Nell and I served the Lord as opportunities came our way. In addition to being pastor and interim pastor in various churches, working with the local associations and conventions (both English and Spanish), there were many other opportunities, during which we came across a multitude of persons who were working for our Lord in many different ways. To illustrate, permit me to share a few examples. First, in the area of teaching, in addition to the local church, I was asked to teach for Southwestern and Golden Gate Seminaries as well as Wayland University, besides directing and teaching in the CLD (Contextual Leadership Development), in classes that included students from diploma to graduate level. All these students have blessed me and touched my life in many ways. I marvel at how God has used them as pastors, teachers and servants to carry out his eternal plan.

God also worked through mission trips. I will use two as illustrations. The first was a group of forty persons sponsored by Albuquerque Central Baptist Association that went on a mission trip to Córdoba, Argentina. It was wonderful to see God working both in Albuquerque and Córdoba: people prayed, gave, went and received; souls were saved; churches were strengthened; construction advanced on a number of building projects, but, more importantly, God was glorified. Just recently, twenty-two years later, four persons who were members of Friendship Baptist Church at that time told me that their lives and their commitment to service had been changed forever by that experience.

The other example is a six-year medical and evangelistic partnership between Del Norte Baptist Church and Nicaragua. The success of the endeavor can only be explained in the light of God's guidance and the power of the Holy Spirit in the lives of willing believers. The members of Del Norte worked together through prayer, giving and going. On every trip, the group was joined by members from other churches. The Nicaraguan side was also a miracle consisting of missionaries, pastors, doctors, nurses and dedicated believers. Souls were saved, the sick were healed, churches were established, lives were changed and, most of all, God was glorified. Once again, we see how God can do his work when his servants yield their lives and talents to him.

The last twenty-one years spent in New Mexico brought us many blessings. We want to thank all the people, churches, associations, conventions, students and everyone who touched our lives. As I told the men's department when I spoke at the Spanish Convention in June 2012, I had taken my first and planned to take my last breath in New Mexico. However, that was not to be the case because we were moving to Evanston, Illinois due to circumstances beyond our control.

In November 2011, I was knocked down and run over by an SUV in a parking lot. I ended up in the hospital with a mangled left foot that required surgery, a long-term injury to my right knee, and MRSA. The doctor told me that I was very fortunate not to have lost my foot, my leg or even my life. Our family felt that, because of this situation and other existing health issues, we should consider relocating near one of our children, Nancy being the most practical choice. We prayed for guidance.

The way that God worked it all out was another miracle. An apartment became available in the same building where our daughter lives. By pooling together all of our savings, my insurance policy, the money from the accident and a small loan, we were able to buy the apartment and make it livable. La Nell and I spent part of May and June there signing papers and making arrangements for paint and repairs. We also found a Baptist Church that we could attend and that was interested in helping us begin a work in Spanish. I would be able to pay expenses and taxes while I taught at Wayland, which wanted me to teach as long as I could. In the space of four months, we put our house on the market, sold it, finished up my teaching responsibilities and moved to Evanston, Illinois.

That was the material part; the spiritual was even more amazing. I thought about God calling Moses at eighty years of age to lead the Children of Israel and wondered if he might use us to begin a work in Spanish in Evanston. As it turned out, he had already made provisions. In our first meeting to learn about the Spanish-speakers in area, I met Christian Castro through a mutual friend. We decided to start weekly Bible studies alternating between our homes, but before we began an opportunity to rent a place in the Reba Ministry Center opened up, so we began Sunday morning Bible studies there. Christian was a member of Iglesia Bautista Filadelfia, a small church that met on Sunday afternoons in a rented space in an English-language Baptist church about a thirty-minute drive away from Evanston. The church was without a pastor, so it invited me to speak and later to fill that position. Larger quarters were required and, unable to find an adequate meeting place nearby, the church decided to join with the new work and go forward under the same name. Christian and I worked together and soon he became the co-pastor.

Because of our declining health, I felt that the time had come to resign, which I did effective July 31, 2016, after four years as pastor. The church called and ordained Christian Castro and he is doing a wonderful job. La Nell and I are grateful to have had a small part in the work here. We remain members of the church and do what we can as our health allows—after all, we are both in our nineties.

This church is our spiritual family. In this small community God is making one body out of many groups and backgrounds (people from Guatemala, El Salvador, Cuba, Mexico, Venezuela, Colombia, Peru, Argentina and the U.S.). What God has done in the last five years is remarkable: there have been ups and downs, trials and victories, deaths, sorrows, miracles, sins, repentance, forgiveness and cleansing, a deepening of fellowship and concern one for another, plus a great desire to serve those living around us and a willingness to answer God's call to service. God is weaving a tapestry of unity to bring glory to his name—a microcosm of what he is doing throughout the world. We pray that the church will be useful in carrying out God's purpose here.

The book shares our story and how it has become a small part of God's plan. Now, as I look back over these years, I would like to challenge you to yield yourself to God's calling. He not only invites everyone to receive pardon, salvation and eternal life, but also to participate in his plan. In his wisdom, he gives gifts to his children according to their needs, to be used as instruments to glorify his name, to edify the church and to reach out to the lost world. His call is one of service, not for honor or position, following the example of Jesus.

Let me urge you to respond to God's invitation. If you have never done so, find peace and purpose by starting a new life through faith. If you already did but have grown distant for whatever reason, return to him. Don't let yourself be deprived of your relationship with God and fellow believers or of God's daily blessings. If he is calling you to some specific task, consider it a privilege, obeying no matter where it leads or what it costs: you will be blessed and will become a blessing to others.

Now I would like to share what I understand about God's eternal plan. I have a growing conviction that we need to know why God created humankind, what his plan and purposes are, and how he has used, is using and will continue to use people as instruments to accomplish this eternal plan which was his from the beginning of time.

What I know about God comes from my personal experience with Biblical revelation, the leadership of the Holy Spirit and interaction with other believers. As I share various passages with you, I will be quoting from the New International Version.

When I think back to 1964, as we were on the ship returning to Argentina after our furlough to begin a new era in our ministry, in one way it seems like ages ago and in another only yesterday. However, during the period covered by this book there have been many changes in the world: scientific, social, cultural and spiritual, as well as in the methods, programs and technology used, yet God has not changed for "he is the same yesterday, today and forever" (Hebrews 13:7).

I never cease to be amazed at how God carries out his eternal plan for the world. Jesus taught us how God unfolds it through the Trinity (Father, Son and Holy Spirit). Jesus said, "My Father is always at his work to this very day, and I [the Son], too, am working" (John 5:17-23). The religious leaders of his day felt so threatened that they wanted to kill him: not only was he breaking their traditions, he was even calling God his own Father, claiming to be one and the same. Jesus gave them this answer: "I tell you the truth, the Son can do nothing by himself: he can do only what he sees his Father doing, because whatever the Father does the Son also does." Jesus also promised to send the Holy Spirit to continue the work. Jesus said, "I will ask the Father, and he will give you another Counselor (just like me) to be with you forever" (John 14:16). "I will not leave you orphaned. I will come to you" (verse 18). He explained the participation of believers in carrying out God's eternal plan by saying, "As the Father has sent me, I am sending you" (John 20:21). See also Acts 1:8, John 17:20-26 and Matthew 28:20.

God has used and continues to use all kinds of people, methods and circumstances to carry out his eternal purpose. We must realize that it is a great privilege to be called and used. We must also know that we, as his people, with the gifts and talents that he has given us, however we use them, are only instruments in his hands. We can do nothing without the presence and power of Jesus in our lives through the working of the Holy Spirit.

As examples, let us review how God called and used four very different persons, methods, situations and needs to carry out his plans and his will, in preparation for sending his Son to create a new humanity and a new earth as he had intended from the beginning.

First, there is the case of Abraham. The peoples of the earth were living in idolatry and rebellion against God's will and purpose. God called Abraham to leave Ur of the Chaldeans to go to the land of Canaan. He made a covenant to bless Abraham and make of him a great nation so that he and that nation would bless the rest of the world. From his descendants would come the universal Redeemer— Jesus Christ. Through many ups and downs, sin and disobedience, forgiveness and redemption Abraham's descendants arrived in Egypt and remained there for more than 400 years (see Genesis chapters 12-50). In Hebrews 11:8-19, the author sums up how God worked through Abraham's faith to realize his purpose. God worked through people, whom He had called, to equip his chosen nation as an instrument to redeem humankind.

Second, God called and used Moses to free the people of Israel from slavery in Egypt, mold them into a nation and lead them to worship the one and only true God. He arranged for Moses to be born in a devout Hebrew family, but to be raised and trained in Pharaoh's palace. Moses was hardened by an impulsive murder committed in an attempt to defend his people. Then God led and protected him as he fled to the desert. He was allowed to become a part of a priestly family, know a wise father-in-law and learn about the arid region where he would guide his people for forty years. Moses was a wise, meek and noble leader, but he was also a sinner. His anger cost him dearly, yet God used him to do mighty things, as he became one of the outstanding men of history, whose obedience allowed God to work through him to bless not only Israel but the whole world as well.

Third, making a long leap into a critical period in Israel's history—socially, politically, and spiritually—for both the Northern and Southern Kingdoms in the eighth century B.C., to the golden age of the prophets, we find the call and ministry of Isaiah, known as the prince of the prophets. God wanted a servant who could look up and see him in his glory, power, majesty and holiness, and at the same time see the sins of the world about him and its need, who would be willing to be cleansed of his own sin and answer God's call to service. When God asked, "Whom shall I send?" and "Who will go for us?" Isaiah answered, "Here am I. Send me!" (Isaiah 6:8-9). Isaiah delivered God's message of that day, a message of condemnation, hope, forgiveness, salvation, a new humanity and an eternal kingdom with Jesus as King.

Fourth, Romans 10 shows us the converted Paul challenging all believers to answer the call of God, basing his message on Isaiah chapter 6. After declaring that salvation is possible to everyone who believes, regardless of ethnic origin, he asks how people can believe if they have not heard, how they can hear if someone does not preach to them, and how a person can preach without being sent. He challenges us to heed the call to go, give and pray for others to be sent to share the good news. Once the message is preached, the result must be left in God's hands.

After God had created His wonderful universe and all that is in it, including all living creatures he said, "Let us make man in our image, in our likeness.... So God created humankind in his own image, in the image of God he created him; male and female he created them" (Genesis 1:26-27). His purpose was for us to be like him, have fellowship with him, and enjoy the wonderful universe that he had created, caring for it, cultivating it and populating it. However, due to humankind's disobedience and consequent inability to carry out God's plan and purpose, all of creation suffered: the earth was polluted and humanity's close fellowship with God was broken. Paul says, "The creation waits in eager expectation for the children of God to be revealed...." (Romans 8:18-23). Because of sin (the original word literally means "missing the mark") that had warped the universe, God put into action his preordained plan of forgiveness and redemption through Jesus, giving fallen humanity the choice of becoming part of the new humanity through the new birth made possible by the work and power of the Holy Spirit in those who believe and commit themselves to God, thus becoming his children not only physically but also spiritually.

Of course, all of us would like to know more about the treasures that God has in store for his children. Up to now we only have glimpses of that glory: "No eye has seen, no ear has heard, no mind has conceived what God has prepared for those who love him" (1 Corinthians 2:9). In his time, God will finish his work of redemption and transformation and will begin his eternal reign; he will be our God and we will be his people (Rev. 21:1-6). We know that when we accept Jesus as Savior and Lord, we are born again and become the children of God. We do not know yet all that signifies but we do know that we shall be like him because we will see him as he is (1 John 3:1-3; Philippians 3:20-21; 1 Peter 1:3-12; 2 Corinthians 5:1-5).

While we are waiting for the final revelation and the consummation of the ages, we must seek to do God's will, live in the present and serve as God's instruments, guided and empowered by His Holy Spirit. John tells us that we are all sinners, but if we confess our sins God is faithful and just to forgive our sins and to cleanse us from all unrighteousness (1 John 1:9-10). He also tells us that the ideal is not to sin but, because we do, the Father sent the Redeemer, His Son Jesus, not only for us but for the whole world (1 John 2:1-2). As we stated above, one of God's reasons for creating humankind was to have fellowship with him. In John's words, "This is the message we have heard from him and declare to you: God is light; in him there is no darkness at all. If we claim to have fellowship with him yet walk in darkness, we lie and do not live by the truth. But if we walk in the light, as he is in the light, we have fellowship with one another, and the blood of Jesus, his son, purifies us from every sin" (1 John 1:7).

As we strive to live in the world and be God's instruments, we must remember that God is love. We must love as he loves and carry his love into the world, not just in theory, but in action and in truth (1 John 3:17-18). Jesus said that the greatest commandment is "Love the Lord your God with all you heart and with all your soul and with all your mind—and the second is like it: 'Love your neighbor as yourself'" (Matthew 22:37-38). He also said, "Love one another as I have loved you" (John 15:12).

To sum up how we should live, we must remember to keep his commands: "We know that we have come to know him if we obey his commands—if anyone obeys his word, God's love is truly made complete. This is how we know we are in him: Whoever claims to live in him must walk as Jesus did" (1 John 2:3-6).

As I think of how I should live, a little chorus that I learned as a child comes to my mind. This is my prayer:

> To be like Jesus
> To be like Jesus
> All I ask—to be like him
> All through life's journey
> From earth to glory
> All I ask to be like him

God not only invites us to receive pardon, salvation and eternal life, but also to be a part of his plan. Serving our Lord is not easy task but it is very rewarding. Jesus said that there would be trials and difficulties, but he promised to be with us and in us to give us power to face and overcome any thing that tries to prevent us from becoming instruments to carry out God's plan.

When I was struggling during my first pastorate, wondering why God had called me to a task that seemed beyond my possibilities, he used people and things to help me. One hymn, "Here Am I, Send Me," was a special blessing. It has four wonderful stanzas, each with a great message; the third has stayed with me through the years. It says, "If you cannot sing like angels, if you cannot preach like Paul, you can tell the love of Jesus, you can say he died for all; if you cannot rouse the wicked, with the judgment's dread alarms, you can lead the little children to the Savior's waiting arms."[129]

I urge you to take time to be with Jesus, let him abide in you and you in him. Do all for the glory of God and seek to serve others. May God bless you all!

---

129 *The Broadman Hymnal* (Nashville: Broadman Press, 1940), 407.

About the Author

Nelda Bedford Gaydou was born and raised in Argentina by missionary parents from the U.S. Growing up, she lived in Rosario, Comodoro Rivadavia and Buenos Aires. She attended the university in the U.S., earning degrees in English Literature, History and Spanish Literature. Besides her native English and Spanish, she speaks French and Italian.

Nelda and her husband live in the mountains of Córdoba, Argentina, and share a beautiful view with three Labrador Retrievers, only blocks away from their two youngest children and four grandchildren, while their firstborn lives in Texas.

Her previous book, *To the Ends of the Earth: High Plains to Patagonia*, won the 2017 International Book Award for General Biography. Upcoming projects include a family memoir on dementia, a collection of biographical stories for children based on her father's experiences in Dickens, Texas in the 1930s, and Spanish versions of the biographies.

Progressive Rising Phoenix Press is an independent publisher. We offer wholesale discounts and multiple binding options with no minimum purchases for schools, libraries, book clubs, and retail vendors. We also offer rewards for libraries, schools, independent book stores, and book clubs. Please visit our website and wholesale discount page at:

www.ProgressiveRisingPhoenix.com

Progressive Rising Phoenix Press is adding new titles from our award-winning authors on a regular basis and has books in the following genres: children's chapter books and picture books, middle grade, young adult, action adventure, mystery and suspense, contemporary fiction, romance, historical fiction, fantasy, science fiction, and non-fiction covering a variety of topics from military to inspirational to biographical. Visit our website to see our updated catalogue of titles.

9 781946 329417